The Two-Soul'd Animal

The Two-Soul'd Animal

Early Modern Literatures of the Classical and Christian Souls

James Jaehoon Lee

NORTHWESTERN UNIVERSITY PRESS
EVANSTON, ILLINOIS

Northwestern University Press
www.nupress.northwestern.edu

Printed in the United States of America

10 9 8 7 6 5 4 3 2 1

ISBN 978-0-8101-3926-8 (paper)
ISBN 978-0-8101-3927-5 (cloth)
ISBN 978-0-8101-3928-2 (ebook)

Cataloging-in-Publication data are available from the Library of Congress.

To Suzanna, Harrison, Hudson, and our future

CONTENTS

ACKNOWLEDGMENTS

This book began in a coffee shop in Berkeley as a passing thought about defining the soul in Longinus's sublime aesthetics and Michel Foucault's late classical ethics, which I hastily scribbled in the margins of Kant's Third Critique. The evolution of the idea—from an essay on the sublime eventually published in *New Literary History*, to the present book, parallels the intellectual and personal transformations I have undergone while writing these pages. I am indebted to all of the mentors, colleagues, and friends who have supported and sustained me as this project grew from its infancy as a marginal comment.

Every page of this book has been sharpened by the advice and encouragement of Victoria Kahn, who always pushed me to think and to write more precisely. She has been a dedicated mentor, and I thank her for shaping me into a scholar. David Landreth has been a wonderfully patient and open teacher and friend. I thank him for his willingness to entertain the wildest ideas and to help me untangle complex logical knots at moments of impasse in the writing of this book. He urged me to be more expansive in my thinking, and his support of my career has been meaningful to this day. At Berkeley, Janet Adelman set the foundation for this book by reminding me on numerous occasions, partly in jest, not to neglect the soul when studying the history of the body. I miss her greatly. Maura Nolan and Deborah Blocker encouraged me to engage more deeply with the historical dimensions of my arguments, and their advice has added richness and depth to each chapter.

At Grinnell College, I enjoyed many lively conversations with Steve Andrews, Erik Simpson, Shuchi Kapila, Tim Arner, Sandy Moffitt, and the late Richard Fyffe, who all gave me new ways to think about the relevance of the two souls beyond the early modern period. Susan Clarke has been a wonderful mentor who helped me to imagine how this book could take shape. I am grateful for my continuing collaboration at the intersection of the early modern and the digital with Blaine Greteman, who offered creative ideas to enliven each chapter. Masha Raskolnikov introduced me to the intellectual possibilities of Renaissance and medieval literature at Cornell University. In many ways, this book is a response to the foundational questions that she posed to me. This book has benefited at every stage from the ideas of Luke Terlaak Poot, Christopher Fan, and Rebecca Schonberg, who engaged in timely conversations as I tested and revised my ideas during a happy period of my life.

I am indebted to Jay Twomey, Xuemao Wang, Arlene Johnson, the Department of English and Comparative Literature, and the University Libraries of the University of Cincinnati for providing me with the time and resources to complete this book. Through the course of this project, Paul Dilley, Daniel Shore, Bill Ingram, Kevis Goodman, James Turner, A. A. Long, Jennifer Miller, Jonathan Culler, Andrew Galloway, Rayna Kalas, Jim Huff, Gordon Gray, and Taite Darlington all asked useful questions and provided crucial historical or theoretical advice at the right time. Reid Barbour's suggestions substantially strengthened my arguments on John Donne's writing and life. I am grateful to Gianna Mosser and Henry Carrigan at Northwestern University Press for their belief in this project and for transforming this book into its present form. Jessica Hinds-Bond and Kemi Adeyemi allowed my words to breathe, and I cannot thank them enough for their careful stewardship of my work. I thank all of the students in my seminars on the afterlives of the classical soul at the University of California, Berkeley, and at Grinnell College. I vividly remember their creative and insightful comments and observations.

To this day, my parents Hyung Sup and Jongsuk Lee remain my most meaningful mentors. I am profoundly grateful for all of their sacrifice, and this book only came to life because of their faith in me. Jason Lee, Syng-Yon Kim, Melissa Clarke, and Thomas Parks all surrounded me with a generous and supportive environment necessary to complete this research. Ruby Lee has made me contemplate the animal soul time and again.

My wife, Suzanna, has always been my best and most perceptive reader and interlocutor, and my sons, Harrison and Hudson, give me hope for the future. These three souls create wonder and joy in my own, and I dedicate this book to them.

Chapter 4 was previously published in *Studies in Philology* 113, no. 4 (fall 2016), as "John Donne and the Textuality of the Two Souls." I thank the journal and the University of North Carolina Press for providing this previous venue to present my argument.

The Two-Soul'd Animal

Introduction

✦

The Two-Soul'd Animal

> This is the doctrine of the sanctity of life, which they either apply to all animal and even vegetable life, or limit to human life . . . Man cannot, at any price, be said to coincide with the mere life in him . . . What then distinguishes it essentially from the life of animals and plants? . . . It might be well worthwhile to track down the origin of the dogma of the sacredness of life.
>
> —Walter Benjamin, "Critique of Violence"

> In our culture, man has always been thought of as the articulation and conjunction of a body and soul, of a living thing and a *logos*, of a natural (or animal) element and a supernatural or social or divine element. We must learn instead to think of man as what results from the incongruity of these two elements, and investigate not the metaphysical mystery of conjunction, but rather the practical and political mystery of separation . . . And perhaps even the most luminous sphere of our relations with the divine depends, in some way, on that darker one which separates us from the animal.
>
> —Giorgio Agamben, *The Open: Man and Animal*

In 1672 Thomas Willis, the Sedleian Professor of Natural Philosophy at the University of Oxford, one of the first fellows of the Royal Society, and celebrated today by scientists as the originator of the term "neurology" and as the "legendary" founder of "clinical neuroscience," introduced his ideas on the animal soul in his Latin treatise *De Anima Brutorum* (*The Soul of Brutes*) by voicing anxiety:[1]

> For that I assert a Man (as the Mad-man in the Gospel possess't with a Legion) to be indued with many distinct Souls . . . But indeed in these Disquisitions (which the Anatomy of the Brain, and its Appendixes, hath lately and more exactly shown) as we have enter'd into a by-way, and not before trodden, there was a necessity to lead thee,

> thorow some sharp and stony ways, beset with bushes and thorns, which might offend thee. And indeed I know not, whether it will be pleasing to all, that instituting the something Paradoxical Doctrine of the Animal Soul, that I should assign to that Soul, by which the Brutes as well as Men live, feel, move, not only Extension, but Members, and as it were Organical Parts, yea peculiar Diseases, and proper means or methods of Curing them; and that moreover, I should form this, which is meerly Vital, and different from the Rational, and subordinate to it, and so Man, a Two-soul'd Animal, and as it were a manifold *Geryon*.[2]

At face value, it is hard to see what would make such a text on comparative nervous structures so potentially offensive to his erudite readership, but Willis found it necessary to preemptively fend off attacks, since his early efforts to define "neurologie" had led him to conclude that analyzing the soul was an unexpectedly "great and difficult thing, and full of hazard." In publishing his work, Willis admitted that he "fears the Censures of the Church" for his potentially "pernicious or heretical" views, along with the rebuke of his scientific peers, who by this time would have included luminaries such as Robert Hooke, John Locke, and Robert Boyle. Willis even went so far as to direct an address to the archbishop of Canterbury, pleading that the latter would "suffer your Grace for my greater Safety, to extend your help to me."

What would provoke such handwringing in anticipation of a text dealing with a seemingly abstruse topic in Latin? In his address to the reader cited above, Willis explains that recent "disquisitions" on the brain have "lately and more exactly shown" what he has increasingly come to recognize as a "sharp and stony way, beset with bushes and thorns." The problem he takes up in his work is the "paradoxical doctrine" of the "bipart or twofold" soul tangled up in the traditions of both ancient and modern systems of thought. As he suggests, the investigations of the Royal Society inherited these precedents, which to his mind have "proved these two distinct souls, to be together" in the human. The simultaneous presence of the "Animal" or organic soul that is shared by all animals, including humans, composed of the faculties and "Organical Parts" permitting the body to "live, feel, move," and the Christian soul that defines the human's relation to God, turns man into a "Two-soul'd Animal" that is monstrous like a "manifold *Geryon*." Willis voices fear about the paradox of the "bipart or twofold" soul that haunts man with the possibility of being a "Two-soul'd" monster, and about what such a paradox could hold for his nascent efforts to establish a coherent science of the mind.

Willis quite earnestly speculated that the monstrous presence of "two souls in man" could still be "agreeable to a good life." In his career, he never came to define how one would be able to recuperate such a "good life" from such a condition. He concluded, rather, by reformulating the complex tradition of the soul as a question: "for by what knitting together, can two independent souls subsist in the same body?" This question at the end of the seventeenth century echoes a similar sentiment voiced by Marsilio Ficino some two centuries earlier, that the idea of two souls turns the human into a "monstrous octopus."[3] From Ficino's octopus to Willis's "*Geryon*," *The Two-Soul'd Animal* traces the evolution of a vibrant conversation on the soul that expressed itself as a nagging doubt that haunted early modern English theologians, but which also prompted humor and erotic speculation by authors such as William Shakespeare and John Donne. Indeed, against an intellectual backdrop characterizing the two-souls dilemma in early modern culture as a site upon which definitions of the human were staged, prominent English authors such as William Shakespeare, John Donne, Sir John Davies, and John Milton offered a positive definition of the two souls as the basis of a new form of Christian freedom. Their literary works created a rhetorical space that became a laboratory of the soul, as it were, in which to experiment and play with the generative possibilities of the soul at the boundary of the classical and Christian traditions.

And so the varied discourse defining the human soul's dual inflections in all of their complexity comes to preoccupy not just early Royal Society investigators such as Willis, but also poets, clergy, philosophers, and legal theorists of the Renaissance world. The condition of "two souls in man" inherited from the ancients serves as the prelude to what Willis ultimately called "neurology," which is a term familiar to us today. *The Two-Soul'd Animal* works backward from this historical terrain to trace the multiple poetic, rhetorical, and theological vectors that collided to form the multifarious concept of the "soul" in the early modern era. It discusses how sixteenth-century humanism, Protestant theology, and natural philosophy viewed the presence of two souls in one body with a blend of suspicion, confusion, and curiosity. All of the English poets and dramatists that I will consider attempted to recuperate a generative vision of the two souls as a productive occasion to define the poetics of a vernacular folk psychology conferring on the Christian subject a new dimension of agency in a Protestant theological context where choice was all but foreclosed.

Two Souls in One Body

The Two-Soul'd Animal argues that the Renaissance imagination of the "human" was a crowded subjectivity precisely as Willis describes to vivid effect, with two souls—one animal and one spiritual—crowding the same body, uneasily coexisting and making man ill at ease in his own skin. The legacy of the humanist ideal of *hominis dignitate* (the dignity of man) was not defined by the conventional dualism of body and soul. Nor was it imagined exclusively in terms of a materialist monism that had been popularized by recent scholarship on anatomy and humoral physiology. Rather, a central problem of early modern culture was the dualism of two souls, created in the conflicting vocabularies of Aristotelian and Christian faculty psychology, which Willis acknowledges in his debt to both ancient and modern, theological and scholastic, traditions of thought.[4]

In order to understand the extent of the discursive field that bounded the English literary authors I examine, a brief definition of the philosophical and theological context of the time is necessary. On one hand there was the Aristotelian tripartite model of the soul, one based on the three organic faculties of intellection, sensation, and nutrition. In his foundational account in *De Anima* (*On the Soul*), Aristotle defines the soul as the "principle" of embodied life: "The soul is in a sense the principle of animal life."[5] For Aristotle, the soul emanates from the function of the body's organs: "The soul may therefore be defined as the first actuality or form of a natural body potentially possessing life; and such will be any body which possesses organs . . . the soul is the origin of the characteristics we have mentioned, and is defined by them, that is, by the faculties of nutrition, sensation, thought, and movement."[6] In Aristotle's comprehensive definition, the soul marks the actualization of the natural body's potential for life; it is the form of the body's matter.[7] Therefore, any natural body that is living must necessarily possess a soul. In defining the soul as the constitutive relation of actuality and potentiality, form and matter, Aristotle places an important condition for the possibility of the living soul; the soul must be the form of a body possessing organs. The soul is therefore embedded in the body's organs, which for Aristotle, make up the most basic unit of life. The functions or "characteristics" of the soul in question are defined by Aristotle as the faculties of nutrition, sensation, thought, and movement. Aristotle's model of the soul is complex because it is continually constituted in a self-reflexive feedback loop: "the soul is the origin of the faculties we have mentioned, and is defined by them." In Aristotle's circular definition, the soul is the "origin" of the faculties, and in turn the faculties it originates feed back to define the soul-as-origin. In this recursive logic, the soul is both the cause and effect of life, the creator of the faculties and the thing that is defined by the very faculties it creates. At its core, Aristotle's soul is a biological principle defining life.

On the other hand, there was the Christian understanding of the soul as an immortal, immaterial, and transcendental substance, although Christian theology had a great debt to Aristotle's model through the teachings of Church Fathers like Saint Augustine and later Saint Thomas Aquinas, who saw value in the organic soul as a technical vocabulary to describe human biology. Garrett Sullivan has recently described this Christian debt to a pagan soul as an "integration": "The idea of the tripartite soul is derived primarily from Aristotle's *De Anima*, albeit with significant elaboration and modification over the centuries, most notably in the tethering of the rational faculties to the immortal, non-organic soul—a development that enabled the integration of the Aristotelian conception of life into Christian belief systems, both Catholic and Protestant." As Sullivan suggests, Catholic and Protestant theologians alike incorporated an Aristotelian understanding of the soul into their belief systems. But this Christian debt to the classical soul was always vexed since, in Christian doctrine, the soul seeks to shed its tethers to the very living functions of the body that compose the Aristotelian soul. From the teachings of the early Christian fathers to the present day, the soul is the principle defining man's spirituality, the promise of immortality, and the possibility of salvation.[8] Aristotle's definition of the soul moves in the opposite direction, with the soul as the "principle of animal life" embedding man's faculties in a network of the shared characteristics binding all living things into a densely intermeshed chain of being. We can begin to see the fault lines emerge between these two models of the soul, in which two fundamentally different "principles" define human nature: the organic principle of "life" binds man to a universe of other living things, while the "spiritual principle" lifts man beyond the bodily plane of the flesh in this world to a closer relationship with God.

The Two-Soul'd Animal illuminates an early modern debate, provoked in part by the theological controversies contributing to the conflagration of the Reformation, that recognized the extent to which Christian thought had defined the human in terms of these two incompatible models of the soul. Throughout the sixteenth century, Catholic and Protestant thinkers as diverse as Pope Leo X, Martin Luther, John Calvin, William Perkins, and Richard Hooker began to realize that these two souls fundamentally contradicted one another. During the Reformation, as we shall see in the following chapter, the ideas of human agency and Christian liberty were dissected at the fault line between free will, contingency, and predestination. Reformation theology asserted that the soul was, in part, in an enslaved condition of "self-hatred" (*odium sui*).[9] This Protestant view of the soul caught between the poles of slavery and freedom would prove foundational in the two-souls debate as it moved to the English context.

Even in the most laudatory treatises celebrating the soul's power in the early modern period, we can find acknowledgments of the presence of two souls in one body. As Robert Mason admits in his 1605 *Reason's Academie*, the latest knowledge "discovered by learning" has revealed a "double life in man"—one "in this world, in respect to his mere sensitive parts," and "the second, in another world . . . immortal, and never finishing, never ending."[10] How to bridge the two souls composing the "double life in man" is the source of a considerable confusion in the Renaissance mind, with Robert Burton paradigmatically describing the problem in his enigmatic *Anatomy of Melancholy* as one that can only raise "doubt" about the stability of the soul:

> The common division of the soul is into three principal faculties—vegetal, sensitive, rational, which make three distinct kinds of living creatures: vegetal plants, sensible beasts, rational men. How these

> three principal faculties are distinguished and connected, *humano ingenio inaccessum videtur*, is beyond human capacity. . . . Many doubts arise about the essence, subject, seat, distinction, and subordinate faculties of it. For the essence and particular knowledge, of all other things it is most hard (be it of man or beast) to discern, as Aristotle himself, Tully, Picus Mirandula, Tolet, and other neoteric philosophers confess.[11]

The faculties of the soul organize the hierarchy of living beings, with the faculty of reason positioning humans at the apex. However, the relationship between the faculties, and the essence of the soul itself, is "beyond human capacity," leading a long tradition of philosophers and theologians into a state of "doubt" and confusion about the condition of our souls. The acknowledgment of the two souls provoked a good deal of questioning, leading Christian thinkers to ask: How can we, as God's perfect design, have two redundant and yet contradictory souls? And how could the core of the religious subject possibly be defined by a psychological paradox? As a result, the "soul" was an intrinsically unstable term that was being renegotiated in Renaissance culture.[12]

These questions and doubts about the slippage between the two souls arose because the Christian integration of classical psychology was an imprecise fit. As Katharine Park has argued, classical faculty psychology was important in early modern culture because it was widely appropriated as a biological, and not primarily a theological, principle.

> The "organic soul"—the principle responsible for those life functions inextricably tied to the bodies of living beings and immediately dependent on their organs. These functions ranged from the vital operations of digestion and reproduction through sensation and emotion to the higher cognitive functions of imagination and memory. . . .[13]
>
> Separate but related, the faculties occupied a static hierarchy of dependence and nobility, ranging from the lowest faculty of nutrition to the highest faculty of intellect . . . The lowest, called the vegetative soul, included the functions basic to all living things: nutrition, growth, and reproduction. The second, the sensitive soul, included all of the powers of the vegetative soul as well as the powers of movement and emotion and the ten internal and external senses. The intellective soul, finally, included not only the vegetative and sensitive powers—the organic faculties—but also the three rational powers of intellect, intellective memory . . . and will.[14]

The three primary faculties of nutrition, sensation, and intellection encompassed all living functions from digestion and reproduction to the higher cognitive processing of imagination, memory, and reason. Throughout the medieval and Renaissance periods, Aristotle's organization of the soul's living functions in terms of its faculties was the primary way of explaining human biology. His definition of the soul was organic—bound by the function of the body's organs and divided into three faculties—and it accounted for all living functions, from the most visceral autonomic processes of respiration and digestion to the workings of the brain. If the classical model of faculty psychology became modified over the centuries from the time of Aristotle into a framework that could "integrate" classical conceptions of life with Christian beliefs, as Garrett Sullivan has suggested, these changes cumulatively twisted the primarily biological scope of the organic soul to force the classical model to conform to the increasingly spiritual exigencies of Christian doctrine.

The potential mismatch between the two souls was a direct inheritance from the medieval tradition of Thomas Aquinas, Albert the Great, Peter Lombard, and Bonaventure, who all sought to integrate "Aristotelian metaphysics in new ways" into Christian doctrine by concentrating "not merely on the technical philosophical solutions implicit in their work but also on the explicit confusions and tensions."[15] In the specific context of the soul, Caroline Walker Bynum has demonstrated how the "body-soul nexus" both "fascinated and confused" medieval commentators of Aristotle, triggering "anxiety" and creating a "zone of tension" about how "one substantial form" of the soul could "account for the nature and thus the identity of person."[16]

Much of this fascination mingled with confusion and tension was created in the thirteenth century by Saint Thomas Aquinas, who implanted the Aristotelian definition of the soul into the core of the Christian idea of personhood. Aquinas's mixture of the patristic tradition of the soul he inherited with the logic of Aristotle's faculty psychology was "both an ingenious solution" and led to "some complex problems."[17] Aquinas drew upon Aristotle's *De Anima* as a way to address a question that began with the early Church Fathers: what will happen to the body's internal organs when the soul is in heaven? Augustine influentially declared his certainty that the internal organs must rise with the soul with the virtuous reincarnated as transparent bodies, with their viscera visible in a sublime unity.[18] The idea that the inner organs could be resurrected became a thorny problem in the medieval period, since as Walker Bynum has suggested, this logic joins material parts of the body involved in some of the least spiritual functions of the human with the soul as a shared locus of salvation.

Aquinas's problematic solution adopted Aristotle's faculty psychology as a way to unify the human's material and spiritual substance into an integrated model of soul that could encompass the different organic and immaterial parts of the self. Aquinas accomplished this integration by adopting Aristotle's "hylomorphism," the view that every living being is a composite of form and matter. In Aquinas's system of thought, Aristotle's vocabulary allows us to understand the "soul as form" to the body's matter in a way that "accounts for identity" and "that makes continuity of the fleshly stuff of body unnecessary."[19] In this definition of a literally "formal identity," Aquinas asserts that the "substantial form in man, cannot be other than the rational soul."[20]

Equally important in the medieval framing of the two-souls debate was the influence of Averroes in medieval and Renaissance psychology. During Thomas Aquinas's second term as master of theology in 1268 at the University of Paris, he framed his ideas as a direct response to Averroist definitions of the soul.[21] Indeed, many of Aquinas's most controversial ideas on the organic soul are directly developed in dialogue with Averroes's commentaries on *De Anima*. Ibn Rushd (1126–1198), commonly known by the Latinized version of his name, Averroes, was a twelfth-century commentator on Aristotle whose influential work spread across the Latin West in the thirteenth century and went on to spur several generations of "Averroist" thinkers who embraced his unique brand of Aristotelianism. Early humanist understandings of the soul viewed the rational faculty through an Averroist lens by drawing a distinction between the pure intellective and the cogitative parts of the soul that received and processed sensory information from the body. With the rise in the thirteenth century of universities in Paris and Oxford, and with Aristotle firmly implanted at the core of the curriculum, Averroes's commentaries became required reading in the effort to demystify Aristotle's more puzzling texts, including *De Anima*. In this intellectual context, Averroes came to be known as the "commentator" and was routinely read alongside Aristotle.

In many ways, the rise of the two souls in the Italian Renaissance as a distinct intellectual and theological problem can be attributed directly to the great influence of Aquinas and Averroes on later humanist philosophers. In the fifteenth century, Renaissance humanist definitions of the soul grappled with both Aquinas and Averroes and their interpretations of *De Anima*. What had previously been taken to be a unified faculty of reason was cleft in two by the Averroist humanist philosophers. For example, Alessandro Achillini posited that the intellect was "universal . . . incorporeal, inorganic [i.e., with no corresponding anatomical seat] and incorruptible."[22] By contrast, the cogitative faculty "is of a particular nature and it is the sentient power (*sensus*), a faculty in the body, with an anatomical basis, and it is the cogitative soul."[23] According to Jacopo Zabarella, in Averroes's system "a human being is human because of the cogitative faculty, and not because of the intellect."[24] In this revised model of the human rational power, immortality was understood as the "extent to which the cogitative power was able to join" with "the intellect" in an eventual psychological union. On earth, according to Paul of Venice, "a human being is not human in an absolute sense because of the cogitative soul, nor is he such because of the intellective soul, but as a result of both souls at the same time."[25]

Taken together, the Renaissance Averroist interpretation of the faculties composing the human defined the soul as a "whole . . . constituted by the intellect, and the sensitive and vegetative principle."[26] As a result, the human was split into "semi-souls," or *semi-anima*, with the organic soul composed of the cogitative, sensory, and vegetative faculties, and with the intellect as the soul's pure, immaterial, inorganic, and immortal aspect. Achillini synthesizes these ideas by positing the human as a "very composite form" with two natures: "one is material and derives from the cogitative faculty, the other is divine and derives from the intellect."[27]

This complex blending of Aristotle, Aquinas, and Averroes in defining the early modern understanding of the soul provoked a range of confused responses. Marsilio Ficino in particular questions why the faculty of reason needed to be divided into semi-souls by pondering the ramifications of a pure intellect descending down to and mingling with the level of the organic, embodied faculties. He parodies the complicated involutions of this psychology as a "divine mind, like a lackey, who will everywhere accompany this bumbling little man who hardly ever uses his own mind."[28] For Ficino, the two facets of the rational faculty proposed by his Averroist contemporaries could only be characterized as "an ontological monstrosity."[29] Despite his mockery, Ficino is an important figure in this conversation because his influential writings nonetheless made the two-souls dilemma an issue at the heart of the humanist movement in general, and not just a theological issue. Ficino places the relationship between the two souls in his definition of Neoplatonist psychology in this way:

> The motion of plants originates from the powers of nutrition and generation and is terminated in the sufficient nourishment of the plant itself and reproduction of its kind. The same is true of the powers which we and the brutes have in common with the plants. The motion of irrational animals, which characteristically pertains to sense, arises from the sensible form and the need of nature and . . . moves toward the fulfillment of bodily needs.[30]

Ficino's Neoplatonist hierarchy of living beings defines each organism by the faculties it possesses: the life of plants begins and ends with the "powers of nutrition and generation," while "irrational animals" are defined by the faculty of "sense" and the "fulfillment of bodily needs." What differentiates humans and places them on a higher plane than animals and plants is the faculty of reason: "Consequently, the rational soul in a certain manner possesses the excellence of infinity and eternity. If this were not the case, it would never characteristically incline toward the infinite."[31]

Unlike plants and animals, whose living functions "originate" and "terminate" in their lower faculties of nutrition and sensation, Ficino asserts that the "rational soul" permits the human to strive beyond the boundary of the body toward "excellence . . . and eternity." Ficino's humanist appropriation of classical faculty psychology seeks to ennoble the faculty of reason as a transcendent substance "inclining" the human "toward the infinite" in excess of the mortal and corporeal faculties of growth and sense that determine the fates of lower organisms in the chain of being.

Renaissance humanists went beyond Catholic and later Protestant theologians to articulate an intimate link between the classical soul and the possibility of human agency. If, for Reformation theology, the soul was in a state of abject slavery, then for worldly humanist philosophers, the soul was precisely the opposite: it was the site of human freedom. The association of psychology with action was perhaps most memorably promised in Pico della Mirandola's claim that the tripartite faculties of the soul confer on man the "freedom of choice . . . as the maker and molder of thyself . . . in whatever shape thou shalt prefer." The freedom of choice that he proposes is a form of self-work upon the faculties of the soul: "At man's birth, the Father placed in him every sort of seed and sprouts of every kind of life. The seeds that each man cultivates will grow and bear their fruit in him. If he cultivates vegetable seeds, he will become a plant. If the seeds of sensation, he will grow into a brute. If rational, he will come out a heavenly animal."

The humanist emphasis on the soul as the seat of agency drew from the *Nicomachean Ethics*, in which Aristotle defines "action" as structured by the operations of the organic faculties. Ultimately, Aristotle defines action as an effect of the soul mirroring the organization of the faculties themselves: "there are three things in the soul which control action and truth—sensation, reason, desire" (1139a18–1139b). These classical systems were attractive ways to define the Renaissance idea of human choice since they offered to early modern humanists, theologians, and natural philosophers a comprehensive and "quite complex account of the actions" through the vocabulary of faculty psychology and humoral physiology.[32]

The Renaissance idea of the soul as the locus of agency was profoundly influenced by the humanist rhetorical ethos, which emphasized that language, and specifically poetry, was the "highest and lasting climax" of the human mind.[33] This sentiment is emphatically defined in Aristotle's *Politics*, where he stresses language as the factor that ennobles the faculties of the human soul: "Among Living Beings, only man has language. The voice is the sign of pain and pleasure, and this is why it belongs to other living beings . . . But language is for manifesting the fitting and the unfitting and the just and the unjust . . . to have the sensation of the good and the bad is what is proper to men as opposed to other living beings."[34] According to Aristotle, man is a linguistic animal. Humans alone possess the power to rationally discern "moral qualities" from sensory particulars through the voice and a linguistic system of signs that can perceive "good and bad and right and wrong" from sensory data. More generally, the use of language and the voice as a way to understand the rational operations of thought and ethical decision-making becomes a central linguistic tenet of early modern natural philosophy and theology. We can find a pointed example in the definition of the soul articulated by Pierre de la Primaudaye in his influential

Academie Francaise, which reflects the Aristotelian logic we have seen in the *Politics*:

> For as wee saide in the beginning of our speech, our soule vseth thoughts and discourses, which cannot bee declared so long as it is inclosed in this tabernacle of flesh, without speech, wordes, and names, by meanes of which, she bringeth foorth and publisheth that which was inclosed and hidden in the secrete closet of her vnderstanding.
>
> [Note: Speach representeth all the partes of the soule.] But in men, voyces framed into wordes are signes and significations of the whole soule and minde, both generally and specially, namely of the fantasie and imagination, of reason and iudgement, of vnderstanding and memory, of will and affections. Wherefore it is an easie matter to iudge by his speach howe all these partes are affected, namely, whether they bee sound, or haue any defect in them. For if a man be dull witted, or haue his fantasie and imagination troubled, and his memory slowe and heauy, he shall haue much adoe to speake that which he thinketh and conceiueth in mind, and haue as we vse to say.[35]

For Primaudaye, language "represents" the faculties of the soul through signs, allowing for the proper functioning of imagination, reason, memory, and the higher powers of the mind. Taken together, the early modern discourse of faculty psychology defined the rational faculty that enables human agency as immanently linguistic. This linguistic psychology is important because it set the stage for an English theological and literary discourse that understood the soul's powers of reasoning and choice in terms of language.

A Vernacular English Discourse of Malleable Souls

The two-souls debate was an erudite battle fought in the halls of the clergy and the academy on the European continent. A key figure in shaping this theological discourse was Martin Luther, who was dismissive of Aquinas's thinking on the soul, since he identified him as the individual who was "responsible for the reign of Aristotle, the destroyer of godly doctrine."[36] Luther altered the tenor of the two-souls issue in substantial ways by voicing his preference for Aristotle's *Rhetoric* and *Poetics* over *De Anima* as sources from which Christian readers could profit. Ironically, the humanist Aristotelians in the Averroist tradition concurred with Luther's interpretation of Aristotle's canon, since he emphasized rhetoric, poetics, and exegesis as the core activities in the philosophical reflection on the soul.

By the time that the two-souls dilemma migrated to the English context in the late sixteenth century, the terms of the debate expanded quickly beyond

Chapter 1

✦

The Two Souls as a Problem of Christian Freedom

In a series of lectures beginning in 1500 on Aristotle's definition of the soul in *De Anima*, a professor of natural philosophy at the University of Padua, Pietro Pomponazzi, concluded that Aristotelian principles could not be used to prove the immortality of the Christian soul. Pomponazzi argued that using *De Anima* as the basis for defining the soul, which had been the canonical position of the Catholic Church since at least Saint Thomas Aquinas, could only lead one to the conclusion that the human soul was mortal. Although Pomponazzi stated at the end of his *Tractatus de immortalitate animæ* (*On the Immortality of the Soul*) that "we must say that the question of the immortality of the soul is a neutral problem," his claims and their repercussions turned out to be anything but neutral.[1] Pomponazzi's lectures and book incited a public outrage with a degree of violence unusual even for the Renaissance. Pomponazzi was accused of heresy by numerous Vatican figures, and a movement of clerics and academics called for him to be burned at the stake for his outrageous views. The leaders of several Italian cities informed Pomponazzi that he would either be burned by the public authorities, or be "handed over to the boys in the street to stone and pelt him with dirt."[2] The Venetian doge forbade the sale of his book and ordered all published copies of his text to be burned in a public ceremony. Pomponazzi feared for his life and withdrew to the relative safety of Bologna.[3]

At issue was not just the heretical nature of Pomponazzi's findings, but his very right as a philosopher to consider the question of the two souls. The Vatican condemned Pomponazzi for "playing the philosopher without due care" in asserting that philosophical logic demonstrates the mortality of the soul. The church's ultimate goal was to modify the pedagogical strategies of "every philosopher who teaches publicly in the universities" by "strictly forbidding teaching contrary to the enlightened truth of faith." Pomponazzi's treatise on the soul thus became a touchstone in a larger debate about the responsibility of lay philosophers and writers to confirm a doctrinal stance. The Vatican's confirmation of the immortality of the soul as the bedrock of church law represents the culmination of the seething public controversy initiated by a single professor of philosophy on a seemingly obscure scholastic subject.

these learned and largely Latinate realms. This was a move that was linguistic and material as much as it was geographic. The Elizabethan-era clerics John Woolton and William Perkins, who brought to English congregations the Protestant notion that original sin was a "disorder" or a "deformitie" afflicting the faculties of the organic soul, published vernacular English treatises on the soul and translated Latin texts for English readers.[37] As John King has suggested, the first wave of English religious translators "self-consciously contributed to the construction of the prevailing view that Protestantism and print go hand in hand" by exploiting "the power of the printing press to effect religious and cultural change" in the English vernacular.[38] Scholars such as Tessa Watt, Jaime Goodrich, and Brian Cummings have reminded us that we should not underestimate the importance of Renaissance material culture in shaping the contours of the two-souls debate in England, particularly the rise of the printing press and book culture.[39] The growing use of the printing press as a way to disseminate vernacular English texts and translations on faculty psychology introduced the proper stewardship and care of the soul to an increasingly literate Anglican audience beyond the narrow confines of the Latinate discourses of the church, universities, and learned societies. With the expansion of print technology in late sixteenth-century England, a growing industry of translations introduced important Continental treatises on faculty psychology to a vernacular English audience, including Primaudaye's *French Academic*, books by John Calvin, and the *Essais* of Montaigne, all of which came to shape the English conversation on the soul. As we shall see, this expansion of the textual discourse of the soul into a popular vernacular English readership is an important part of the story I have to tell.

As in the case of the Continental thinkers, the possibility of two souls also triggered confusion for sixteenth-century English philosophers across numerous discourses. Sir Walter Ralegh paradigmatically states in his *Treatise of the Soul* that the "two kinds of souls" ensure that "the substance of the soul is hardly known."[40] In the domain of natural philosophy, Sir Francis Bacon recognizes in the *Advancement of Learning* "two different emanations of souls": a "rational soul, which is divine" and which draws its origin "from the breath of God" as described in Scripture, and "the other from the wombs of the elements," which is "irrational" and "common with brutes" as described in the classical faculty psychology of Plato and Aristotle.[41] According to Bacon, many thinkers had "variously reported" and "laboriously enquired" into the different "substances and faculties" of the soul, but the presence of two souls led to a "maze" of confusion rather than a "straight way" to a unified model of the soul reconciling the classical and Christian traditions.

Amidst the theological and humanist thinkers who characterized the two-souls dilemma in terms of a maze-like confusion, "disorder," and "contagion," prominent English authors rethought the relationship of the two souls in the space of the literary. Elizabethan and Jacobean poets and playwrights could plausibly engage the issue of two souls as a question of human agency because, as Mary Thomas Crane has argued, by 1600 in England, the words "act" and "action" were already subtly shifting from the domain of humanist ethics to the language of performance.[42] This evolution in the terms of the psychological discourse toward theatrical and literary modes of representation was made possible by the dual functions of the classical organic soul as the psychological nexus responsible for both rational agency, which the humanist movement embraced, and aesthetic experience, which was familiar ground for poets and rhetoricians. The organic soul was central to Renaissance theories of poetic cognition derived from classical and humanist rhetoric and taught to English schoolboys. Sensation, emotion, and imagination, characterized by Cicero and Aristotle as the motions of the sensitive soul stirred by poetry and rhetoric, were adjacent to the intellectual soul's volitional powers enabling reasoned choice—intellect, memory, and will—which Augustine, Averroes, and Aquinas had all identified as the faculties of Christian agency placing man in a station above brute animals and plants.

The English authors studied in *The Two-Soul'd Animal* place these two interpretations of the organic soul's faculties—one rhetorical on the plane of aesthetics, the other theological on the plane of ethics—into contact as a way to construct a new mode of Christian agency by rewriting how the two souls define the subject in the malleable rhetoric of literary language described by Cicero and Aristotle. These writers attempted to shift the terms of the two-souls debate as a productive occasion to redefine a constitutive blending of classical and Christian psychologies in the literary domain. The vocabulary mobilized by their literary works as they parse through the problem of two souls in one body differs dramatically from the theological and philosophical tone of crisis we have seen, moving to a far more positive affective register of curiosity and even subtle humor. In the hands of a playwright like Shakespeare, the presence of two souls in one body ceases to be an anguishing dilemma and instead takes on the playful spin of a joke in *Twelfth Night*: "shall we rouse the night-owl in a catch that will draw three souls out of one weaver? Shall we do that?"[43] And John Donne transforms the wrenching spiritual crisis of the sixteenth century into a flirtatious reverie in his poem "Extasie," drawing the reader into the metaphysical climax of an erotic psychological reverie by which his poetry "interanimates two soules" shaped by "faculties" that "knit / that subtile knot, which makes us man."[44]

By lingering in this rhetorical space of playful literary inquisitiveness about the soul, the English authors studied in *The Two-Soul'd Animal* all used the soul as a way to experiment with the idea of Christian freedom at a time when the ideas of agency, choice, and freedom were being renegotiated in fundamental ways in the wake of the Protestant Reformation. I take the domain of the literary in this historical context as being not narrowly mimetic or aesthetic, but rather as a type of laboratory of the soul, a unique space for experimentation so as to reconceive the idea of the soul as the locus of agency and to articulate a novel vision of Christian freedom when these terms were shifting. By reclaiming an experimental space within the bounds of their literary creations to explore the points of contact and tension between the two souls in a tentative, playful, or even subversive way, their texts clear a space for a vernacular English model of the soul that broke from the Latinate discourse by rewriting how the dual psychologies define the subject in the malleable rhetoric of literary language. They assert, contra the prevailing Protestant doctrine, that the contents of the soul are not fixed, but can be rewritten by the devotional subject exercising his powers of rational choice. Their innovation lies in shifting the theological problem of the two souls into the domain of the figural and the textual. For them, the rhetorical figures composing the literary text are not simply representations or approximations of the theological abstractions defining the soul. Rather, literary language delimits a suspended medium of ideation, allowing the poet to work within the labyrinth of the psychological problem in a speculative way that can embrace the manifold paradoxes and possibilities of the soul, which the deterministic parameters of logic or empirical observation cannot tolerate.

Across their disparate genres and within their unique intellectual and literary projects, these English authors strive to transform the soul from the metaphysical basis of salvation, conventionally analyzed during the Reformation in the domains of theology or philosophy, into a malleable substance described in classical and humanist rhetoric in terms of the capacity of its faculties to be struck and reshaped through the sensory and passionate experience attending the writing and reading of literary language. Taken together, their works articulate a vernacular rhetoric of the two souls grounded in a model of textuality that turns the psychological dilemma of the sixteenth century into the basis of a novel post-Reformation vision of spiritual plasticity, which gives to the Christian subject the power to edit the soul's substance precisely as a text's type can be reset, or as its language can be rewritten.

Body and (Animal) Soul: The Critical Conversation

The Two-Soul'd Animal enters into a lively recent scholarly conversation on literary representation and the ethics of the body/soul relationship in early modern culture mediated through a materialist lens. This critical discourse has established the classical organic soul as a central component of the early modern poetics of embodiment, cognition, and devotion. Ramie Targoff's *John Donne: Body and Soul* (2008), Noel Sugimura's *"Matter of Glorious Trial"* (2009), and Garrett A. Sullivan Jr.'s *Sleep, Romance and Human Embodiment* (2013) have all recently developed, in their different ways, the ground that Gail Kern Paster broke with *Humoring the Body* (2004).[45] Paster's articulation of a "history of embodied emotions" in which "the psychological had not yet become divorced from the physiological" persuasively demonstrated that in Shakespeare's time "psychology and physiology are one."[46] Sullivan's work in particular is important for its effort to link the vegetative faculty of the soul with the literary genres of the romance and epic, setting an important precedent for embedding early modern psychology into the literary domain. All of these works on faculty psychology and humoral physiology have persuasively demonstrated that the early modern literary field was a vibrant place in which authors such as Shakespeare, Donne, and Milton engaged in critical assessments of the body/soul interface and offered counter-narratives to the dominant discourses of the soul espoused by theology and natural philosophy. *The Two-Soul'd Animal* builds upon this body of work recognizing early modern literature as an important proving ground for pre-Cartesian theories of psychology and embodiment, but complicates their claims by shifting from the dualism of body and soul to the far less familiar psychological dualism of two souls, classical and Christian.

In respecting the nuance and complexity of the soul as it was defined historically, *The Two-Soul'd Animal* attends to the different threads defining the soul's specifically psychological, material, and spiritual valences while being mindful not to flatten the myriad facets of the soul into a purely material phenomenon or object of dissection and humoral diagnosis. Paster's important suggestion that "psychology and physiology are one" has inspired a wide range of sensitive readings which, in placing the two domains into contact, nonetheless risks conflating both by collapsing the distinction, however blurry, between the two. To take but one influential example, Michael Schoenfeldt's important work on "psychological inwardness" as a "bodily condition" draws from Nietzsche's exhortation that the "soul is only a word for something about the body."[47] In a similar method, Jonathan Sawday's *The Body Emblazoned* (1995) and Richard Sugg's *The Smoke of the Soul* (2013) have focused on the prominence of anatomy and physiology in early modern discourses of the body, but in a way that verges on transmuting the soul into the body by studying the "materiality of the soul" and the "physiological nature of the soul."[48] The soul was certainly interlaced with the body's materiality in the early modern period to a surprising extent, particularly to the eyes of the modern reader. But the soul's mysterious power lay in its paradoxically dual spiritual and material nature that was not reducible to either state of being. *The Two-Soul'd Animal* persistently places Renaissance psychology and physiology into tense and almost uncomfortable contact, precisely as the authors with which I engage would have struggled as they traced the fault lines of the soul/body interface, without equating them as "one" along the lines of Paster's methodology.

Understanding the premodern soul's multiple valences in all of their complexity requires us to attend to how faculty psychology links the human to the lower animal faculties. Laurie Shannon is one of several scholars who has recently built upon Paster's allusive analysis of "identification across the species barrier," using posthumanist and ecocritical reading strategies as a productive way to understand the early modern epistemologies differentiating animal faculties from the human.[49] In her study *The Accommodated Animal* (2013), Shannon critiques the "animal/human divide" in an "unabashedly political vocabulary" that is used to define how "animals possess their own subjective investments in the world."[50] By refocusing our gaze on how the early modern world defined the human in relation to the animal as a question of the political, she has set the stage for considering how the faculties of the soul defining the plant, animal, and human can shape the idea of Christian subjectivity and the subject's agency. I take my cue from Shannon's provocative argument that places the question of the "incompletely human" historical subjects squarely in the domain of the political. Accordingly, *The Two-Soul'd Animal* focuses on the literary effort to transform the presence of vegetal, animal, and rational faculties in the body into the foundation of a new vision of a Christian subject position that embraces this hybrid psychological composition as the basis of spiritual agency.

In tracing the contours of the two-souls dilemma in the early modern English context, I am drawing upon fascinating work in adjacent fields that can only enrich our understanding of the history of the soul. Leslie Lockett's *Anglo-Saxon Psychologies in the Vernacular and Latin Traditions* (2011), which analyzes a "hydraulic" model of the soul much like Paster, Masha Raskolnikov's *Body Against Soul* (2009), and Sarah Rivett's *Science of the Soul* (2011) have all richly contextualized the relationship of faculty psychology with religiosity both before and after the early modern period.[51] In the domain of the history of ideas, Fernando Vidal's *The Sciences of the Soul* (2011) and Susan James's *Passion and Action* (2000) are broader intellectual histories that focus largely on philosophical discourses of the soul, and though they do not include literary analyses of the early modern period, they show that such consideration is due.[52]

All of these historical and philosophical works have framed the current analysis in important ways by demonstrating how the organic model of the soul inherited from Aristotle was transmitted, interpreted, and appropriated in manifold intellectual discourses in the medieval, eighteenth-century, and transatlantic historical contexts bracketing the Renaissance and Reformation. Yet particularly problematic in recent philosophical and historical scholarship on the soul, including work by Susan James, Philip Pettit, Jonathan Lear, and even Jacques Derrida, is a tendency to jump in time from Thomas Aquinas in the medieval scholastic context to the era of Thomas Hobbes and Rene Descartes, or even more jarringly from Aristotle to Freud.[53] This methodology completely bypasses the Reformation and its aftermath, which fundamentally revised the Christian subject's relationship with the soul as the basis of spiritual life and salvation. *The Two-Soul'd Animal* attempts to remedy this historical gap by tracing the complex line from Aquinas and Thomist thought, through the Reformation and the early modern period, leading us to the era of Hobbes and Descartes by the end of the present analysis. *The*

Two-Soul'd Animal uses literary texts as a way to bridge the seeming philosophical or theological gaps in the historical narrative of the early modern soul, and takes a synthetic view of the soul's history at the intersection of poetics, theology, and science in the Renaissance world.[54] It does not simply use poetry and drama to illuminate philosophical movements or to testify to a broader discursive moment, but argues that the anxiety about the two conflicting models of the soul in the sixteenth and seventeenth centuries set the stage for a debate between poetry, religion, and natural philosophy, which allows us to tell the story of the power of poetry and rhetoric to transform the early modern subject that no previous study has fully recounted.

The Two-Soul'd Animal subsequently embraces the methodological expansion of what Barbara Fuchs calls the "religious turn" in literary criticism by linking the material and spiritual dimensions of the early modern soul. In a recent review of early modern literary criticism, Fuchs has suggested that "the religious turn has become predominant in the field," with studies on medicine, the body, poetry, nationhood, and gender all "turning to religion as a critical term or even a heuristic."[55] This book unites a materialist reading strategy defining the organic soul as a function of the body, developed by scholars such as Paster, Schoenfeldt, Sullivan, and Shannon, among others, with the theological controversies of the soul understood in the Renaissance as the basis of devotion and Christian spirituality. Katharine Craik and Tanya Pollard have stated that there is a need to correct the tendency of "literary studies of the emotions and the body [that] have focused primarily on their textual representations, rather than taking seriously the complex and intimate reciprocity between books, bodies, and selves."[56] Literary texts from the Renaissance were not simply mimetic representations of bodily or psychological states; rather, they more decisively imagined that the word and the text could mold the subject in fundamental ways through the resources of classical and humanist theories of rhetoric and poetics. *The Two-Soul'd Animal* takes up Craik and Pollard's call, but does so by shifting to the psychological interplay between the text and the *soul* that was constitutive of the early modern religious subject. The central question of the story to come is how textuality and rhetoricity came to shape ideas of the soul as the basis of Christian selfhood in the early modern world in a way that does justice to the "complex and intimate" literary practices developed by the English authors I consider.

A Literary History of the Two-Souls Problem: Shakespeare, Davies, Donne, Milton

Chapter 1, "The Two Souls as a Problem of Christian Freedom," excavates the historical origins of the two-souls dilemma as a theological crisis in the wake of the Protestant Reformation, during the first decades of the sixteenth century. Sixteenth-century religious thinkers attempted to respond to Thomas Aquinas's recognition in the *Summa Theologiae* that "it would seem that besides the intellectual soul there are in man other souls essentially different from one another, such as the sensitive soul and the nutritive soul." In this chapter, I focus on Pietro Pomponazzi's controversial claim that the classical organic soul is not ennobling, as Neoplatonist thinkers would have it, but rather leads to a basic confusion about human nature: "man is clearly not of a simple nature, since he includes three souls—the vegetative, the sensitive, and the intellective—and that he claims a twofold nature for himself, since he exists neither unqualifiedly mortal nor unqualifiedly immortal but embraces both natures." I track the explosive response to Pomponazzi's assertions in the immediate Catholic context, but also as a way to understand the subsequent Protestant interpretation of the presence of two souls in one body, which viewed the organic faculties as the scar of original sin emblazoned upon each person. The Protestant model of the classical soul as scar comes to shape the commonplace Elizabethan understanding of original sin as a "disorder" or "contagion" afflicting the organic soul, resulting in a fractured or split psyche within the Christian subject. The Elizabethan clerics responsible for translating the Protestant doctrine of the two-souls issue for a broad vernacular English audience transformed the abstruse psychological crisis into a problem to be negotiated on the terrain of popular rhetoric and vernacular textuality, which profoundly influenced all of the authors studied in the subsequent chapters.

Chapter 2, "Hamlet's 'Soulbending Sovereignty' and Shakespeare's Rhetorical Soul," takes as its cue recent suggestions of Stephen Greenblatt and Joshua Scodel that Shakespeare's drama attempted to carve out a fraught space for freedom within the political constraints of the authoritarian Elizabethan and Jacobean world.[57] I propose that Shakespeare imagined the idea of freedom in religious terms, and his plays participated in a vernacular folk psychology of the two souls that led him to articulate a new mode of Christian liberty. In *Hamlet*, Shakespeare specifically rejects the extremely oppressive, but widely employed, body of tropes defining the soul in terms of imprisonment, bondage, binding in chains, and servitude. Shakespeare reverses the Protestant line of thinking, and turns the susceptibility of the Aristotelian soul to be disrupted and altered by theatrical fiction and stirring rhetorical address into the positive freedom of the Christian subject to redefine his or her soul in ways not constrained by the bondage of God's law. Hamlet is therefore not paralyzed between thought and action, as the story normally goes. Shakespeare's *Hamlet* represents the most striking attempt to resolve the early modern paradox of two souls in the rhetoric of theater. Shakespeare identifies the power of rhetoric to disrupt and reshape the workings of the organic soul's faculties as a form of agency giving individuals the ability to redefine how the soul composes them as Christian subjects unshackled from the chains of psychological servitude.

Chapter 3, "Sir John Davies and the Lyrical Psychology of the English Commonwealth," reads Davies's widely read poems of the 1590s, *Nosce Teipsum* and *Orchestra*, alongside his prose legal tracts on common law and Ireland to unexpected effect. This chapter complicates the assumption that Davies was a conservative legal theorist justifying imperial expansion and the violent suppression of native populations based on common law principles. In his poetry, Davies proposes to synthesize the two souls into a political harmony, and a more useful model for a commonwealth, through the meter and rhythm of lyric poetry. The metrical regularity of poetic language gives structure to the otherwise chaotic motions of the organic soul, compelling its faculties and passions to "dance" in an organized unity, in precisely the same manner that individuals in a disorganized mob unite by consent to form a commonwealth. By figuring the soul's faculties as lyric instruments (for example, a lyre, or as a versified text to be written and recited as a beautiful song), the organic soul can enjoy the rhythmic metrical unity of "consent" as the Christian soul does. He applies this idea to his own legal thinking by imagining the English nation as a collective "dance" of citizens regulated by the periodicity of poetic meter, and not as the traditional model of the "body politic" led by the king as the rational faculty governing over the unruly body.

Chapter 4, "Be Thou *Verbum*: John Donne's Printerly *Techne* of the Soul," takes as its point of departure Donne's 1627 sermon that redefines ontology as a form of textuality: the will to "print a book" must be reconceived as the desire "*to be*" a book. Donne's materialist statement of *imprimo ergo sum* in the final years of his life represents the culmination of a lifelong project, spanning his early poetry to his final sermons, that was haunted by the two-souls paradox. From his early *Songs and Sonnets*—which likened the two souls to two lovers through a vocabulary of graphical traces such as etchings, carvings, and circles—to the *Second Anniversary*, which figured the two souls as complementary dual faces of a reversible inscribed sheet, Donne finally arrived in his late sermons at his master metaphor of the printing press. Donne's works translate the paradox of two souls into a question of textuality, shifting the problem of the psyche into the linguistic medium of the poet and preacher. Donne's innovation lies in moving the contradiction of two souls away from the terrain of theology, natural philosophy, or medicine by showing how technologies such as printing and engraving offer an alternative material vocabulary to think about the two souls in a way that was not irreducibly paradoxical. Moreover, the metaphor of print opens the possibility of a psychological agency to rewrite the soul as a mode of publication. Donne suggests that the soul figured as a printed text or engraving is fundamentally unstable, since it is open to multiple iterations of editing, revision, and reprinting; but this instability is a positive attribute, since it introduces a form of malleability immanent to the human psyche.

Chapter 5, "From Animal to *Anima*: Milton's 'Living Soul' and the Promise of Discursive Reason," demonstrates how John Milton differs from the other authors studied in the book because he does not view the two-souls problem as a constitutive difference defining the Christian subject that needed to be addressed, remedied, or exploited. Milton asserts in *Paradise Lost* and *De Doctrina Christiana* that the classical organic soul *is* the Christian soul described in Scripture, but it is one that needs to be refined and converted to a more spiritual form capable of attaining salvation over the course of one's life. For Milton, language, or what he terms "discourse," is central to this process: he argues that the substance of the soul is linguistic, and that language as the matter of reason enables this conversion into a spiritual form. For Milton, it is the organic soul's intrinsic instability and its capacity to be continually reshaped through the processes of "discursive reason," and not its stable essence, truth, or goodness, which ultimately draws us closer to the state of angels.

The "Intimate Caesura"

In the epigraph to this introduction, I invoke Giorgio Agamben and his suggestion that the "articulation of the concept of life has a foundational moment" in the history of Western thought.[58] Just as God created life through a divine speech act in Genesis, Agamben identifies a moment of parallel significance from classical antiquity, Aristotle's definition of the soul in *De Anima*, as the generative locus of "life." In many ways, Agamben's focus on *De Anima* as a decisive moment takes up Walter Benjamin's musing, noted in the epigraph, that "it might be well worthwhile to track down the origin of the dogma of the sacredness of life" that differentiates man "essentially from the life of animals and plants." However, as Agamben observes, Aristotle's foundational articulation of the soul as the principle of life is not a definition in any formal way: "it is important to observe that Aristotle in no way defines what life is: he limits himself to breaking it down, by isolating . . . a series of distinct and correlated faculties or potentialities (nutrition, sensation, thought)."[59] The Aristotelian legacy of defining the soul in terms of its faculties constitutes the human according to a logic of internal psychological difference, instead of the positive assertion of a working definition. Agamben, however, recognizes the historical power of the Aristotelian model of the divided soul as "a mobile border within living man," since, ironically, throughout medieval and early modern systems of thought, "without this intimate caesura the very decision of what is human and what is not would probably not be possible."[60]

Before Descartes, this "intimate caesura" of the divided soul was the terrain upon which the idea of the "human" was negotiated. Agamben proposes a "new way" to imagine the human in a more complex manner than the familiar "conjunction of a body and soul, of a living thing and a *logos*, of a natural (or animal) element and a supernatural or social or divine element" to which we too easily appeal. He urges us instead to think of the human as an emergent property of "what results from the incongruity of these two elements" that resist conjunction. In tracing the evolution of the "practical and political mystery of separation" within the soul, the chapters that follow tell the story of this constitutive ontological disjunction—our "intimate caesura"—that defined the human throughout the medieval and early modern periods. In recounting this story, my point is to reveal how "even the most luminous sphere of our relations with the divine depends, in some way, on that darker one which separates us from the animal."[61]

In this chapter, I argue that debates about the two souls were reinvigorated in sixteenth-century Europe when readers such as Pomponazzi, and later Martin Luther and Philip Melanchthon, revisited how Aristotle, Averroes, and Aquinas defined the classical faculties in a Christian context. Pomponazzi's critique of Averroes and Aquinas came at a time when the idea of the soul itself was changing at the onset of the Protestant Reformation and its interrogation of the basic tenets of the Christian faith. Pomponazzi's identification of the problem of two souls in the composition of the individual Christian subject set the terms for a vibrant cultural debate dominating much of sixteenth-century philosophy and theology. The controversial line of thinking he triggered has been insufficiently acknowledged in the literary and philosophical history of the period. For the purposes of the present analysis, this chapter will outline the problem at the center of the book's narrative as a whole. How did the presence of two souls become a cultural crisis in early sixteenth-century Europe? How did this debate migrate to England, and why would a seemingly esoteric theological debate find its way into the texts of some of the most prominent early modern authors writing in the English vernacular?

From Paul to Aquinas: Aristotle in a Christian Worldview

To understand why Pomponazzi's positions were so controversial, we need to first place his ideas into context, particularly in relation to patristic and medieval debates about salvation and the nature of the soul. The biblical precedent was set by Saint Paul in 1 Corinthians 15, where he describes resurrection and salvation by employing a metaphor of the seed, drawing on the language of organic growth as located in the faculty of nutrition. As a result, "for most of Western history, body was understood primarily as the locus of biological process."[4] Paul's use of plant metaphors of growth and change caused a good deal of consternation in the medieval period, because the "organic processes of nutrition and growth are treated as threatening to the nature of things," since growth can quickly lead to decay.[5] Indeed, the early church figures, including Augustine, Gregory of Nyssa, and Origen, equated "procreation and nutrition" with "putrefaction and death," and with damnation associated with "eternal digestion." By contrast, this fear of the faculty of nutrition's power to grow and change the shape of the body as an inevitable slipping into the decay and digestion of the self recasts salvation as the "triumph over the food chain."[6]

The obsession with growth governed by organs of the faculty of nutrition changes dramatically with the twelfth-century shift to the *soul* as the locus of Christian selfhood. As Caroline Walker Bynum has suggested, "the acquisition and appropriation in the early thirteenth century of key Aristotelian concepts, such as substance, meant that basic ideas of nature and human nature had to be reconsidered."[7] Thomas Aquinas precipitated this shift by rejecting Paul's organic seed metaphor as the privileged bodily figure of resurrection in favor of an alternative idiom in which the soul constituted the core of human identity. Aquinas's *Summa Theologiae* (ca. 1265) was the "established and accepted synthesis of Aristotelian and Christian doctrine" touching upon all areas of doctrinal thought, but very specifically on the nature of the soul.[8] Aquinas's work was in large part a response to and expansion of *De Anima*. As Susan James has suggested, "Aquinas takes over Aristotle's philosophy as he understands it and incorporates it into a systematic account of the place of humanity in God's creation."[9] Aquinas was motivated by the need to align the authoritative texts of a pagan Greek philosopher with the teachings of Scripture and the early Church Fathers. Could the soul promised in the Old and New Testaments be reconciled with the Aristotelian soul? Were the Christian and classical souls different, or could the Aristotelian soul be recuperated into the Christian fold?

In probing these questions, Aquinas adopts much of Aristotle's logic, including the model of the soul as the form of the body's matter, and the idea that the powers of the soul are organized into the three faculties of nutrition, sense, and reason. Aquinas's doctrinal task lay in synthesizing the finite scope of the three faculties bounded by the human body and its capacity for life—what we would today call biology—with the infinite scale of God's power and the promise of the soul's immortality beyond embodied life. His solution to this logical knot relied upon a redefinition of the sensitive faculty that humans, God's chosen creations, share with all animals.[10] He observes that animals may not have the capacity to reason as humans do, but they nonetheless exhibit behaviors that mimic volitional actions that are recognizable to us. Such behaviors are a response to external stimuli mediated by the sense organs in both humans and other animals, but these sensory inputs are processed differently. For lower animals, the senses are organized and processed by the *estimatio naturalis*, an involuntary mechanism that propels an animal to respond to an external stimulus, but in a way that is not intentional or conscious. Aquinas's famous example is that of a sheep seeing a wolf who instinctively responds to the visual cue of the predator as a prompt to flee.

By contrast, humans employ a subtly different power in the sensitive faculty in such situations; a "particular reason" that is not merely a mode of involuntary estimation, but rather a form of cogitation and reasoning embedded within the faculty of sense itself, serving as a type of bridge between the raw senses and the higher powers of memory and imagination in the rational faculty.[11] This sensory search engine of sorts processes information more quickly than the deliberate and logical reasoning processes of the intellect and in certain circumstances can be very useful in hastening action. When conflicts emerge between differing emotions, memories, and sensory stimuli, they do not mark some flaw within the higher faculty of reason, or between reason and sense. Instead, conflict is localized to the "particular reason" of the sensitive faculty. For loftier questions beyond the urgency of fight or flight, the faculty of sense relays its information to the rational faculty for contemplation of "universal" logic by the "agent intellect," as opposed to the merely "particular" logic housed by the senses that is closer to the instinctive, pre-rational response of animals.

We can see glimmers of why Aquinas's revision of Aristotle was attractive in the medieval world, since it synthesized the classical and Christian models of the soul. Aquinas concedes, following Aristotle, that humans do share faculties in common with animals and plants. What differentiates humans are two different inflections of reason, one sensory and one intellective, housed in different faculties of the soul and directed to different ends. The "particular reason" of the sense faculty is closer to the state of animals, derives its function from the sense organs, and concerns itself with the brute functions of living in the physical world. Far nobler is the "agent intellect" of the rational faculty that thinks of universals beyond life and beyond the material world.[12] The "particular reason" leans closer to Aristotle's pagan understanding of reason, while the "agent intellect" corresponds to the promise of truth beyond the mere precarity of life, as promised by Scripture. This Thomist solution attempted to unite the best qualities of both souls: the Christian soul was now intrinsically rational, and the rational soul was now immortal and capable of being redeemed. The passionate and animalistic conflicts and perturbations of the soul that Aristotle identified were now sequestered in the pseudo-rational "particular reason" of the sensory faculty.

As a result of the separation of intellect from particular reason, Aquinas distills human identity into the soul: "Beatitude is the perfection of man as man. And since man is man not through his body but through his soul . . . it follows that man's beatitude does not consist chiefly otherwise than in an act of soul and passes from the soul on to the body by a kind of overflow."[13] Departing from the Pauline organic logic of growth embedded in the body's nutritive functions, Aquinas brings us to an idea of the self defined exclusively by the soul, with the body as a "kind of overflow" from it, and in which "man is man . . . through his soul." Aquinas isolates human identity in even narrower terms by suggesting that human individuality is contained exclusively in the intellective power of the rational faculty. Aquinas's influential views led to a decisive shift in the fourteenth century to the primacy of the soul in the theological discourse and curriculum of the major universities.

Aquinas's views were not without controversy, however, because a conservative backlash from 1270 to 1290 contested his idea of the soul as discrete from organic matter, which made the body's materiality a small part in the composition of Christian identity. The dramatic about-face Aquinas stimulated—from Paul's organic seed metaphor rooted in the physical processes of the faculty of nutrition that dominated much of the early medieval theological conversation, to an immaterial idea of identity narrowly located in the intellective powers of the rational faculty—led many Christian thinkers in the late medieval and early Renaissance periods to call for a middle way between the extremes of materialist growth and pure intellect.

Renaissance Averroism and Pomponazzi: The Two Souls and Christian Freedom

The Islamic philosopher Averroes became a useful counterpoint between the poles of Paul's seed and Aquinas's intellect in the Italian Renaissance. Averroist interpretations of the soul, particularly as a lens to rethink Aristotle and Aquinas, became popular from the thirteenth century and into sixteenth-century Italy. These accounts set the tone for much of the humanist discussion on the nature of the soul. P. O. Kristeller has suggested that the wide-ranging body of scholars who adopted an Averroist strain of thought constituted a school of "secular Aristotelians," and more recently, the Averroist impact on the early modern understanding of the soul has gained attention as an area of study.[14] The roster of secular Aristotelians with an Averroist bent includes foundational figures of Renaissance humanism such as Agostino Nifo, Alessandro Achillini, Giovanni Pico della Mirandola, and Paul of Venice. The importance of Averroes in the Renaissance discourse of the soul made Aristotle's *De Anima* a core text of the university curriculum.[15]

Given the vitality of Averroist thought in the Italian Renaissance, it is fair to say that the presence of two souls in one body only became a problem in the early modern period because of the broad impact of Averroist readings of Aristotle's *De Anima*, particularly in the theory of semi-anima or divided souls, which are split between the cogitative and intellective facets of the faculty of reason. The Renaissance Averroists expanded the scope of Averroes's own line of reasoning by widening the split between the organic, material, and the inorganic, immaterial parts of the soul to all of the faculties beyond reason, including sensation and nutrition. In an early Renaissance articulation of this Averroist logic, Paul of Venice invokes in his *Libros De Anima Explanatio* (1415–20) the idea of a double soul: "The human being, apart from the partial faculties (vegetative and sensitive), has two total faculties, i.e. the sensitive cogitative, which is generable and corruptible, and performs functions of inherence and information, and the intellective one, perpetual and eternal, which informs but does not inhere."[16] Critical to this idea of "two souls" was Averroes's claim that the cogitative faculty was defined by its relationship with the lower faculty of sense, and not with the intellect: "the cogitative faculty is the culmination of the representative activity of the senses." Jacopo Zabarella takes up this idea in declaring that the cogitative faculty is the unique *forma informans* (formal principle) of the human, "which defines the genus 'animal' as a human species, so that a human being is human because of this faculty, and not because of the intellect." In making this claim, Zabarella refers to Themistius's observation that there is "placed in man another soul, subject to multiplication."[17]

Critically, the Averroist division of the soul's faculties set the stage for the work of Pietro Pomponazzi, who as professor of philosophy at Padua worked alongside Alessandro Achillini. Pomponazzi's lectures on the immortality of the soul attempted to bring together on one hand the Averroist psychology drawing the distinction between the cogitative and intellective facets of reason with the Christian thought of Aquinas on the other, which elevated the power of the intellect above all else. Pomponazzi sought to place these two lines of thought on the soul's faculties into provocative contact, so as to investigate the possibility of proving the immortality of the soul promised by Scripture and by Paul in Corinthians.

Pomponazzi precipitated a furor as he sought to demonstrate that both the Thomist and the Averroist solutions to the simultaneous existence of the classical and Christian soul were based upon flimsy logic: "unless I am mistaken, the Commentator [Averroes], St. Thomas, and whoever thinks that Aristotle judged the human intellect to be truly immortal are far from the truth."[18] For Pomponazzi, putting the Christian soul, assumed to be immortal and immaterial, into the place of Aristotle's faculty of reason necessarily places the Christian soul into relation with the two lower organic faculties of sense and nutrition because Aristotle's idea of intellect relies upon the body for its proper function.[19] Pomponazzi writes, "The intellective soul is the act of a physical and organic body. Since, therefore, in its being the intellect is the act of a physical and organic body, it will thus also depend in all its functioning on some organ, either as subject or object. Hence it will never be totally released from some organ."[20] In Pomponazzi's reading of Aristotle, the intellectual soul owes a great debt to the lower faculties of the body. The intellect is "the act of a physical and organic body," and as such its ostensibly immaterial cognitive activities "depend in all its functioning on some organ." The unexpected effect of the Thomist solution therefore is that the mortal and material operations of the body's organs are turned into the necessary adjunct of the putatively immortal and immaterial rational Christian soul. Rather than lift the Aristotelian rational soul onto a higher plane of Christian immateriality and immortality, Pomponazzi argues that the Thomist solution has the unfortunate side effect of dragging the immortal and immaterial Christian soul into a necessary relation with the fallen, flesh-bound state of the body. In the Thomist solution, the Christian rational soul becomes trapped in the materiality and mortality of the body's organs, and cannot ever be "totally released" into a purely immaterial or immortal state.

Following the Thomist solution to its logical conclusion, then, simply mires the Christian soul in the body's fallen organs. Based on this conclusion, Pomponazzi argues that Aquinas's medieval solution unifying the Aristotelian and Christian souls cannot be upheld. Pomponazzi suggests that one must acknowledge that the human possesses two different natures that cannot be unified into a single idea of the soul.

> Man is clearly not of simple, but of multiple, not of certain, but of ambiguous nature, and he is to be placed as a mean between mortal and immortal things . . . For in performing the functions of the vegetative and of the sensitive soul, which cannot be performed without a bodily and perishable instrument, man assumes mortality. However, in knowing and willing, operations which are held to be performed without any bodily instrument, since they prove separability and immateriality, and these in turn prove immortality, man is to be numbered among the immortal things.[21]

Human nature cannot be unified, and must be understood as "multiple," encompassing both mortal, physical characteristics alongside immaterial activities such as knowing and willing. The inaccurately "simple" and "certain" solution proposed by the medieval scholastics must be replaced by an understanding of the human that is "multiple" and "ambiguous." The Aristotelian soul's faculties of sense and vegetation require a "bodily and perishable instrument," and therefore they assume a mortal, physical condition. By contrast, Aquinas insisted that the rational soul works "without any bodily instrument," and its purity enables humanity to strive toward the plane of "immortal things." However, Pomponazzi counters that each person is a composite of mortal and material faculties on one hand, and immortal and immaterial faculties on the other, which cannot be deemed pure or unified in any simple way. "From these facts the whole conclusion can be drawn, that man is clearly not of a simple nature, since he includes three souls—the vegetative, the sensitive, and the intellective—and that he claims a twofold nature for himself, since he exists neither unqualifiedly mortal nor unqualifiedly immortal but embraces both natures."[22]

Moving away from the medieval solution, Pomponazzi reimagines human nature in a more complex way than a simple separation between two parts of the soul. He introduces the different logic of two intermeshed souls that cannot be separated. The human includes three faculties or powers of the soul—the vegetative, the sensitive, and the intellective—two of which are mortal and physical, and one that should be immortal and immaterial. However, in using the term "include" to describe the relation between the three Aristotelian faculties, there is no clear boundary delimiting the rational faculty from the sensitive and vegetative faculties, and all three must be combined in a confused mixture of mortal and immortal qualities. We must therefore "embrace both natures," recognizing the physical embeddedness of the mortal and immortal souls, evoking the image of two intermeshed bodies locked in an "embrace" where it is impossible to discern where one individual ends and the other begins. Pomponazzi pushes the two souls into an uncomfortably close contact, "claiming" both souls as a possession, swallowing up the rational powers into the domain of the mortal faculties by "inclusion," and ultimately insisting upon the physical embrace of two souls in a situation where spatial separation is impossible. The faculty of reason does not reside on a pure plane of immortal and immaterial ideation, since the physical embrace between the two souls locks the powers of reason into the workings of the organic faculties of the classical soul. By this point, Pomponazzi's claim that the rational Christian soul can "never be totally released from some organ" becomes clear. The physical organs of the Aristotelian faculties consume the immortal Christian soul and will not easily let go of their embrace—the soul will "never be released."

In making such a controversial claim about the mortality of the human soul, however, Pomponazzi realizes that the existence of a mortal soul would suggest that all religions, all philosophers from Socrates to the Renaissance, and indeed "the whole world is deceived and that a widespread belief (of the immortal soul) is completely false."[23] He suggests, however, that this provocative claim is part of his point since, quite ironically, facing one's mortality allows one to attain a state of true Christian virtue, whereas unquestioning belief in the lie of the soul's immortality leads to a state of abject servility. He explains, "Those who claim that the soul is mortal seem better to save the grounds of virtue than those who claim it to be immortal. For the hope of reward and the fear of punishment seem to suggest a certain servility, which is contrary to the grounds of virtue."[24] Those who believe in the immortal soul are motivated only by the "hope of reward" and the "fear of punishment." Such a crude basis for ethical decision-making sinks the human down to the level of the animal or the slave who is merely motivated by fear of the whip or the hope for pleasure. Hoping for immortal reward in heaven and fearing immortal punishment in hell are not truly free or virtuous grounds for ethics, since the motivation of reward/punishment operates at the level of crude animal instinct. Thus, believing in the immortal soul drags the human down to a level of base "servility" that is antithetical to Christian freedom. Pomponazzi specifies that believers in the immortal soul are servile since they confusedly exhibit "uncertain action, and without any end," which cannot be the basis of ethical agency.[25]

By contrast, he praises the freedom of the mortal human to choose by harnessing the powers of the soul's faculties. Against the "servile" believers of the soul's immortality, Pomponazzi prefers the true virtue of the person who questions this received truth and entertains the possibility that the soul is mortal:

> Wherefore the human soul has some of the properties of the Intelligences and some of the properties of all material things; whence it is that when it performs functions through which it agrees with the Intelligences, it is said to be divine and to be changed into a God; but when it performs the functions of beasts, it is said to be changed into a beast . . . Some have said that man is a great marvel, since he is the whole world and can change into every nature, since to him is

> given the power to follow whatever property of things he may prefer. Therefore the ancients were telling the right fable when they said that some men had been made into gods, some into lions, some into wolves, some into plants, some into stones, and so on; since some men have attained intellect, some sense, some the powers of the vegetative soul, and so on. Therefore those who place bodily pleasures above moral or intellectual virtues rather produce a beast than a god; those who put riches first, rather gold; whence the former are to be called beasts, the latter insensate.[26]

In many ways, this passage represents the culmination of Pomponazzi's argument. Pomponazzi proposes that the recognition of the soul's mortal nature leads to true human freedom, in contrast to the servility of reward and punishment occurring with the false promise of the immortal soul. He therefore defines Christian freedom as the ability to configure the three faculties of the organic soul into different arrangements as one "prefers." In Pomponazzi's model of freedom, each human has the power to choose and configure the faculties of his soul either in pursuit of an ethical life, or in pursuit of bestial pleasures and sin. Therefore, when individuals strive to perfect their intellectual faculties, they are "said to be divine and changed into a God," whereas individuals who "place bodily pleasures above moral or intellectual virtues" spiral downward into the subhuman state of a sensory "beast." Even further, those who "put riches first" sink into the "insensate" state of an inanimate object without a soul, such as gold. The transformations of each type of individual correspond directly to the three organic faculties of the Aristotelian soul. In each of these cases, individuals have the power to choose the specific faculty of the organic soul they "prefer" to use as a template in defining the ethical trajectory of their lives. The power of choice in Pomponazzi's model is defined as the selection of the mortal organic faculties of the Aristotelian soul, and humans are unique among living creatures insofar as they can "change into every nature" according to this freedom of the soul. Pomponazzi emphasizes that such possibility of human change is a form of agency, driven by the power of choice; that a human possesses "the power to follow whatever property of things he may prefer." Man's "great marvel" lies in the possibility of freedom to the extent that one can "prefer" and "change" the various properties of his soul. In these moves, Pomponazzi redefines what is worthy of wonder in the human soul. No longer is the possibility of immortality or even salvation beyond life the primary "marvel" and "power" of the human soul. The human soul is a "great marvel" and holds a unique station above animals since it has the capacity to "prefer" the operations of some faculties over others, and has the power to modify the condition of the soul's faculties in a free way.

For Pomponazzi, then, concepts such as freedom and servility are not defined in relation to God or a king. Rather, the ultimate power of the mortal human soul lies in our relation to the state of our own faculties and in the ability to choose and be changed by the selection of such faculties. Acknowledging that the faculties of the soul are mortal quite surprisingly leads humans to a state of freedom in relation to their own souls, as opposed to the "servility" and "uncertain action" guided by the fictitious ruse of the immortal soul. Pomponazzi's argument was revolutionary both in the substance of its critique of unquestioning Catholics, who are cast as impotent slaves in this narrative, and also in its audacious presumption that a scholar could interrogate and revise the doctrinally established Thomist definition of the soul in a way that bypasses the authority of the church. In the decade before the Reformation, Pomponazzi began a process of questioning who has the right to think and to speak about the soul. For his part, however, he chose at the end of his text the path of "servility" in order to save his life in the face of the angry mobs who he knew would seek to burn him at the stake for heresy: "And therefore these are the things that seem to me must be said in this matter, yet always submitting myself in this and in other matters to the Apostolic See. At Bologna, in the fourth year of the Pontificate of Leo X. To the praise of the indivisible Trinity, etc."[27] In the final lines of his text, Pomponazzi himself chooses a path of "submission" to the Apostolic See and Pope Leo X, opting for subjection under Vatican law.[28] Such a move, however, was insufficient to offset the outrage. The scandal incited by Pomponazzi's teachings triggered a major crisis in church thought, with dozens of texts and pamphlets attempting to refute Pomponazzi's logic. Pomponazzi's work set the terms for a debate over the nature of the two souls that would continue throughout the sixteenth and seventeenth centuries, as theologians, natural philosophers, poets, and rhetoricians would struggle in their own way to answer the basic question asked by Pomponazzi that provoked anxiety: is the mortal state of the classical organic soul the condition for Christian freedom? Pomponazzi's work thus established the two-souls problem in Continental Europe and England as more than a theological issue, but more vitally as an issue renegotiating the idea of Christian freedom.

The Vatican's Response

Pomponazzi's work provoked a great deal of anxiety, since it implied that the bedrock of Christian doctrine, the immortality of the soul, was proved on flimsy logical grounds, and as such, Christian faith was built like a house of cards. The public furor over Pomponazzi's thinking ultimately incited a vigorous response from the Vatican, culminating in the Fifth Lateran Council meeting under the leadership of Pope Leo X in the St. John Lateran Basilica in Rome. On December 19, 1513, the council published a polemical papal decree on "the nature of the rational soul."[29] The papal bull confirmed the immortality of the soul by citing both Aristotle's *De Anima* and scriptural authority. The Lateran Council's decree states that Pomponazzi's assertion of the mortal soul called into question the basic truth of Christian doctrine: the possibility of salvation and the reward of afterlife.

> Whoever hates his life in this world, will keep it for eternal life and when he promises eternal rewards and eternal punishments to those who will be judged according to the merits of their life; otherwise, the incarnation and other mysteries of Christ would be of no benefit to us, nor would resurrection be something to look forward to, and the saints and the just would be (as the Apostle says) the most miserable of all people.

If the soul were indeed mortal, the entire Christian religion would be a lie. Without the promise of immortality, the "incarnation and other mysteries of Christ would be of no benefit to us, nor would resurrection be something to look forward to." Calling the immortal soul into question would turn the holiest Christians, the saints and the just, into simply "the most miserable of people."

Although the explicit purpose of the papal decree aimed to renounce Pomponazzi's position and force a change of pedagogical method in universities, the Lateran Council's document does not question the basic logic that made Pomponazzi's work so controversial: that the human possesses two souls, one mortal, and one immortal, and the combination of the two drags the immortal Christian soul into the flesh-bound condition of the mortal Aristotelian soul: "For the soul not only truly exists of itself and essentially as the form of the human body, as is said in the canon of our predecessor of happy memory, Pope Clement V, promulgated in the general council of Vienne, but it is also immortal . . . this is clearly established from the gospel when the Lord says 'They cannot kill the soul.'" According to these two parallel definitions proposed by the Lateran Council, the soul is "the form of the body," using Aristotle to cast the soul as the form of the body's mortal state, while on a second, parallel track that is structured grammatically by a "but . . . also" clause, the soul is understood as immortal. Thus, the soul is pulled in two directions within this definition: on one pole toward the body and its mortality, and on the other pole toward immortality. Even as the Lateran Council insists that "truth cannot contradict truth," its definition of the immortal soul counterposes two equally true souls existing within each Christian subject.[30]

The division of the soul within the Lateran Council's own definition of the immortal soul reveals why Pomponazzi's thinking provoked such a violent controversy. Pomponazzi argues that two souls are built into the Christian definition of the soul, with a mortal soul defined in the classical tradition and an immortal soul based on Scripture. The Lateran Council's own proof of the soul's immortality demonstrates the extent to which these two souls exist implicitly in the canonical definition of the soul. Although medieval Christian thinkers had acknowledged the presence of two souls, no one prior to Pomponazzi had adequately recognized its consequences. In taking Pomponazzi's provocations seriously enough to merit a formal response, the Vatican brought the question of two souls into the foreground of theological debates in the years just before the Protestant Reformation, drawing attention to the fact that the existence of two souls was a major problem destabilizing the unity of Christian thought.

The Protestant Soul: Grace, Free Will, Bondage

In 1517, four years after the Catholic Church's official dispute with Pomponazzi, Martin Luther triggered the Protestant Reformation with the publication of his 95 Theses. Luther was familiar with Pomponazzi's work, and indeed accepted Pomponazzi's interpretation of Aristotle and the soul as an accurate understanding of the issue.[31] Luther did not accept the full consequences of Pomponazzi's claims, however, and the Protestant response to Pomponazzi's problem of the two souls differed substantially from the official Vatican reaffirmation of church law. Unlike the Catholic scholastic tradition, which tried to unify the organic faculties of the Aristotelian soul with the immortal Christian soul into a single hierarchy, Protestant doctrine turned the Aristotelian faculties into the diseased substance of man's fallen condition, differentiated from the immortal Christian soul as the locus of grace and salvation.

Luther's definition of the soul was sharpened in his debate with Desiderius Erasmus and Johann Eck on Christian spirit and the possibility of free will. Erasmus and Eck drew a strong distinction between the flesh and the spirit, locating human agency in the purity of the spirit. Luther rejected the notion that the Christian "spirit" signified the rational faculty of the soul.[32] Rather, for Luther, the entire man, encompassing both "flesh" and "spirit," composed the substance of God's grace.[33] Luther believed that this more expansive view of grace beyond the narrow confines of reason was necessary because after the fall, the rational faculty was "limited in its spiritual ability and clouded in its knowledge of the sacred."[34] As a result, grace was not isolated to spirit and rational choice, but also needed to take the flesh and its fallen nature into account.[35] Luther's view was that the entire human, both flesh and spirit, was subject to God's judgment, and therefore salvation or damnation shaped his understanding of free will. It is Luther's ironically more capacious view of grace encompassing all of the body and soul that leads him to critique Erasmus on free will.

For Luther, the fallen soul's disorder could be characterized most accurately as a state of simultaneous freedom and abjection, which he describes in his 1520 *Christian Liberty*:

> I shall set down the following two propositions concerning the freedom and the bondage of the spirit: A Christian is a perfectly free lord of all, subject to none. A Christian is a perfectly dutiful servant of all, subject to all. These two theses seem to contradict each other. If, however, they should be found to fit together they would serve our purpose beautifully. Both are Paul's own statements, who says in I Cor. 9, "For though I am free from all men, I have made myself a slave to all." What can it profit the soul if the body is well, free, and active, and eats, drinks, and does as it pleases? For in these respects even the most godless slaves of vice may prosper.[36]

The Christian experiences the states of freedom and bondage at once, without contradiction. In Luther's example, if the body is well and free, or suffers as a "slave of vice," this does not affect the soul. By contrast, faith is a free choice to enter into a "royal marriage" with Christ, who is the "bridegroom" to the soul as bride.[37] For Luther, this is the condition of "true and spiritual liberty, making our hearts free" through the operations of "natural reason." For Luther, the faculty of reason may lead the human to strive freely to attain this "royal marriage" of grace but, by contrast, the fallen "disorder" of the lower faculties pulls us toward the slavery of vice, struggling against the rational spirit that may voluntarily accept faithful union with Christ. All of the faculties, whether spiritual or material, are subject to grace in Luther's system, and therefore Protestant theology problematized the idea of freedom into a struggle between a rational choice to freely enter a "marriage" with grace, and a fallen "will in bondage," a compulsion to be enslaved by sin. Protestant thinkers redefined the lower faculties of the soul, in their "disorder," as the scar of the fall.[38] In the dominant Protestant account of the two souls, the fallen "disorder" and disruption of the soul's lower faculties locked in conflict with the faculty of reason's power of choice and striving for grace defined the Christian subject in a state of psychological paralysis, if not contradiction, in Luther's eyes.

Philip Melanchthon's definition of the soul was important in the Protestant context, because while Luther was stridently anti-Aristotelian, Melanchthon by contrast was the most learned Protestant Aristotelian. Melanchthon sought to reconcile Lutheran tenets with the psychology of Aristotle and Galen in order to move beyond the psychological impasse between free will and self-bondage that emerged in the wake of the dispute between Erasmus and Luther. Melanchthon is particularly significant among the Reformers in his belief that knowledge about classical faculty psychology, and specifically Aristotle's *De Anima*, was critical for any theologian to understand the nature of the soul, and its potential for volition and will. He writes, "The theologian who does not know those most erudite discussions on the soul, on the senses, on the causes of volition and affections, on knowledge and on the will, lacks a great instrument."[39] Melanchthon's views are all the more surprising because "the soul, the senses, appetites, affections, knowledge, and the will are all topics which had traditionally been treated in the universities in reading Aristotle's *De Anima*."[40]

When compared to Luther's decisive rejection of Aristotle, Melanchthon's effort to understand the contours of classical psychology is all the more notable among his Reformation peers. Melanchthon makes it clear, however, that while he takes Aristotle's model of the soul seriously, he finds little use in that philosopher's focus on all living souls, including those of plants and lower animals. Melanchthon, by contrast, considers only human souls in his commentaries on *De Anima*. His narrow focus on the human soul represents, according to Kusukawa, "a novel claim when reading the *De Anima*" that interpreting the human through an Aristotelian lens is not just profitable, but indeed "necessary for understanding the Christian soul."[41] Because of this logic placing an understanding of Aristotle's pagan psychology as a necessary step in defining the Christian soul, Kusukawa has suggested that Melanchthon's treatise "was a Christian and indeed Lutheran reading of Aristotle's *De Anima*."[42]

Since all of the soul's faculties were subject to grace and damnation in Luther's system of thought, Melanchthon saw the need to more precisely account for how the operations of the lower organic faculties of sense and nutrition could fit into Luther's comprehensive vision of grace. The Thomist and Averroist models he inherited did not suffice for his purposes, and so Melanchthon dedicated his efforts to articulating a coherent Lutheran definition of the soul through a careful reading of *De Anima*, which he acknowledged as the most complete integration of the faculties into a cohesive understanding of the human. Melanchthon adopts Aristotle's tripartite model of the soul with the rational faculty, but with the addition of Galen's assignment of the soul's powers to organs:

> [In the] tripartite division of the human soul . . . there are three functions of the human soul which each have their seat in the bodily organs: the rational soul which regulates voluntary motions and supplies motions to the sense has its seat in the head; the sensitive soul which supplies motions to the sensitive appetites and has its seat in the heart; and the nutritive soul which nourishes and gives growth to the human body has its seat in the liver. Galen's division of the soul is thus linked with the functions of the human body.[43]

Melanchthon supplements Aristotle's organic psychology by embracing Galenic anatomy, and particularly Galen's specific assignment of anatomical locations to individual faculties and powers of the soul. Anatomy becomes important for Melanchthon because his understanding of the soul is shaped by the dispute between rational will and the uncontrollable movements of the body's organs and limbs that house the lower faculties.

> Freedom in the divine will, and in rational creatures, angels and men, is a faculty of the will, which is able to act or not act, or to act either in one way or another . . . It is first of all true that men are not able to achieve complete obedience to the law of God, nor be free of sin and death . . . But there is some freedom left, since God wants a distinction between a free agent and agency without plan or freedom to be understood to some degree, and wants it known that he is the freest agent, not bound by any causes. He even wants us to control our outward actions with some vigilance and labor of our own.
>
> This therefore is the true rule. It is absolutely certain that, in this weak nature of man, even in those who are not regenerate, enough freedom was left for controlling motion, that is, restraining the outer members lest they do any outward deeds hostile to the law of God . . . Furthermore Paul expressly says that the righteousness of the flesh which is the performance of external works by natural forces, is in harmony with the law of God. When he affirms that such justice can exist in those who are not regenerate, it is clear that it is a certain freedom of the will that rules the outer limbs. Also, God gave the human race magistrates and laws, so that the outer limbs may be restrained. This entire governance, indeed the very voice of laws would be completely useless if the outer limbs could not be restrained. Thus it must be admitted that there is some freedom . . . Since this governing of external actions is to some extent in our power, God wants us not to be slothful or slack, but to force our limbs by his law and the fear of punishment as if they were harsh chains.[44]

Melanchthon paradoxically links his definition of freedom as that which is only found in creatures possessing the rational soul to the notion of "complete obedience" by the lower faculties. In the fallen state, humans can only experience a partial trace of the complete freedom enjoyed by God. God has "left" a small remainder of freedom in order to permit humans to understand to some degree what concepts such as "agent," "agency," and "freedom" signify. Humans retain "enough freedom left" to force the lower faculties and their anatomical loci into a state of obedience to the rational soul. For the Christian subject, obedience to God's law requires the free use of the organic faculty of the will to bind the motions of the unruly lower faculties. For Melanchthon, the faculty of the will is free to bind its own organs in "harsh chains."

The psychological conflict between the volition of the rational faculty and the fallen nature of the lower faculties becomes the source of the common Protestant narrative which claimed that the disturbed workings of the soul's faculties evinced man's deeply rooted corruption after the fall. Without this psychological backstory, Luther, Calvin, and Melanchthon sound merely punitive. But within the context of the two-souls problem, we can see that Protestant theologians attempted to take into account all of the faculties of the soul with their inherent complexities and contradictions in the fallen world, in a more comprehensive view of the soul than Aquinas or even Erasmus, who sought to isolate grace and freedom narrowly within the faculty of reason.

For these reasons, the Protestant soul and its faculties were entangled, leading to the widely employed body of tropes defining the Christian subject in terms of binding in chains. Luther argues that this psychological struggle between the different parts of the soul binds the Christian idea of selfhood to such an extreme extent that it takes on the characteristics of a prisoner or captive. In *De Servo Arbitrio* (1525; *The Bondage of the Will*), Luther insists that the Christian soul "has no 'Free-will,' but is a captive, slave, and servant, either to the will of God," located in the faculty of reason, "or to the will of Satan," located in the unruly and involuntary impulses of the nutritive and sensory faculties and their fallen organs.[45] Taken together, Luther re-terms "free will" into the more accurate notion of a "will in bondage," describing a Christian soul that "when it is free, it binds itself and goes of its own accord into bonds!"[46] Therefore, in the Protestant model exemplified by Melanchthon, Luther, and Calvin, the importance of the soul's faculties has shifted in a fundamental way. If for Pomponazzi the acknowledgment of two souls in one body can lead to an unfettered Christian freedom, the Protestant reformers added a level of complexity to the idea of a difficult freedom where the rational choice of the intellect is at every turn circumscribed in the fallen state by the impulsive operations of the lower faculties and their tendency to sin.

"Yet All Things May Be Imprinted": The Two Souls in Vernacular English Print Culture

Apart from exerting a profound effect on Lutheran doctrine, Melanchthon is important for our purposes because of his major impact on early Tudor England and the formation of the Anglican Church. During the reign of Henry VIII, German Lutherans and the Tudor court began a series of negotiations on the trajectory of church reforms in England. A "breakthrough" in the Protestant effort to sway Henry occurred in 1535, with Melanchthon dedicating his new edition of the *Loci Communes* to Henry "in consideration of his interest in the Gospel, and his appreciation of learning and the arts."[47] The gesture and the book itself were important in stimulating Henry's momentum toward initiating the English Reformation. As John Schofield has suggested, the effect of Melanchthon on "Henry and the English talks cannot be overestimated," not only for the act of political goodwill, but also because in Melanchthon's writings Henry found a more moderate set of positions that softened Luther's tenets by joining the possibility of "good works" to "salvation and eternal life for the first time in a Lutheran" text.[48] Melanchthon's influence on the

English Reformation was profound. His logic stating that good works are "pleasing and acceptable" was directly written into the Thirty-Nine Articles of 1563 delineating the tenets of the Anglican Church. Henry preferred Melanchthon's interpretation to Luther's and, through Cromwell, he altered the university curriculum at Oxford and Cambridge by expunging the works of the church doctors and canon law and adding in their stead Melanchthon's writings as the authorized Protestant account of the soul.[49] In a peculiar convergence, then, Melanchthon's reading of *De Anima* took on the status of Anglican doctrine in the second half of the sixteenth century.

Melanchthon therefore served as a crucial theological bridge between the Continental debate about the soul's faculties and the English Reformation. These Reformation ideas on the soul gained prominence through the work of Elizabethan-era clerics such as William Perkins and Richard Hooker, who played a significant role in introducing the largely Latinate two-souls debate to a vernacular English audience through their translations and commentaries of early sixteenth-century Catholic and Protestant texts. By translating the theological issue of the two souls from Latin into the common language of English, these Anglican figures opened up the question of the soul to a wide popular audience. The earliest figure involved in the dissemination of the two-souls problem to an English audience was John Woolton, the bishop of Exeter. In 1576, he simultaneously published two vernacular English texts that described the problem of two souls: *A Treatise on the Immortalitie of the Soule* and the *New Anatomie of the Whole Man*.[50] Woolton's two texts were not simply translations of Protestant antecedents, however, and they ultimately took on a life of their own in shaping English debates on the soul. Woolton declared his texts to be the first systematic treatises on the soul in the English language, since "none have hitherto written anything in our Englishe toung of so worthy an Argument."[51] The accuracy of Woolton's claim notwithstanding, his texts were popular, and they had a large impact on the English response to the problem of two souls. Woolton's major contribution in introducing the psychological problem to an English audience involved his revision of the fall—our original innocence, our fallen state, and our ultimate salvation.

In Woolton's narrative voice, prior to the fall, the "Image of God in man" was constituted by a harmony between the faculties of the organic soul, which Woolton locates throughout his texts in the brain (the mind and will) and the heart (the senses and emotion).[52] In Woolton's account of the prefallen faculties, there was no need for coercion, since all operations of the soul embodied the law of God in their very operation:

> In the hart all affections and appetitions did obey his minde and will, neither was there dissention in any thing. So that there was a Divine harmonie of the minde, will, and harte. For as the minde did rightly knowe god and his wyll: so the hart and the will did thinke

> one thing . . . And every orgaine parte and instrument of mans substance had facultie infused into them by god, that they were both willing and hable to doo the thinges required by god at their hands, which god according to the law of obedience had imprinted, and as it were stamped in Reasonable natures. There was also in this image of god in man, a preheminencie and superioritie above all other inferior creatures, both in reason and quicknes of senses.[53]

It is precisely the ease of obtaining this harmony of the faculties that Woolton emphasizes in the pre-fallen human. Woolton associates each "orgaine parte" of the body's anatomy with a "facultie" infused by God. In this case, the word "facultie" describes both the powers of the Aristotelian soul assigned to each organ, and the natural aptitude and facility with which the organs are able to follow the law of God.[54] In combining these two definitions of the word "facultie," Woolton exploits the fact that the Latin *facultas* and *facilitas* were basically two forms of the same words defining a sense of easiness. If early modern English usage largely preferred the definition of "facultie" as a power of the soul, Woolton reclaims its Latin definition describing "ease" or "facility." Thus, the "facultie" infused into each organ describes how the powers of the soul are rooted in the body's organs, but also how such organic powers function with a natural and easy harmony with the law of God. The body's "orgaine partes" infused with the faculties are fully "willing and able" to perform the things "required by god." The faculties of the soul, based in the body's organs, are the basis of the "willing" obedience to God's law "imprinted" and "stamped" within the pre-fallen human.

Things change after the fall, and its effects are felt most acutely in the faculties of the soul:

> I feele in my members another law, fighting against the lawe of God, O miserable man that I am, who shall deliver me from the death of this body, &c. In mans hart the love of god is utterly extinct, and flames of raging affections doe burne . . . For the very nakednesse, whiche man did see in him selfe most evidently: doth not onely signifie the outwarde, but also the inwarde deformitie both of body and soule. By means therefore of Adams fall the image of God was destroyed in mans nature, all his powers and faculties were either depraved or utterly loste. He was spoyled of all his gyftes, in minde, will, and hart.[55]

Woolton's logic here faithfully adapts Luther and Melanchthon's anatomy and physiology of the fall, in which the physical effects of original sin are felt most powerfully in the disjointed state of the two souls. In his account, Adam and Eve were not only ashamed of their "outwarde" nudity, but more importantly, "nakednesse" defines the "inward deformitie" scarring the fallen soul.

Woolton specifically defines the fallen inward nudity as the depraved state of the "powers and faculties" of the Aristotelian soul. The internal nudity of the soul destroys the image of God traced onto the soul, and leads the "powers and faculties" of the Aristotelian soul to function in a "depraved" way contrary to the pre-fallen law of obedience. The specific gift in question is the harmony of the organic faculties; the concord of the mind and will of the rational faculty with the heart of the sensitive faculty have been lost. For Woolton, following his Protestant influences, the transformation of the soul's "powers and faculties" from the embodiment of the harmonious law of obedience into a deformed and depraved state of affection and emotion represents the most tragic sign that humans have changed after the fall.

Ultimately for Woolton in *The New Anatomie of the Whole Man*, the "eternitie" of the soul requires a "willing obedience and service" (fols. 47–48) to the natural law inscribed upon our fallen organs. For Woolton, the relation of the mortal organic soul and the immortal "veritie and stabilitie" of the Christian soul requires "willing service" to the natural law that is always already inscribed within us. Such "willing service" is not coercive, nor is it a state of pure freedom. Woolton's willing service describes a condition of voluntary servitude to God's natural law implanted in the organic faculties of the classical soul. For Woolton, the problem of two souls leads fallen humans to freely serve.

The idea of "willing service" is not narrowly Woolton's alone, however, since the sentiment echoes the simultaneous state of Protestant freedom and slavery proposed by Luther. The English context of the late sixteenth century extends this line of thinking, with the influential Puritan William Perkins going so far as to say that a disease of the faculties is the only reason why fallen humans resist the law of God: "Wherefore it remaines that originall sinne is nothing else but a disorder or euill disposition in all the faculties and inclinations of man, whereby they are all caried inordinately against the law of God."[56] The basic substance of the soul's faculties has not changed, but their "disposition" has. The "disorder" of the faculties leads fallen humanity to move in two opposing directions, with the lower faculties resisting the law of God by binding the body's organs in chains of sin, while at the same time the "willing" rational powers of the soul strive to attain a state of grace.

Printerly Sentiments

What does differ from the Continental Protestant view in the account of English clerics such as Woolton and later Richard Hooker is the nuanced addition of a logic of *printing* at the core of their vision of the two souls. Woolton's logic insists that the immortality of the soul comes to depend on the fallen, mortal organic faculties as the substrate upon which natural law is "imprinted" and "stamped." In a fascinating move, Woolton turns the mechanics of the printing press into the means of God etching natural law onto our fallen organic faculties. We can now register the subtle shift that Woolton applies to the problem of two souls. If for Pomponazzi the immortality of the soul was a political lie, and for Melanchthon the immortal soul was a reward for a life of self-discipline, Woolton transforms the immortality of the Christian soul into a very specific act of printing natural law onto the organs of the Aristotelian soul. The most famous moment in Anglican theology espousing this view can be found in Hooker's *Of the Laws of Ecclesiastical Polity*:

> The soule of man being therefore at the first as a booke, wherein nothing is, and yet all thinges may be imprinted; we are to search by what steppes and degrees it riseth vnto perfection of knowledge . . . Beasts are in sensible capacitie as ripe euen as men themselues, perhaps more ripe. For as stones, though in dignitie of nature inferior vnto plants, yet exceed them in firmenesse of strength or durability of being; and plants though beneath the excellency of creatures indued with sense, yet exceed them in the faculty of vegetation and of fertility: so beasts though otherwise behind men, may notwithstanding in actions of sense and phancie go beyond them; because the endeuors of nature, when it hath an higher perfection to seeke, are in lower the more remisse, not esteeming thereof so much as those things do, which haue no better proposed vnto them. The soule of man therefore being capable of a more diuine perfection, hath (besides the faculties of growing unto sensible knowledge which is common vnto vs with beasts) a further hability . . . the ability of reaching higher then vnto sensible things . . . When once it comprehendeth any thing aboue this, as the differences of time, affirmations, negations and contradictions in speech; we then count it to haue some vse of naturall reason. Whereunto afterwards there might be added the right helpes of true art and learning. . . . So as following the rules & precepts . . . of an Art which teacheth the way of speedy discourse, and restraineth the minde of man that it may not waxe over wise. Education and instruction are the meanes, the one by use, the other by precept, to make our naturall faculty of reason, both the better and the sooner able to judge rightly betweene truth and error, good and evill.[57]

For Hooker, man's soul is a book capable of being "imprinted" by education, with the capacity to think and to judge according to the logic of speech and discourse that composes the pages of his being. As a child, man's soul is "as a booke, wherein nothing is, and yet all thinges may be imprinted." Hooker describes a soul that is modeled upon the organic faculties, with the process of rising into the "perfection of knowledge" determined by the powers of the soul that define each rung of life. As "beasts" are perfectible through their faculty of sense, and "plants" excel at the level of their "faculty of vegetation and of fertility," humans have the further ability to reach beyond the faculties of sense and vegetation to the "natural faculty of reason." This mode of reason for Hooker is not primarily cognitive, but pedagogical and linguistic. Through a lifetime of spiritual teaching and learning, man can gain the ability to process and judge "affirmations, negations and contradictions in speech" by learning and practicing "the way of speedy discourse." Hooker imagines the human faculty of reason as situated on the hierarchy of faculties in the classical model of the organic soul, perfectible through a linguistic education mediated by discourse, and the result is the power to judge and to reason ethically in language.

Both Hooker and Woolton embed within the description of the soul's relationship with God a direct acknowledgment of the print medium that enabled them to disseminate their spiritual teachings to a broad lay audience. The larger Anglican turn to print, books, speech, and education is significant because it represents a shift from the conventional medieval trope of God writing the heart to a metaphor that reflects the technology of education at the time—the printing press.[58] The printers and publishers of Woolton, Perkins, and Hooker were in fact responsible for a large share of the expanding vernacular print discourse translating Latin, Continental, and classical texts that could now be introduced into circulation in English culture.[59] The Anglican clerics who published their religious work therefore enjoyed such a marked level of success and popularity not only because of the inherent interest provoked by their topics, but also because of the new audiences they could reach through the print medium and the energy of printers and stationers, through which their texts could be reprinted in successive editions to meet growing demand, as was the case with the surprisingly eager readership that Woolton, Perkins, and Hooker's texts all found. It is a testament to the importance of the press in not just disseminating but also shaping the ideas of these Anglican clerics that they went so far in their writings as to use the press itself as a useful trope to describe the workings of the soul. The apotheosis of this line of Anglican thought is the religious prose of John Donne, whom I discuss at length in the fourth chapter.

The print medium allowed Anglican preachers to expand the reach of their spiritual teaching beyond the space of the pulpit and court and into the homes of lay English readers. Indeed, many of the titles introducing the Anglican theology of the soul, and the problem of two souls inherited from Pomponazzi and the Reformation, explicitly targeted households with texts such as *Godlie Private Prayers for Householders to Meditate Upon, and to Say in Their Families* (12 editions between 1577 and 1609); *Certaine Sermons Appointed by the Queenes Majestie, to Be Declared and Read, for the Better Understanding of the Simple People* (11 editions between 1559 and 1595); *How to Read, and in Reading, How to Understand . . . the Holie Bible* (1594); and the translation of Saint John Chrysostom's *Phisick for the Soule*

(1570 and 1578). All gained a wide readership and built a literate audience that grew increasingly knowledgeable about the soul.

The Anglican turn to a printed vernacular discourse teaching commonwealth subjects about the nature of the soul represented the primary way in which English authors such as Shakespeare, Donne, Davies, and Milton themselves learned about the seemingly abstruse philosophical and theological intricacies of the two-souls dilemma. Based on what we know about the education of Renaissance schoolboys and the reading practices of these particular authors, it is fairly unlikely that these figures encountered Pomponazzi or Melanchthon in the original Latin, although Milton may be a pointed exception. The far more probable scenario is that these authors would have become familiar with the controversial workings of the two souls through teachings on the management and care of the soul as the core of the Christian subject, which Anglican theologians disseminated in the form of the spiritual manuals mentioned above, in their larger push to expand into a vernacular audience across England. In contrast with Pomponazzi, then, who faced retribution from the Vatican for his attempt to bring the discussion of the soul into the academy, English authors were able to exploit the technology of the printing press to disseminate the production of knowledge about the soul to a broad readership.

The consequences of this expansion and eventual integration of the psychological question of the two souls into the vernacular literary culture of early modern England are manifold and important to the narrative that will unfold over the course of the following chapters. First, access to a vernacular English print discourse of the soul gave anyone with the ability to read the right to think about the soul and apply the spiritual teachings contained in the sermons to one's existence and "household." Second, the Anglican clerics we have considered began a shift to thinking about the faculties of the classical soul in terms of books, writing, speech, and print as a reflection of the textual medium which enabled them to disseminate their own teachings in the first place. It should come as little surprise, then, that the English authors who learned from this Elizabethan discourse of the soul adopted this textual vocabulary in their own appropriations, critiques, and responses to the two-souls problem at the heart of the Christian subject. If the expansion of the printed text from Latin into English in the late sixteenth century allowed every literate Christian to learn about the nature of the soul for the purposes of pastoral care, so too did this intellectual access give commoners as well as poets and playwrights beyond court and the halls of the academy the right to puzzle over and contest the paradoxes and conflicts inherent within their own souls. The problem of the two souls became a recurring theme in time because, of course, the stakes were quite high: could we attain salvation with two contradictory souls at the core of our being, particularly after the controversies of the Reformation?

Against this intellectual backdrop, the English authors I have chosen among many others articulate some of the most capacious and ambitious responses to the two-souls problem in early modern culture. Rather than accepting a prescribed fate of psychological paralysis caught between freedom and abjection dictated by mainstream Protestant thought, the English poets studied in this book argue that the faculties of the soul, insofar as they are described in textual terms, can be rewritten. The possibility of this reinscription can modify the nature of the soul and the possibility of the subject's sense of Christian freedom. The subsequent chapters will therefore read some of the most prominent early modern English authors with new eyes, reconceiving their works as an effort to rewrite the soul itself, so as to reimagine how the tense contact of the classical and Christian models of the soul could serve as the catalyst or spark for a free Christian subject in the decades after the Reformation.

Chapter 2

✦

Hamlet's "Soulbending Sovereignty" and Shakespeare's Rhetorical Soul

> In the first decades of its performance, Hamlet's signature action may have been not paralyzing thought but frenzied motion.
>
> —Margreta de Grazia, *"Hamlet" without Hamlet*

William Shakespeare's *Hamlet* (composed 1600–1602?) represents one of the most striking accounts of the two-souls conflict in Elizabethan England, and for this reason it serves as an ideal way to reorient our focus from the theological and historical frame of the Reformation to the literary and theatrical response. Shakespeare's outsized impact on the English literary tradition and the influence of his works during his time make his drama an ideal case study to demonstrate the extent to which the two-souls dilemma made its way from the rarefied Latinate halls of the church and learned societies into the popular English discourse of Elizabethan playhouses and print shops. Shakespeare used the space of the theater as a type of laboratory of the soul, in which to play with the limits and affordances of the classical and Christian conceptions of soul, placed consistently and intentionally into provocative contact in the bodies and experiences of his characters. Where the Anglican tradition of spiritual teaching aimed to smooth over, or at least explain away, the disjunction between the two souls, Shakespeare experiments in his plays with the generative and destabilizing limits of the self, where the tension between the Christian and classical souls allows for an exhilarating reimagination of how the soul defines human life. Within Shakespeare's corpus, *Hamlet* is the most deliberate in its staging of the struggle to resolve the early modern paradox of two souls in the space of the theater. It is Shakespeare's most intense and sustained articulation of a specifically vernacular English discourse of the soul.

Shakespeare responded in his plays to the vernacular theology that proposed an ethics of the self defined by the diseased corrosion of the organic soul that is the scar of the fall in every human. Shakespeare's innovation, and how he differs from the vernacular psychologies of his contemporaries, lies in his turn away from the dominant theological and ethical discourse of suppressing and disciplining the soul's volatile passions. By contrast, Shakespeare conceives of the soul quite differently by appealing to the vocabulary of classical rhetoric. In the lessons of his humanist rhetorical education, Shakespeare would have found a popular and influential vision of a linguistically inflected soul drawn from the pages of classical sources such as Aristotle, Cicero, Quintilian, and Horace—authors who composed the core of the Renaissance schoolboy's education.[1] Shakespeare grounds his understanding of the soul in the classical techniques, targeting and shaping the contours of the soul by directing its persuasive language to stir and to arouse the passions seated in its faculties.[2] Through this rhetorical model of the soul, Shakespeare in effect enunciates a praise of the soul's passions so as to define a new form of Christian freedom. The rhetorical soul and its faculties are susceptible to, but made malleable by, the stirring effects of language, in vivid contradistinction to the conventional Protestant narrative of the fall as a psychological scar.

This chapter reads *Hamlet* as a limit-case of early modern psychology, and not the paragon of tragic convention. We are recentering our critical gaze on the play's great preoccupation with the composition and fate of the soul, which has largely been lost in the age-old debate about the psychology of Hamlet's proto-modern mind. His psychology, as I shall argue, is not primarily defined by "pure consciousness" or "the premier Western performance of consciousness," as suggested by Jonathan Bate and Marjorie Garber, respectively.[3] Hamlet's psychology draws profoundly from the much older tradition of the classical organic soul, and its power to define the Christian subject in a fraught Protestant world.

Although *Hamlet* culminates with Prince Hamlet's eventual murder of his uncle, the prince spends much of the play vacillating in his resolve to avenge his father's murder, and this deferral of action has become a central question for generations of the play's readers. For all of the late twentieth-century emphasis on the "modernity" of Hamlet's selfhood and the depth of his "consciousness," Hamlet's "delay," as pointed out by Margreta de Grazia, has cast him as an indecisive, abject subject characterized by overthinking paralysis rather than freedom or agency. As Samuel Johnson famously describes the prince, he is "rather an instrument than an agent."[4] Some of the most sensitive readers of *Hamlet* have in the past several decades focused their critical energies on reversing Johnson's dismissive logic by reevaluating the status of Hamlet's agency. To these "subjectivity" critics, Hamlet's rich interiority marked him as an exemplary type of agent, appropriate for Shakespeare's changing world, and signaling the shift to the "modern" era. So the now-familiar story about *Hamlet* goes.[5] More recently, Shakespearean scholars have added a layer of historicist nuance to Hamlet's place in the story of the modern subject, by more seriously considering the materiality of the Galenic humoral system in defining the Renaissance mind and soul. So, as Gail Kern Paster has influentially posited, affective states and cognition in Shakespeare's works were themselves a "quality of matter," and for Michael Schoenfeldt, "the purportedly immaterial subject is constituted as a profoundly material substance" in the early modern context.[6] Richard Sugg's investigations on the "positively embodied versions of the soul" have unearthed an early modern "experience of the soul" that could "be surprisingly physical," while Donovan Sherman has focused on the manner in which Shakespeare introduces "the soul into the elements," a process by which "souls become things." Christopher Crosbie, in a similar line of reading, has explored the economic dimension of the vegetative faculty as "an outlet for thwarted material fecundity."[7]

The common thread linking these various reading strategies reconfiguring the subject's body/soul relationship is a shared vocabulary of the "material" basis of human embodied experience. Stephen Greenblatt, in *Hamlet in Purgatory*, stakes out a different understanding of the "material" shaping the Shakespearean subject. From his considerably different vantage point, Shakespeare's model of the soul is a palimpsest of the theological debates and texts he inherited from the Reformation: to understand the soul in Shakespeare's play, "we only need to recognize how alert he was to the materials that were being made available to him." The materials in question were not the physical fluids and substances of the body, but rather the "theological struggles" from which "Shakespeare's play . . . is in part one of the unintended consequences."[8] The "soul" as it was defined in Shakespeare's time, I think, cannot be divided between theological and physiological poles, toward which the scholarly reading strategies described above have subtly drifted. Rather, Greenblatt's suggestion that the question of the soul was the site where "important forces had been busily struggling for decades," and that Shakespeare appropriated the "weakened or damaged institutional structure" of the soul as a proving ground for his social critique, seems to be far more accurate. The soul in early modern England could only be characterized as an intense "struggle," and could no longer be considered a coherent thing or substance in itself, with the idea of soul itself undergoing successive waves of change, critique, and revision. Within this struggle spread across Elizabethan England, Shakespeare's *Hamlet* is a spiritual palimpsest of multiple conflicting models of soul compressed within the vexed protagonist.

The oscillation and tension between the materialist model of the soul indebted to classical humoralism and faculty psychology on the one hand, and the fate of the Christian soul and its contested definition in the turmoil of the Reformation on the other, offers Shakespeare a generative moment to experiment with the manifold possibilities and problems attending the two souls. Based on his education, however, and even if we correct Ben Jonson's overstated assumption of Shakespeare's "small Latin and less Greek," it is nonetheless fairly unlikely that Shakespeare read *De Anima* or Galen's *On the Natural Faculties* directly.[9] A far more probable inference, given the humanist curriculum of his time, would be that he drew from the rich and nuanced description of the soul's faculties in texts on rhetorical eloquence and the art of poetics, in which the soul is the target of persuasive speech and the locus of *movere*, Cicero's influential rhetorical goal to move an audience to a certain position of judgment by stimulating their passions and by provoking the activity of their souls' faculties into a heightened state of motion.[10]

This rhetorical soul explicitly identifies the wide range of passionate appeals to the vegetable, sensitive, and rational faculties as defining the soul as intrinsically vulnerable and unstable when confronted with the instruments of well-executed, persuasive address. In this instability, however, the soul is malleable. It is this extensive description in the English translations of classical rhetorical manuals that gives to vernacular playwrights and readers like Shakespeare a widely recognized and influential system of thought on the operations of the soul's faculties, and a precise technical vocabulary on how to mold and work upon the classical soul with language and through its effects upon the passions. The rhetorical soul is a double-edged sword, for its emotional instability is precisely what enables its plasticity in language. This dual nature represents why rhetoric's contact with the soul's faculties is such an important logic in *Hamlet*. By exploiting the robust vernacular rhetoric of the classical soul, Shakespeare imagines an alternative to the ubiquitous and gloomy condition of the diseased and bound Protestant soul.

The unstable but pliable rhetorical soul opens up a site of a new vision of post-Reformation spiritual freedom by unfettering the faculties of the organic soul depicted as suspended between the states of simultaneous abjection and freedom in the Protestant narratives of Luther, Calvin, and Melanchthon, and later in the English context of Woolton, Perkins, and Hooker. Shakespeare creatively experiments with a different form of Christian agency forged in the intensity of the rhetorical soul's passionate, sensate, and embodied reaction to language. In this sense, my reading of *Hamlet* concurs with the recent appraisals by Greenblatt and Joshua Scodel of Shakespeare's plays as an exemplary proving ground of early modern conceptions of freedom.[11] However, this novel mode of Christian freedom should not be confused with an unqualified praise of passion, as delineated in early modern culture by Richard Strier.[12] Rather, as Scodel asserts, Hamlet's is a difficult freedom, and the rhetorical plane of agency recuperated by Shakespeare in the tragedy is an agitated, disordered state of the soul that gains its freedom precisely as a result of its instability.

This counterintuitive logic is perhaps why Hamlet has provoked confusion and fascination in so many generations of readers and scholars because, as T. S. Eliot has suggested, *Hamlet* is "most certainly an artistic failure" because of its "puzzling" nature, "disquieting" ethical conclusions, and "unstable condition."[13] The incoherence of the soul that moves Hamlet away from the pole of conventional heroism and subverts our expectations of equilibrium in character development or psychological unity, beyond the simple "antic disposition" of his madness, represents Shakespeare's unexpected achievement.

For Hamlet's agency, in quite a contrast to the Protestant narrative of the fallen soul, inheres in the intensity of a freedom built from the fragments of the rhetorically induced disorder of the soul.

The Rhetorical Soul in the Early Modern Vernacular: "Soulbending" Sovereignty

Shakespeare's effort to recuperate a sense of freedom from the soul's disorder is all the more surprising since he was writing in an "intellectual milieu in which the passions were regarded as an overbearing and inescapable element of human nature, liable to disrupt any civilized order . . . unless they were tamed, outwitted, overruled, or seduced."[14] According to the tenets of the dominant early modern ethical and behavioral discourse, the passions, if not suppressed altogether (according to the neo-Stoic argument), should be "shaken (but not stirred)," as Gail Kern Paster puts it, and should be kept "within the bounds of moderation."[15] According to this familiar line of reasoning advocating for temperance, "there is no reasonable creature consisting of soule and bodie, in whose mind contrarie motions are not incamped . . . swallowed up in seas of disquietness."[16] This doctrine of temperance was made popular through a popular discourse of translations that introduced Continental texts such as Juan Huarte de San Juan's *Examination of Men's Wits* and Guillaume de Salluste Du Bartas's *La Sepmaine* to a broad English readership. One of the most widely read accounts of this ethic of affective self-constraint was found in the 1594 and 1618 translations of Pierre de la Primaudaye's influential *Academie Francaise*, of which the latter was printed by John Legat, the printer of William Perkins's strident theological treatises.

> They are called perturbations of the soule, which if they be not mastred by reason, doe so carie the soule hither and thither, that in the ende they constraine the reasonable power thereof to giue ouer all authoritie and libertie. . . . The best of them all, and they which came nearest to the knowledge of the truth were the Academiks, whose first authors were Socrates and Plato, who, as we heard yesterday, alwaies taught, that our true good consisteth in the tranquilitie of the soule, voide of all perturbations, and in stead of them adorned and enriched with all vertue, which is the proper substance and matter of Philosophie, and therefore called the onely permanent good of the soule.[17]

The "perturbations of the soule" are not pernicious in themselves, but pose a threat only insofar as they circumscribe the "authoritie and libertie" of the soul's "reasonable power." In effect, the main problem is one of the soul's agency: do the passions "carie the soule hither and thither," or does the rational faculty enjoy this volitional power to choose and to act? The popular solution posited by Primaudaye, and echoed in countless early modern behavior manuals, is an ethical one that invokes the classical authority of Plato and Socrates: "our true good consisteth in the tranquilitie of the soule, voide of all perturbations." Goodness requires a purgation of the soul, evacuating its aesthetic capacity so it is void of the passions.[18]

Against the prevailing psychological and ethical discourses that sought to moderate the turbulent motions of the classical soul, Shakespeare in *Hamlet* draws our attention to one classical discipline where the passions of the soul were taken seriously as a positive tool in quite a different light: rhetoric. This rhetorical vocabulary would have made sense to Shakespeare, since his education was largely one suffused with "the language of Renaissance humanism" and focused on "exercising rhetorical techniques learned from ancient and modern" rhetoric manuals.[19] Rolf Soellner, and more recently Sarah Dewar-Watson and David Beauregard, have persuasively made the case that Shakespeare, despite his "small Latin and less Greek," would have had considerable familiarity with Aristotelian philosophy, with Soellner specifically insisting in relation to classical conceptions of the soul that translations of Aristotle and his Renaissance commentators gave Shakespeare "most of the descriptions for the operations of the soul."[20] Shakespeare's knowledge of Aristotelian psychology is a thorny question, however, since *De Anima* remained untranslated in English in the sixteenth century, and it is unlikely that he read that text itself or one of the Latin commentaries on *De Anima* produced by learned societies or universities.

So how indeed did Shakespeare learn about classical faculty psychology, and more specifically the Aristotelian conception of the soul, which recurs so frequently as a vocabulary for defining the human across his plays, and which serves as a crux in shaping *Hamlet*, as I am arguing here? The most obvious answer is that it is likely that Shakespeare had his most sustained and lasting engagement with different models of the classical soul through his rhetorical education at the "excellent free grammar school" of the King's New School.[21] We can find evidence of the rhetorical soul throughout the major classical texts of the humanist curriculum. Within the Aristotelian tradition, the *Ars Rhetorica* (*Art of Rhetoric*) rather than *De Anima* held the greatest influence on vernacular English accounts of the soul. As Brian Vickers and Lawrence Green have argued, Aristotle's *Art of Rhetoric* was read in early modern English culture primarily as a meditation on the soul, while Quentin Skinner suggests that even a voice skeptical of Aristotelian eloquence like Francis Bacon thought of the *Rhetoric* as "mainly a work on the 'affections' or passions of the soul," and not just a treatise on the art of persuasion.[22]

We can find the logic of the rhetorical soul in Cicero's *De Officiis* and *De Oratore*—both influential texts in the Renaissance curriculum. In *De Officiis* (*On Duties*), Cicero draws upon the common conceit of man as differentiated from beasts by the distinct faculties assigned to each: "In no other particular are we farther removed from the nature of beasts . . . for they are not endowed with reason or speech."[23] For Cicero, speech is distinctly human and marks us as reasoning creatures, but speech is also intimately bound up in the rhythms of the sense faculty. "It is, then, not hard to know that there is a certain rhythm in a speech: for the senses decide that . . . And verse itself was not invented by *à priori* reasoning, but by nature and the senses, and these last were taught by carefully digested reason what was the fact; and accordingly it was the careful noticing and observation of nature which produced art."[24] Linguistic speech, then, is important for defining the human soul because it conforms to the workings of the soul's rational and sensory faculties. It is not surprising that some of the most influential sequences from *De Oratore* (*On the Orator*) depict eloquence as a mastery of the soul's faculties and passions and not primarily "philosopher's definitions" or "the supreme good." Cicero explains:

> Wherefore the speaker will not be able to achieve what he wants by his words, unless he has gained profound insight into the characters of men, and the whole range of human nature, and those motives whereby our souls are spurred on or turned back. . . . Who lastly can by his eloquence either arouse or calm, within the souls of men, whatever passion the circumstances and occasion may demand . . . in such way does he range over men's souls, and explore their feelings and thoughts, that he needs no philosophers' definitions, and does not inquire in his discourse whether "the supreme good" is subjective or objective, whether it is to be defined as virtue or pleasure, or whether these two can be wedded together.[25]

The skilled rhetorician can manipulate the "souls of men" from "within," and his discourse "ranges over men's souls" in order to "achieve what he wants by his words." As a result, in the Ciceronian model of the soul so popular in Elizabethan England, the orator's eloquence makes him the "soulbending sovereign of all things."[26] It is unsurprising to claim that the legacy of Cicero in early modern England posited rhetoric as a master discourse, but it is quite surprising, within the context of *Hamlet*, to recognize the extent to which Cicero's works in the early modern period identified rhetoric as the master discourse of the *soul*.

Even in Neoplatonist strains of thought, we can see this classical model of the rhetorically inflected soul. For example, Plato's *Phaedrus* insists that the "rhetorician's . . . whole effort is directed to the soul" when he claims:

> Evidently the man whose rhetorical teaching is a real art will explain accurately the nature of that to which his words are to be addressed, and that is the soul, is it not? . . . So it is clear that Thrasymachus, or anyone else who seriously teaches the art of rhetoric, will first describe the soul with perfect accuracy and make us see whether it

> is one and all alike, or, like the body, of multiform aspect; for this is what we call explaining its nature. . . . Since it is the function of speech to lead souls by persuasion, he who is to be a rhetorician must know the various forms of soul.[27]

The influence of the Platonic imagination of the rhetorical soul can be found throughout Thomas North's 1580 translation of Plutarch's *Lives*, which was one of Shakespeare's primary source texts for classical material in his plays. According to North, Pericles showed "that rhetorike and eloquence (as Plato sayeth) is an arte which quickeneth mens spirites at her pleasure, and her chiefest skill is, to knowe how to move the passions and affections thoroughly, which are as stoppes and sounds of the soule, that would be played upon with a fine fingered hande of a conning master."[28]

Thus, in translations of the classical rhetorical treatises that lay at the core of the Renaissance schoolboy's humanist education there exists a latent, but nonetheless pervasive, vernacular English pedagogical discourse on how the faculties of the soul can be shaped and molded for the ends of persuasion and aesthetic experience, precisely as Hamlet articulates in response to the players. Leonard Barkan concludes from the evidence of Shakespeare's rhetorical education that the "marks of all these processes and influences are written everywhere in Shakespeare's text."[29] As John Walker points out, many of the key scenes in the comedies defining the soul and its faculties in the classical tradition occur in classrooms. "In *Love's Labour's Lost*, Nathaniel, the schoolmaster, analyzes Dull's psychological deficiencies in Aristotelian terms, and in the *Comedy of Errors* (II.i), Luciana's lecture to Adriana is based on the classical idea that men are distinguished from animals because they have souls . . . as more highly developed sense perceptions."[30] And indeed, the training of the Renaissance schoolboy is all the more appropriate as a context for Shakespeare's tragedies because Hamlet defines himself in act 1 as a student:

> O all you host of heaven! O earth! What else?
> And shall I couple hell? O, fie! Hold, hold, my heart,
> And you, my sinews, grow not instant old,
> But bear me stiffly up. Remember thee?
> Ay, thou poor ghost, whiles memory holds a seat
> In this distracted globe. Remember thee?
> Yea, from the table of my memory
> I'll wipe away all trivial fond records,
> All saws of books, all forms, all pressures past
> That youth and observation copied there,
> And thy commandment all alone shall live
> Within the book and volume of my brain,
> Unmixed with baser matter. Yes, by heaven! (*Hamlet* 1.5.92–104)

It has been popular in recent years to read this sequence in terms of the Renaissance student's commonplace book.[31] According to this line of reading, Hamlet defines his intellect and memory as a text "copied" in the commonplace book of his mind. Here he specifically identifies the organic locus of cognition, the "book and volume of my brain," as a text. Describing the organs of the rational faculty is significant because Hamlet follows the Galenic model embraced by Protestant thinkers such as Melanchthon, and later Woolton, who identify the brain as the anatomical seat of the rational faculty. Hamlet's mind is not immaterial or untethered from the body's organs, as Aquinas would have it, but is embedded within matter. The matter being described specifically appropriates Aristotle's metaphors of the soul as "form," "pressure," and "matter."[32] Apart from the abstruse particularities of *De Anima*, the figure of the wax seal was pervasive in early modern vernacular rhetorics, with Henry Peacham suggesting that metaphors themselves functioned "as pencils" upon the "wax seal" of the mind, and with Cicero in *De Oratore* describing how the training of the soul's faculties requires the "imprinting" of the mind "as a wax writing tablet and the letters written on it."[33] Underlying the model of the wax tablet and the commonplace book as templates for the rational faculty is the more fundamental Renaissance topos defining "speech" as the "representation" of the soul's faculties, as we have previously seen in the 1594 translation of Primaudaye, in which words represent the "signes and significations of the whole soule." Hamlet's tablet of the mind therefore reflects a broader early modern rhetorical model in which the rational faculty was a textual medium that one has the power to write and rewrite precisely as a sedulous student would during the course of his drills. Hamlet identifies himself as a student, and this move permits us to rethink how he defines the faculties of his soul within the framework of Renaissance rhetoric as something that the student has the power to physically edit. In recasting the organs of his reason and memory in terms of the schoolboy's tablet, Hamlet positions himself within the early modern rhetorical discourse that conceived of the soul in terms of a palimpsestic textuality allowing the student to train and mold his faculties.

This is significant for our purposes because while the erudite early modern ethical and medical discourses, which were largely translated for a scholarly audience from Continental languages or Latin, proposed a model of rigorously training the soul into a posture of rational temperance, a parallel vernacular counter-discourse of the soul in humanist rhetorical education advocated for precisely the opposite by exploiting the propensity of the soul to be perturbed by passionate "conceits" and "speeches" as a way to mold the soul's faculties.

The humanist education in the classical arts of rhetoric has been inadequately recognized as a robust vernacular discourse of the soul, in which Shakespeare would have been well-versed, and which offered to him a technical vocabulary to work through the problems of the classical soul in a

Christian world on the English stage. Shakespeare probably did not read *De Anima*, but he was familiar with Cicero and Quintilian, and in these classical sources from his boyhood teachings he would have found a rich discourse on the malleability of the soul. In the context of this vernacular psychology indebted to the humanist emphasis on classical rhetoric and taught universally to English schoolboys, Shakespeare places the theological struggle of the Catholic and Protestant models of the soul into provocative contact with the very different rhetorical model of the soul described by classical rhetoric.

Hamlet and the Ghost: The Captive Soul in a Catholic Afterlife

Hamlet's struggle to resist the bleakness of an enslaved soul by finding an alternative psychological vocabulary becomes all the more urgent in the opening moves of the play, when he learns the grim extent to which his father, and potentially the prince himself, are trapped on a trajectory that will ultimately bind them in a state of imprisonment.

> I am thy father's spirit,
> Doomed for a certain term to walk the night,
> And for the day confined to fast in fires,
> Till the foul crimes done in my days of nature
> Are burnt and purged away. But that I am forbid
> To tell the secrets of my prison house (1.5.9–14)

In the context of the Reformation model of the soul, the ghost's speech exaggerates the enslaved extreme of Luther's discourse that we have already seen. The dead king's spirit is locked in a "prison house," bound and "confined to fast in fires," violently punished in direct proportion to the "foul crimes" of sin performed during his life. Hamlet's father presents a vision of Christian immortality and afterlife defined in terms of binding and punitive suffering. It should be noted that the play never presents the Christian soul's immortality as the blissful reunion of the elect with God in heaven. Moving away from a fantasy of the body as the prison of the soul that would otherwise be free when released from the bonds of the flesh, the king demonstrates that in death, he simply exchanges the prison of the body for another prison of the soul.

The exquisite irony of this scene only becomes evident once we recognize that the prison the ghost evokes, as Greenblatt has noted, precisely matches contemporary descriptions of the *Catholic* conception of purgatory.[34] This peculiar tension between the ghost's narrow interpretation of the Protestant idiom of slavery and imprisonment placed into contact with a decidedly Catholic vision of purgatory is jarring, since Hamlet himself begins the play voicing the somewhat naive assumption that the security of his soul's immortality is self-evident, as he brazenly follows the ghost into the darkness:

> Why, what should be the fear?
> I do not set my life at a pin's fee,
> And for my soul, what can it do to that?
> Being a thing immortal as itself?
> It waves me forth again. I'll follow it. (1.4.64–68)

In this initial encounter with his father's ghost, Hamlet exhibits his absolute certainty in the Christian soul's immortality in his tautological reasoning: "being a thing immortal as itself?" The Christian soul's immortality is confirmed in a comparison to "itself," requiring no proof other than the tautological confirmation that the soul is indeed unshakably immortal. Hamlet's father quickly troubles this sure confidence in the fate of the soul by staging a puzzling contradiction between two warring models of the soul. By moving the fate of the soul to a state of the "bondslave" that must suffer from a regime of punishment, the ghost invokes a vocabulary of imprisonment that forecloses the possibility of freedom to the Christian subject. By contrast, however, his return from the spiritual prison serves to confirm that the Catholic idea of purgatory is correct, in direct contradiction to the prevailing Reformation belief that purgatory, and the system of indulgences upon which it was built, was one of the bases of the corruption motivating Luther and Calvin's original critique of the papacy. These opening moves defining the soul's fate in the first scenes of *Hamlet* are all the more surprising with the Danish prince appealing to "canon" law as the impediment forbidding him from "self-slaughter" (1.2.132), while being a student studying at Wittenberg, the epicenter of northern European Protestantism and the place where Luther famously incited the Reformation with his 95 Theses.

The point here is not to claim, as Sir Edmund Chambers and Ernst Honigmann have speculated, that Hamlet was a Catholic protagonist in a Protestant world, perhaps reflecting Shakespeare's own religious leanings.[35] For the purposes of the present analysis, it suffices to say that the opening scenes of *Hamlet* begin to question, and indeed trouble, the component of Protestant thought in which the organic tripartite soul is the locus of an abject slavery locking the Christian subject into the election of God's will. The return of Hamlet's father affirms that the prison metaphor deployed in Protestant theology is certainly true, but only when ironically situated in a Catholic context of purgatory. In effect, the ghost of Hamlet's father intimately links the fate of the fallen soul with the idea of purgatory—the basis of the system of indulgences—against which sixteenth-century Reformers so stridently defined themselves.

My reading therefore concurs with the assessment of Claire McEachern, who rightly acknowledges that Shakespeare's "theatre is not theology" but that his plays "informed how personhood was understood, and perhaps literary character, was understood in this moment," particularly as it related to "imaginations of an afterlife."[36] Against this historical backdrop, it is unsurprising that Hamlet voices a good deal of confusion about human nature and the fate of the soul as a result of his encounter with the ghost. Put within the context of the two-souls paradox, Hamlet's dilemma is not so much marked by indecision or inaction, but rather by a basic confusion about how his soul defines who he is, since so many parts of his father's story do not correspond to the received wisdom of his Protestant world.[37]

Beyond the long-term consequences inflicted upon the soul that he so vividly conjures, the ghost suggests that Hamlet's more pressing concern is the frightening impact that the irresponsible disclosure of the afterlife could inflict upon Hamlet's organic faculties in the present, and not necessarily his spiritual future.

> . . . But that I am forbid
> To tell the secrets of my prison house,
> I could a tale unfold whose lightest word
> Would harrow up thy soul, freeze thy young blood,
> Make thy two eyes like stars start from their spheres,
> Thy knotted and combined locks to part,
> And each particular hair to stand on end,
> Like quills upon the fretful porpentine.
> But this eternal blazon must not be
> To ears of flesh and blood. List, list, O, list! (1.5.13–22)

Hamlet's torture in the immediate context would be the effect of the "word" upon the organs and fluids of his faculties. The king's ghost is forbidden from recounting the "tale" of the Christian afterlife because of the dramatic effects such a story would have on the faculties of his son's soul as understood in the classical vocabulary of blood, eyes, hair, and ears. The "words" of the frightening "tale" of the Christian soul's punishment would "harrow up" Prince Hamlet's "soul," by triggering the complete uprooting and disruption of the proper function of his faculties, and by pushing him into the animal state of the "fretful porpentine." Hamlet's father insists that "words," "tales," and "blazons," echoing the early modern rhetorical pedagogy we have seen, can directly intervene in and violently disrupt the workings of the organic faculties and can fundamentally change the nature of the soul and its organs. Although he simply repeats the conventional prisoner narrative of the Protestant soul as his own destiny, what inspires terror in his son's potential fate is not the same possibility of roasting in a Catholic purgatory, but rather the profoundly negative rhetorical effect that his "blazon" and "words" would exert on Hamlet's faculties. This "harrowing" effect precisely describes the classical soul's volatile instability at the core of early modern rhetorical pedagogy. Hamlet's father is prohibited from "harrowing" his son's soul because of these reasons, and so too Hamlet will later take this message to heart, by ironically disobeying his father's prohibition to drive his interactions in the rest of the play.

Hamlet's Confusion: How to Define "Man"?

Hamlet, having faced the conflict of the Protestant and Catholic visions of the soul's fate in the first act of the play, voices far less certainty about the status of his soul than he previously boasted in the naive terms of "being a thing immortal as itself." His confusion reveals itself most pointedly as a series of meditations in which the prince begins to work through a range of other views on the soul from the early modern period. Most notably, he falls back upon the language of the classical soul as a counterpoint to his father's vexing account of the afterlife. We can see this process in Hamlet's resulting understanding of "man" as a mixture of "faculties," "form," "reason," animal like characteristics, and motion—all attributes of the soul described by Aristotle in *De Anima*—interlaced with angelic, God-like qualities. Hamlet queries: "What a piece of work is man, how noble in reason, how infinite in faculties, in form and moving, how express and admirable in action, how like an angel in apprehension, how like a god: the beauty of the world, the paragon of animals. And yet to me, what is this quintessence of dust? Man delights not me, nor woman neither" (2.2.288–93). Hamlet works through a range of different ways of imagining "man," from the faculties of the classical soul, to the Christian soul's resemblance to angels and God, ultimately concluding in the frustrating irresolution of the "quintessence of dust." He no longer assumes, as he did at the beginning of the play, that he is exclusively defined by his Christian soul tautologically defined by its immortality. Hamlet attempts to synthesize the Christian and classical souls into a hierarchical chain of being from animals to angels and gods, but this attempted synthesis fails, collapsing back to the level of earthly "dust" rather than rising to the immaterial transcendence of Christian salvation. Hamlet's description of "man" in terms of the "faculties" of reason and locomotion relies upon the grammatical coupling enabled by the copula "is." To the initial question of "what is man?" Hamlet responds that man is the Aristotelian soul defined by the faculties of reason and locomotion, form, and action. The movement to the Christian model of the soul is far less assured, described instead in terms of the metaphorical comparison of "like": "how like an angel . . . how like a god." In moving from the Aristotelian soul to man's spiritual affiliation with angels and gods, Hamlet shifts from the emphatic identity of "is" to the less certain comparative register of "like."

Hamlet's confusion between the two souls therefore hinges on the conflict between declarative constative fact ("is") and the rhetorical approximation of figural language ("like"). He finally evinces his disappointment by describing his negative emotional state: "man delights not me." Hamlet's negative emotional response registers his struggle to find the right language, be it Aristotelian or Christian, to describe the soul. In response to Hamlet's lack of "delight," Rosencrantz suggests that perhaps the tragedians will elicit more emotional "delight" from the prince. Hamlet's initial reaction to the player's Hecuba speech is outrage, since he finds the same fault in the player's performance as he does in the Christian soul: both are figurally "like" something else and do not simply declare a true statement of fact about the human soul. Although Hamlet desires the firm identity established by the copula "is" to describe the two souls (either he is a Christian soul, or he is a classical soul described in Aristotelian terms), he is disappointed to find that both souls are instead composed of fictions and figures.

In his contemplation of "what a piece of work is man," Hamlet appeals to a Renaissance commonplace, extending back to Aristotle's *Politics* and the *Rhetoric*, locating the human power of just and ethical judgment—to avenge or not—in the faculty of the soul's reason. This can clearly be seen in John Wilkinson's popular 1547 translation of Aristotle's *Ethics*:

> The Solle of man hath thre powers, one is called ye lyfe vegitable: in whiche man is partener with trees & with plantes: The second power, is the life sensible in the whiche a man is partener with beastes, for why al beastes haue lifes sensible. The third, is called solle reasonable, by the whiche a man differeth from all other thinges, for there is none reasonable but man. And this power reasonable is sometyme in acte, and sometime in power, frome whence the Beatitude is whan it is in acte and not whan it is in power. . . . The solle of man hath divers powers, as one called the power irracional: that is to say unresonable, wherein a manne differeth not from plantes & brute beastes. And therefore this is not the propre power in manne. For by this power manne may worke his operacion sleaping. The other is the power intellectiue, according to whose work after the forme aforsaid, is good and evell . . . The power racional is to be said in two sortes, the one is the power which is very resonable: that lerneth deserneth and judgeth. The other power, unreasonable, that is to saye, the power concupissible, and is called reasonable as long as it is obedient & under the power of that which is very reasonable, as the good child unto the father, whiche receaveth his correction. [38]

According to this vernacular account of the organic soul, man's rational power is what differentiates him from the irrational powers of plants and animals. It is this reasoning faculty that learns, discerns, and judges in order to reach ethical judgments, much like Aristotle suggests that "Rhetoric is as it were an offshoot . . . of the science of Ethics."[39] Hamlet's situation diverges from the main strain of Aristotelian thought in the early modern period, however, since his ascension up the hierarchy of the soul's faculties in positing "what a piece of work is man" is not sufficient to enable his powers of judgment to evaluate the justness of his father's command to avenge his murder.

Hamlet's logic collapses into the "quintessence of dust" not because of a failure of "reason" or "apprehension," but rather, quite surprisingly, because of a lack of *pleasure*: "and yet to me, what is this quintessence of dust? Man delights not me, nor woman neither." Hamlet's pivot at the end of his speech makes it clear that he regards the stakes of "man" on the plane of "delight," and not reason, and this subsequently shapes his extended interaction with the players. He draws instead from the other, strikingly different, discourse of the organic soul's faculties found in the domain of rhetoric, which is paradigmatically enunciated for our purposes in Nicholas Grimald's 1556 English translation of Cicero's *De Officiis*:

> For in this worlde here beneath, are three kindes of living wightes: wherof some have no more, but life: as plants, herbes, and trees, growing oute of the ground: some have not onely life, but senses also: as sheepe, oxen, & other beastes: ye third comprehendeth bothe these: and ouer life, & senses, hath the souerain ruler, Reason: as in the nature of man we see them all conjoyned. It remains therfore, and meete it is for him, such doings to practise: as may bothe severallie agree with eche of these parts, and generallie with them alltogither. To the parcell inferiour (by which we receiue our nourishment, our growing, & the state of our bodie) wellfare is appointed the uttmost ende: wherin the thing consisteth, we call profitable: which concernes the getting, maintayning, or recovering of helth. *Of the soule, or life endewed with senses, pleasure is the end, that it would enioye.*[40]

Cicero's text describes the same ladder of faculties defining the spectrum of living beings: mere life, such as "plants, herbes, and trees," life with "senses also: as . . . beastes," and "over life, & senses . . . Reason: as in the nature of man we see them all conjoined." Ultimately, however, unlike the prevailing discourse valorizing the triumph of reason, Cicero finds the faculty of reason to be necessary but not entirely sufficient for defining the ends of man, since "of the soule, or life endewed with senses, pleasure is the end, that it would enjoye." This stress on pleasure and delight confirms Quentin Skinner's suggestion that the tradition of Aristotle's *Ars Rhetorica* strove for a "distinctive art of reasoning," emphasizing the powers of judgment and the discernment of the just life as we have seen above, whereas the Renaissance disciples of Cicero and Quintilian were far more interested in the *art* of persuasion.[41] Through his thought process in the "what a piece of work is man" speech, Hamlet subtly shifts from the Aristotelian understanding of how the soul gives substance to the idea of "man" through the rational and ethical power to learn, discern, and judge, to the distinctly Ciceronian model of the soul's faculties as the locus of delight and pleasure.

This nuanced evolution in Hamlet's thinking signals why this speech is so important as a pivot point in the play. Hamlet's change of mind moves us from a human soul made distinct by reason so as to reach ethical judgments surrounding revenge to a soul defined by aesthetic experiences of "delight" and "pleasure." This transition in focus is why the introduction to the players in act 2 is so timely, and is precisely what motivates Hamlet to ask insistently for a "speech straight" away, a "passionate speech." Hamlet's meditation has drifted from the ethical domain of reason in order to decide a just course of action—"there is nothing either good or bad but *thinking* makes it so" (2.2.244–45, emphasis mine)—to his idea to create a "speech of some dozen or sixteen lines which I would set down and insert" into the text of the "Murder of Gonzago."

The "Passionate Speech" and the Monstrous Force of the "Conceit"

The movement to thinking about soul in its aesthetic capacity is by no means a smooth shift in how Hamlet approaches the problem of avenging his father's murder, as demonstrated by the anguish provoked by the "passionate speech" that the player does eventually deliver, as powerfully described in the "rogue and peasant slave" soliloquy:

> Ay, so God buy to you! Now I am alone.
> O, what a rogue and peasant slave am I!
> Is it not monstrous that this player here,
> But in a fiction, in a dream of passion,
> Could force his soul so to his own conceit
> That from her working all his visage wanned;
> Tears in his eyes, distraction in his aspect,
> A broken voice, and his whole function suiting,
> With forms to his conceit? And all for nothing,
> For Hecuba!
> What's Hecuba to him or he to her,
> That he should weep for her? What would he do
> Had he the motive and the cue for passion
> That I have? He would drown the stage with tears,
> And cleave the general ear with horrid speech,
> Make mad the guilty, and appal the free,
> Confound the ignorant, and amaze indeed
> The very faculties of eyes and ears. (2.2.505–22)

Hamlet's reaction to the player's "passionate speech" has frequently attracted critical attention as a way to map Hamlet's complex intersubjective relation with his parents onto the triangle of Pyrrhus, Priam, and Hecuba.[42] More recently, Gail Kern Paster has popularized a reading strategy emphasizing the player's heavy focus on humoral physiology, in the description of Pyrrhus with a dark complexion, in his armor covered in blood, and in his physiological state of being "roasted in wrath and fire." In reading Hamlet's response to the Hecuba speech as an expression of filial intersubjectivity on the one hand and of humoral physiology on the other, these interpretations have glanced across the surface of the most obvious but crucial point about Hamlet's soliloquy: he is most preoccupied with the player's "passionate speech" as a rhetorical fiction, and in the speech he articulates the play's most explicit account of how "conceits" can alter the soul through aesthetic experience, precisely as Cicero describes.

Hamlet is initially horrified by the player's "passionate speech," calling his performance "monstrous." The player's Hecuba speech provokes such a violent reaction from Hamlet precisely because it was extremely successful: the actor was able to wind himself up into a passionate fury, arousing powerful emotions in Hamlet and his spectators. The problem with this effective dramatic performance, and what makes the player so "monstrous," is the fact that his account of Hecuba's grief is fake: it is a "fiction" and simply a "dream of passion." Hamlet berates himself as a "rogue and peasant slave" since he has lacked such fury in response to his father's death. His horrified response to the player centers on their radical difference of agency. He defines himself in abject terms, as a "rogue and peasant slave" with no power to control himself or his reaction to his father's command to murder. In contrast to Hamlet's abject paralysis, the "monstrous" player wields a tremendous power to manipulate every aspect of his being. The player has the active power to "force" his own "soul" through fictional language and rhetoric, in contrast to the abject position of the "slave" describing Hamlet who does not know how to feel and act.

Hamlet is very specific in describing the nature of the player's agency to transform himself by outlining the impact of the rhetorical "conceit" of the "passionate speech" on the player's "soul." He very specifically delineates the effect that rhetoric and fictional language have on the Aristotelian soul's faculties, passion, and organs. The reaction to the player's theatrical rhetoric emanates from the organs of the soul. Hamlet's explanation of the relation of the player's rhetoric to the soul is surprising because it redefines the language of fiction as something with the power to physically change the structure of the soul and its organs. Rhetorical "conceits," therefore, do not only involve the cognitive appeal to passion and reason of conventional classical or humanist rhetoric. Hamlet turns theatrical rhetoric and performance into a way of materially intervening in the physical "function" of the soul's faculties, capable of directly disturbing the listener's organs. Therefore, the player does not simply stimulate a free play of feelings or thoughts; his rhetoric goes so far as to physically change the body: draining the blood from his face, making his visage pale and altering the circulation of his blood, forcing tears to flow from his eyes, twisting his face into contortions, cracking his voice, "cleaving" the sense organs with "horrid speech," and stunning the "faculties of eyes and ears." The language of rhetoric powerfully moves the soul to such an extent that its organs and faculties are torn apart in a passion. Although the rhetorical "conceit" is completely fictional, the effect it has on the soul is violently physical. Hamlet describes a model in which the language of rhetoric and theatrical performance can fundamentally alter the organs of sense, circulation, and affect composing the faculties of the soul.

Hamlet's emphatic declaration that rhetorical "conceit" targets the organs and "faculties" of the Aristotelian soul complicates Paster's claim that the player's Hecuba speech and Hamlet's reaction present a model of early modern subjectivity paralleling Deleuze and Guattari's concept of a "disembodied selfhood" anchored in a "Body without Organs": "nothing more than a set of valves, locks, floodgates, bowls, or communicating vessels."[43] Such an analogy between Hamlet and Deleuze and Guattari is tenuous, since Hamlet is decisively talking about a soul necessarily defined by its organs. For all of Paster's attempts to cast Hamlet as a "body without organs," Hamlet persistently invokes his organs as the basis of his faculties. Paster herself revises her claim, admitting that "the early modern body is a body with organs—indeed organs given discrete psychological functions," in an acknowledgment that the early modern subject was defined by an organic faculty psychology in the Aristotelian tradition.[44] My argument, contra Paster, attempts to restore the early modern understanding of the body's organs as vitally important in defining the early modern soul, and not as a proleptic anticipation of a proto-postmodern "body without organs." Paster's project in general notices the pervasiveness of the language of faculty psychology in Shakespeare's plays, and in *Hamlet* in particular. However, she construes the vocabulary of faculty psychology in early modern England in terms of humoral physiology, and only partially acknowledges the specifically Aristotelian debt of such a materialist psychology. In a way, Paster's work supports my own argument by demonstrating the ubiquity of materialist faculty psychology in Renaissance England, but it does not comprehensively recognize how such a faculty psychology contributes to a new understanding of the early modern inflections of the classical soul, and not the hyper-material fluidity of the Deleuzean body.

Ultimately, Hamlet argues that the "whole function" of the player's soul bends "with forms to his conceit." His diction in this case reconceives the nature of the classical soul, by revising Aristotle's famous definition of the soul as the relation of form and matter in *De Anima*. In Aristotle's foundational definition, the soul is the form given to the matter of a "natural body possessed of organs."[45] Hamlet fundamentally rethinks the nature of the soul by embedding its "form" in the power of the rhetorical conceit. He defines the "form" and "function" of the soul as bending to the structure of the "conceit." Hamlet transforms the concept of "form" central to the

Aristotelian definition of the soul into something inflected by the language of the rhetorical "conceit." The "fiction" of theater possesses the power to change the "form" of the soul, "forcing" the faculties and their associated organs to bend to the shape of the rhetorical "conceit." In lamenting the power of the player's fictional words, Hamlet gives tremendous power to rhetorical address. Fictional rhetoric alters the nature of the classical soul's faculties, transforming the "form" and "function" of the soul into something modulated by a "conceit." Despite his initial refusal to engage in rhetoric's soul-bending force, after his extended reflection in the "rogue and peasant slave" soliloquy, we begin to see a subtle change in Hamlet's growing appreciation of the positive valence of rhetoric's influence on the soul as a way to redress the imbalance of power with his adversaries.[46]

Speaking with a "Miraculous Organ": Passion and Action

We can identify two major consequences of the rhetorical soul in the final three acts of the play. One is directed at Claudius and Gertrude in moments of confrontation, and the second implicates Hamlet's own soul. Based on his observations on the ability of the player's rhetoric to warp and to reshape the faculties of the soul, Hamlet uses this power as one of his primary modes of engaging his family and members of the court, alongside his more obvious and self-declared employment of the "antic disposition." He turns the disruptive effect of rhetoric upon the soul's faculties immediately toward Claudius, in the form of the Mousetrap play, and subsequently in his interrogation of Gertrude, when he "speaks daggers" to his mother in order to probe the maladies of her corrupted soul.

Based upon this new understanding of the soul, Hamlet moves past the paralyzing confusion demonstrated in the "what a piece of work is man" speech, when he harnesses the power of rhetoric as a way to test Claudius.

> Why, what an ass am I! This is most brave,
> That I, the son of a dear father murdered,
> Prompted to my revenge by heaven and hell,
> Must like a whore unpack my heart with words,
> And fall a-cursing like a very drab,
> A scullion! Fie upon't! foh!
> About, my brains. Hum—I have heard
> That guilty creatures sitting at a play,
> Have by the very cunning of the scene
> Been struck so to the soul that presently
> They have proclaimed their malefactions;
> For murder, though it have no tongue, will speak
> With most miraculous organ. I'll have these players

> Play something like the murder of my father
> Before mine uncle. I'll observe his looks.
> I'll tent him to the quick. If 'a do blench,
> I know my course. (2.2.539–55)

Hamlet makes a decisive turn in his thinking "About, my brains" and comes to realize that he can redirect those "words" that defined him as a "whore" as a way to probe Claudius's heart, turning the power of rhetoric away from self-flagellating grief, and toward his uncle as a form of diagnostic procedure. Therefore, the power of the "conceit" to "force the soul" of the player which frustrates Hamlet in the first half of the soliloquy becomes a potent way to judge Claudius by "striking his soul." When the "cunning" of a theatrical performance "strikes" the soul of guilty spectators, the soul immediately "proclaims" its "malefactions" and deeds, in the peculiar idiom of the soul's organs. The agitating power of rhetoric can unearth the deep structure of one's psychology by bypassing rational cognition, and by "striking" the organs of the Aristotelian faculties to such a forceful extent, that they "speak" and "proclaim" the truth in an autonomic physiological and affective response. Hamlet's power to disrupt others and to control his own heart and brain hinges on the capacity of rhetoric to anatomize Claudius's soul. In claiming that he will "observe his looks" and "tent him to the quick," Hamlet is not suggesting that he will pitch a tent to shelter Claudius's soul from the rain. In medieval and early modern English usage, the verb "to tent" defined the act of probing and dissecting an organ during an anatomical procedure.[47] Hamlet therefore describes the power of theatrical rhetoric to disturb the Aristotelian faculties as a form of psychological anatomy, a rhetorical "tenting" or probing of the soul's faculties. If Hamlet is at first frustrated by the extent to which he could not control his passions, faculties, and organs in response to the fictional rhetoric of the play, he realizes that Claudius will not be able to control himself either. Hamlet's initial lamentation about his abject lack of agency as a "rogue and peasant slave" who is powerless in the face of the player's rhetorical "conceit" and "passionate speech" becomes the basis for a decisive course of action that will enable him to judge Claudius.

Through the course of the "rogue and peasant slave" soliloquy, Hamlet comes to embrace the paradox of a mode of *action* provoked by the experience of the soul's *passion*, a contradiction in terms. As Susan James has demonstrated, "passion" and "action" represented the two diametrically opposed poles of the classical soul's function as it was understood in the early modern world.[48] Passion defined the faculties of the soul in their moments of passive receptivity and "suffering." By contrast, action described the role of the three faculties in shaping human agency: the capacity to eat and to reproduce, to move, to think and imagine, to respond to sensory stimuli, and for the rhetor, "to do things with words," to borrow J. L. Austin's expression.[49] Embracing the two far poles of the soul's function and paradoxically fusing them together takes on a new writerly dimension in *Hamlet* that reflects Shakespeare's own dramatic art. Hamlet's capacity to act in relation to the king is literally authorial in nature, by drafting "a speech of some dozen or sixteen lines which I would set down and insert" in the "Murder of Gonzago" (2.2.515–19). In response to the player's performance of the "passionate speech" initially demanded by Hamlet, the prince in turn comes to write his own "speech" composed of "lines" to strike Claudius's soul. Hamlet's authorial agency lies in his power to write the words to disturb the soul of the guilty. His problem, then, is not a "soul unfit for the performance," as Goethe's Wilhelm Meister exclaims in "probably the single most influential interpretation of the character of Hamlet," according to Paul Kottman.[50] The issue at hand arises as a different kind of fitness altogether: how to select the words "fit" to probe Claudius's faculties. And indeed, the player king's speech matches the tenor of Hamlet's own meditations:

> To pay ourselves what to ourselves is debt.
> What to ourselves in passion we propose,
> The passion ending, doth the purpose lose.
> The violence of either grief or joy
> Their own enactures with themselves destroy. (3.2.175–79)

The speech ranges across the self-reflexive paradox of a passion that stimulates action, or in the case of the oration, one that destroys the self with the odd neologism of "enactures."[51] The destructive intent of Hamlet's stated goal to strike Claudius's soul and to "catch the conscience of the king" proves to be effective, with Claudius later lamenting the psychological condition that Hamlet anticipated: "my soul is full of discord and dismay!" (4.1.40).

Since Hamlet's rhetorical "tenting" of the soul is so effective with Claudius, he uses the same procedure in his confrontation with his mother. In act 3 scene 4, Hamlet forces Gertrude to peer into the mirror revealing the nature of her soul:

> Come, come, and sit you down. You shall not budge.
> You go not till I set you up a glass
> Where you may see the inmost part of you. (3.4.17–19)

The "glass" Hamlet has in mind that will be capable of exposing the "inmost part" of Gertrude's soul is a fictional image, "the counterfeit presentment of two brothers":

> Look here upon this picture and on this,
> The counterfeit presentment of two brothers.
> See what a grace is seated on this brow:
> Hyperion's curls, the front of Jove himself,

An eye like Mars, to threaten and command,
A station like the herald Mercury
New lighted on a heaven-kissing hill—
A combination and a form indeed
Where every god did seem to set his seal
To give the world assurance of a man.
This was your husband. Look you now what follows.
Here is your husband, like a mildewed ear
Blasting his wholesome brother. Have you eyes?
Could you on this fair mountain leave to feed,
And batten on this moor? Ha, have you eyes?
You cannot call it love, for at your age
The heyday in the blood is tame, it's humble,
And waits upon the judgment, and what judgment
Would step from this to this? (3.4.54–72)

For generations of psychoanalytically minded critics, Hamlet's confrontation with Gertrude in her closet represents a sort of primal scene, the son's most direct attempt to fantasize about and seize control of his mother's sexuality.[52] However, Hamlet's "glass" up to Gertrude does not reveal her psychology in a psychoanalytical register so much as it exposes her faculty psychology through a sustained speech. The prince in effect delivers an ekphrastic oration carefully describing the aesthetic and ethical consequences of the visual differences within the "counterfeit presentment of two brothers." His speech engages in a close reading, as it were, of the two "pictures," forcing Gertrude to see the psychological corruption of her faculties and organs. Hamlet exploits the power of his verbal description as a commentary critiquing his mother that comes to anatomize or "tent" the faculties of her soul. Hamlet has therefore made a full reversal by this point in the play. If he initially reacts in confusion and anguish upon observing the player's "passionate speech" in act 2, he mobilizes the same rhetorical resources, in this case through the ekphrastic exercise of praise and blame directed at two "counterfeit" pictures, to provoke precisely such a disruption in Gertrude's soul.

Hamlet pushes even further in condemning his mother's acts by engaging in an extended vivisection of her faculties:

. . . and what judgment
Would step from this to this? Sense sure you have,
Else could you not have motion, but sure that sense
Is apoplexed, for madness would not err
Nor sense to ecstasy was ne'er so thralled
But it reserved some quantity of choice
To serve in such a difference. What devil was't
That thus hath cozened you at hoodman-blind?

> Eyes without feeling, feeling without sight,
> Ears without hands or eyes, smelling sans all,
> Or but a sickly part of one true sense
> Could not so mope. O shame, where is thy blush?
> . . . .
> Proclaim no shame
> When the compulsive ardor gives the charge,
> Since frost itself as actively doth burn,
> And reason panders will. (3.4.71–88)

Hamlet specifies that Gertrude's utter failure of judgment, leading her to move from the image of King Hamlet to that of Claudius, reflects the deep-seated infection of the organic faculties that have taken hold of her soul. The rhetoric deployed here specifically repeats the procedure of "tenting" or anatomically probing the humors, spirits, and organs that Hamlet described in act 2 as his way of "striking the soul" of Claudius. Hamlet's choice of the word "apoplexy" to describe the condition of Gertrude's faculties is significant, since the term derives from the Greek *apoplexia*, signifying a "striking or hitting."[53] As in the case of Claudius's soul "struck" by a theatrical performance mirroring his murderous act, Hamlet's "counterfeit presentment" of the brothers' images serves as a way to diagnose the extent to which Gertrude's Aristotelian faculties have been "struck" or "apoplexed" into a state of perversion and sickness. Hamlet's choice of the term "apoplexed" to describe the etiology of Gertrude's disease of the soul specifically identifies a problem in her organs. Apart from defining a "striking" or "hitting," the medical condition of "apoplexy" describes the uncontrolled bleeding of the internal organs. In claiming that Gertrude's faculties of sense, motion, and judgment are "apoplexed," Hamlet specifies that Gertrude's organs are suffering from a profound dysfunction verging on stroke or hemorrhage.[54] In contrast to the faculties of locomotion, sensation, emotion, the common sense, will, and rational judgment working in harmony, the organs responsible for Gertrude's faculties suffer from the severe insult of "apoplexy," causing her faculties to fall apart in a dysfunctional "ecstasy."

The "ecstasy" of her soul has disrupted the clear path linking the lower faculties of locomotion and sense to her higher cognitive faculties of the common sense ("one true sense"), emotion ("O shame, where is thy blush?"), and ratiocination ("what judgment"/"mope" or act without one's wits). Hamlet explains that the rupture between the lower faculties of sense and motion and the higher faculties of affect and judgment has occurred because each of Gertrude's senses has become unhinged from the other adjacent sense organs, in a case of disrupted synesthesia: "Eyes without feeling, feeling without sight, / Ears without hands or eyes, smelling sans all." In a breakdown of the soul's coherence similar to that which we have already seen in the "what a piece of work is man" speech, the interrelated functions of Gertrude's faculties have been dissolved, since the senses and their organs no longer correspond. The problem afflicting Gertrude's soul is a dysfunctional misalignment of her faculties and their organs.

For her part, Gertrude clearly grasps the message of Hamlet's incisive critique:

> O Hamlet, speak no more!
> Thou turn'st my eye into my very soul,
> And there I see such black and grained spots
> As will not leave their tinct. (3.4.89–92)

Hamlet's anatomy of Gertrude's soul "turn'st her eyes into her very soul" in a literal autopsy or auto-optics of her diseased faculties and organs. She specifies that it is Hamlet's language, his "words" and "speech," which serve as the medium disturbing her soul:

> O, speak to me no more!
> These words like daggers enter in my ears. (3.4.95–96)

If Hamlet promises to use theatrical rhetoric to "strike" and "tent" Claudius's soul, in this confrontation with Gertrude, he comes to fully exploit the tremendous power of forceful rhetorical address ("words like daggers") to alter the faculties and organs of someone else's soul.[55] Hamlet verges on stepping too far, however, since the ghost sees the need to interrupt Hamlet's verbal barrage:

> O, step between her and her fighting soul!
> Conceit in weakest bodies strongest works. (3.4.115–16)

Hamlet's rhetorical "conceit" splits Gertrude in two, dividing his mother between "her" and "her fighting soul." Much like the power of the player's "conceit" to "force" his soul to the form of the "passionate speech," Hamlet uses the force of his own rhetorical "conceit" to alienate his mother from her own soul. The "conceit's" ability to anatomize and reshape the faculties of the other's soul actively "works" to divide the other within herself, othering herself from her own soul.[56] Hamlet's "words like daggers" and "conceits" function as a "glass" that reveals to Gertrude her soul's decaying faculties and organs as an alien, exteriorized object to be seen in a mirror; an optical specimen to study and contemplate rather than an immanent part of her self. If in previous moments of the play Hamlet used theatrical rhetoric to disrupt and anatomically "tent" Claudius's faculties in an effort to unveil his guilt, in his later confrontation with Gertrude, Hamlet uses the power of "words" and the "conceit" to alienate his mother from her own soul, harnessing the "conceit" to fracture her in two. In both cases, Hamlet uses the moving power of the fictional rhetorical "conceit" to reshape his primary adversaries, Claudius and Gertrude, into disrupted subjects with shattered psyches. He redirects rhetoric's ability to disturb the soul's faculties as a way to reconstitute others as souls internally divided within themselves, which, in effect, re-creates the basic problem of the presence of two souls in one body. Hamlet's sustained perturbation of the rhetorical soul gives him the power to recast others as subjects defined by auto-alterity, an otherness of the soul within the most intimate recesses of their selves.

The profoundly disruptive effects of the rhetorical "conceit" and fictional language upon the organic soul are precisely the violently negative consequences of which the ghost warned Hamlet in their initial encounter. The king's ghost vividly told Hamlet that he must never narrate the literary "tale" and "eternal blazon" of the Christian soul's punishment whose "words" would "harrow" and shock the faculties of all who listen. Hamlet's father argues that it is important to keep the disruptive rhetorical force of the "tale" and "blazon" segregated from the soul in order to prevent a disturbing "harrowing" of its organs and faculties. Throughout the play, Hamlet increasingly disregards his father's interdiction to keep the rhetorical "blazons" and "words" of the "tale" away from the soul. His arc throughout the play hinges on his growing ability to capture the powerful effect of "harrowing" rhetoric so as to alter and disrupt the souls of others. Hamlet disobeys his father's command, in insisting that the explosive contact between the "words" and "tales" of rhetoric and the soul must occur. The susceptibility of the classical soul to be "harrowed" by rhetoric opens a space for Hamlet to redirect the soul to different ends. But to what ends does he move?

The Self-Inflaming Orator

The second major consequence resulting from Hamlet's recognition of the "soulbending" power of rhetoric is a more fundamental transformation of his relationship to his own soul. He turns the force of rhetoric into a way to self-reflexively reshape the configuration of his own faculties, in effect answering his own previously posited question of "what a piece of work is man" by reworking how his soul defines *himself* as man. By twisting the ethics of "knowing thyself" (which we will examine more extensively in the following chapter on Sir John Davies), Hamlet imagines an alternative ethics of the self founded upon the power of rhetoric that is reflected back onto one's own soul, rather than used to influence and shape others. This self-probing address is, of course, famously the purpose of the "to be or not to be" soliloquy, and is also quite pointedly the goal of his soliloquy in act 4 scene 4:

> How all occasions do inform against me
> And spur my dull revenge. What is a man
> If his chief good and market of his time
> Be but to sleep and feed? A beast, no more.
> Sure He that made us with such large discourse,
> Looking before and after, gave us not
> That capability and godlike reason
> To fust in us unused.

In this sequence from the second quarto edition, Hamlet subtly revises and appends a coda to the unresolved question of "what a piece of work is man" in act 2 scene 2. Surely, he speculates, "man" cannot merely be "a beast, no more," defined by the impulse to "sleep" and the urge to "feed," stemming from the impulses of the vegetable soul.[57] And indeed, man is defined by "such large discourse" that he can conceive of causes and effects, "looking before and after," that bespeaks a "capability and godlike reason." The crucial addition here is that the reasoning faculty takes the form of "large discourse"—in both the linguistic and rational senses of the term—distinguishing the human soul from the bestial functions of the vegetable and animal souls. The proviso of the human soul furnished with "large discourse" also breaks from Hamlet's prior goal of aspiring to the state of "angels," by relocating the "godlike" character in man in the production of discourse, and not a metaphysical rise up the chain of being, which as we have seen, collapsed into the "quintessence of dust."[58]

Hamlet's probing soliloquies are not so much moments of self-fashioning or the invention of a proto-modern subjectivity replete with a deep core of interiority. They are, rather, "discourses" directed at the self, a thought process performed through speech, and most importantly, a type of self-persuasion where Hamlet mimics the classical rhetorical topos of turning the instruments of invention and persuasion onto the self. The most famous example of this strategy can be found in Cicero's *De Oratore*:

> I give you my word that I never tried, by means of a speech, to arouse either indignation or compassion . . . without being really stirred myself, as I worked upon their minds, by the very feelings to which I was seeking to prompt them. For it is not easy to succeed in making an arbitrator angry with the right party, if you yourself seem to treat the affair with indifference; or in making him hate the right party, unless he first sees you on fire with hatred yourself; nor will he be prompted to compassion, unless you have shown him the tokens of your own grief by word, sentiment, tone of voice, look and even by loud lamentation. For just as there is no substance so ready to take fire, as to be capable of generating flame without the application of a spark, so also there is no mind so ready to absorb an orator's

> influence, as to be inflammable when the assailing speaker is not himself aglow with passion. . . . Plato . . . left on record—no man can be a good poet who is not on fire with passion, and inspired by something very like frenzy.[59]

For Cicero as with Hamlet, a "speech" can only be effective on others if it has already inflamed the speaker's own soul. In this recursive feedback loop, the force of rhetoric directed at others so as to "work upon their minds" reflects back to the speaker, "stirring" himself in the process. This model of a self-reflexive rhetoric placing the speaking subject in an agitating relationship with himself, in which he occupies both the positions of the subject and object of rhetorical persuasion and perturbation, matches the arc of Hamlet's soliloquies in general. From his first "O that this too too solid flesh" speech, to the "rogue and peasant slave" and "how all occasions do inform against me" soliloquies, Hamlet's speeches serve as rhetorical attacks on himself, arousing feelings of indignation, lamentation, and anger (precisely as Cicero suggests) so as to incite himself into action. This is by no means a seamless practice for Hamlet, and in many instances he does not practice with himself what he preaches to others, particularly in the case when he lectures the players to "speak the speech" with "a temperance that may give it smoothness" (3.2.1–7) and in his appeal to Horatio soon thereafter to "give me that man / that is not passion's slave" (3.2.64–65). For all of his proclamations to the contrary, however, Hamlet reverses himself and uses precisely the same passionate rhetorical agitation of the soul that he disclaims as his preferred mode of self-address and self-definition.

Part of the reason for Hamlet's complex and wavering opinion about the value of rhetoric's effect on the soul's faculties is its involuntary nature. The plane of agency that Hamlet begins to articulate across his soliloquies is only partial: he is not an agent with the unfettered freedom to act as he pleases. The partial agency that Hamlet recuperates from the effects of rhetoric on the faculties of the soul is momentary and largely uncontrollable. For a brief window of time, the stable equilibrium of the soul, repeatedly emphasized in the normative depictions of the hierarchy of the faculties we have examined, is thrown into disarray by the rhetorical "conceit." Hamlet recognizes that it is precisely this unbalanced state of the faculties that gives him an opportunity to reshape the souls of Claudius and Gertrude, and increasingly, his own soul, into a different conformation, albeit only for a brief instant exceeding the rational control of the self. Hamlet's agency is therefore counterintuitive because it gains its power from being completely involuntary, defined by the explosive response of the soul's faculties to rhetoric, precisely like the uncontrollable "harrowing" of the soul provoked by the ghost's tale.

This involuntary reaction to rhetoric does not give one the positive agency to remold one's soul as one desires according to an ideal state of being, but rather opens up a negative agency to redefine others and oneself through disruption by throwing one's constitutive faculties out of harmony. Unlike Alan Sinfield's reading that counterposes the Calvinist determinism of the Protestant soul against Hamlet's effort to attain a "Stoic tranquility of mind" through the "exercise of rational powers," I argue that Hamlet's ability to resist the punitive binding of Protestant doctrine hinges on his movement away from a state of "tranquility" and reason, to the opposite pole of the rhetorical soul's disordered frenzy that reacts explosively to passionate address.[60] By redefining himself, Claudius, and Gertrude in terms of the very brief window of time in which they all experience the chaotic disarray of their faculties, Hamlet imagines the negative freedom to capture the "soul-bending" force of rhetoric. Hamlet draws upon the early modern discourse of the rhetorical soul to open up the possibility of a fleeting freedom in a Protestant world filled with enslaved souls: the agency to define oneself as a disrupted subject.

Hamlet's Rhetorical Afterlife

Shakespeare's innovation in the context of the early modern two-souls discourse lies in this basic shift from a vocabulary of the captive soul to a tentative recuperation of the positive possibilities resulting from the instability of the rhetorical soul. This rhetorical effect on the soul served as the basis of Shakespeare's own education, in the form of the vernacular English pedagogical treatises on the art of eloquence prevalent at the time. The text of *Hamlet* stages this shift in our understanding of the early modern soul. Shakespeare's main move in *Hamlet*, then, is a provisional break from a theology of the soul that he inherits from the Reformation and that shapes our entry into the play, with the warring visions of Catholic and Protestant afterlives depicted in the first act and subsequently in the "what a piece of work is man" speech. He moves with the Hecuba speech and Hamlet's "rogue and peasant slave" soliloquy to a rhetorical understanding of the soul that reveals dynamic new ways to imagine action.

The result of rhetoric as a master discourse of the soul is a double-edged sword. Rhetoric certainly makes the soul "malleable," as we have seen, and classical texts prevalent during Shakespeare's time would have "called on the orator to mould his audience, to manipulate or 'work them up.'"[61] But the plasticity of the soul through the instruments of rhetoric is not an unqualified benefit, since, as Skinner points out, the susceptibility of the soul's faculties and passions to be bent by rhetorical language recasts the soul to some as "inherently unstable and hence pliable" on one hand, but "volatile" and extremely fickle on the other. The destabilizing effect of rhetoric upon the soul leads "to an exceeding confusion of judgments" and a pell-mell of emotional states, as suggested in Florio's popular 1603 translation of Montaigne.[62]

We can see the pliability of the soul as it slips into an unstable volatility in the final scenes of the play. As a result of his final soliloquy in act 4 scene 4, Hamlet ultimately collapses into violence: "O, from this time forth, / My thoughts be bloody or be nothing worth!" (4.4.9.55–56). Hamlet has gained by this point the ability to arouse himself to a state of "bloody" thoughts, but he cannot control the outcome of his response, and his incitation to violence proves to be all too effective. This consistent self-reflexive provocation into a frenzied state moves the play into the surprising, and seemingly out of character, violent rage that suffuses act 5, beginning with Hamlet's assertion of his royal status: "This is I, Hamlet the Dane," while he leaps into Ophelia's grave to grapple with Laertes. This absurd physical spectacle encoded in the stage directions seems to contradict J. Dover Wilson's suggestion that Hamlet's return inaugurates "the complete Prince; dignified, cool, reflective."[63] As de Grazia has observed, the "gymnastic feat and . . . rhetorical tour de force" of Hamlet's leap has "posed a problem for critics who find a new tranquility in Hamlet after his sea adventure."[64] The intensity of the violence only escalates in the final combative fencing duel, and when Hamlet finally does kill the king, it is certainly not the calm, deliberate revenge of the "man / That is not passion's slave" (3.2.64–65), but a redundant and opportunistic act of violence blinded by rage. Hamlet kills Claudius "twice-over," since he has already stabbed the king with the "envenomed" foil and yet still proceeds to force Claudius to swallow the remaining poison while berating the dying man with a litany of hateful epithets.[65]

> Here, thou incestuous,
>   murd'rous, damnèd Dane,
> Drink off this potion. *Forcing him to drink the poison.*
>   Is thy union here?
> Follow my mother. *King dies.* (5.2.267–69)

The violent excess of the scene stands as an over-literal performance of the passionate force bending the soul's faculties throughout the play. Perhaps the "soulbending" power of rhetoric we have examined finally brings the soul to the point of being broken.

Indeed, the final scene of *Hamlet* is an oration. Hamlet implores Horatio to "report me and my cause aright / to the unsatisfied" by "telling his story" (5.2.317–18, and 328). Horatio follows Hamlet's command to "tell his story" in literal terms, ordering the bodies of the main characters to "high on a stage be placed to the view" and "presently performed" to an "audience" of spectators. Horatio insists that the "story" of Hamlet's life be performed immediately on stage, while the audience's "minds are wild," preventing errors of "plot" from the passage of time. The performance in question, however, is less a theatrical play than it is an oratorical mode recited by a single speaker. Horatio turns Hamlet's afterlife into a rhetorical performance, which must occur while "men's minds are wild," echoing Hamlet's insistence that the power of the "passionate speech" must provoke a "harrowing" of the soul's faculties. In effect, Hamlet's afterlife embodies the disruptive logic of rhetoric's "passionate speech," unfolding in the rhetorical frenzy that occurs when "men's minds" are made "wild" by the performance of Hamlet's life and death.

Hamlet therefore has two afterlives. One, speculatively described by Horatio as crowded with "flights of angels," seems to be overly optimistic. Given that Hamlet's father has confirmed the existence of the "prison house," we might assume that the prince's soul must endure torture and punishment for breaking God's commandment forbidding murder. The second afterlife to which we are more directly exposed is an oratorical performance, transplanting his "dying voice" into the speech of Horatio, capturing the "wildness" of the soul's faculties that he has described for much of the play in his own soliloquies.

For the purposes of conclusion, the oratorical afterlife calls for attention, since it extradiagetically implicates the audience and readers of the play itself. Horatio explains that the "story" to be "presently performed" on stage is an account of "how these things came about"; how the dead bodies strewn about the stage met their violent fates. This story of "how these things came about" is precisely what the playtext of Hamlet itself narrates. Hamlet commands Horatio to recite the story of his life and death, a story that is encoded in the text of *Hamlet* that we have been reading or watching for five acts. Hamlet performs a striking act of metalanguage, implicating the audience or reader in the experience of the main character's rhetorical afterlife.[66] The play's final moments give an account of why the story of Hamlet's life is being told in the first place: the end of *Hamlet*'s plot is the beginning of the play's text, which will be recounted to us, the audience, by Horatio. The audience or reader has been participating in Hamlet's rhetorical afterlife for the entire duration of the play, but we can only realize this at the end of the play, in its account of the play's genesis as a retelling of Hamlet's "story."

If we are to accept that the "audience" gathered by Horatio and Fortinbras to "hear" Hamlet's story interpolates the actual spectating audience or reader, then the "wild minds" in question are our own, and we are suddenly implicated in the disruptive effects of rhetoric on the soul's faculties just as the play's fictional characters have been. In the shock of the final scene's rapid-fire sequence of violence, the audience's stunned reaction demonstrates that our "wild minds" prove to be as susceptible to the power of passionate rhetoric as Hamlet first identified in his encounter with the players. The effect of Hamlet's disruptive rhetorical "conceits" is not only directed at Claudius and Gertrude. Hamlet's rhetorical afterlife, which Horatio "speaks" and "truly delivers" as a speech, has "harrowed" our own faculties, passions, and organs (stirring confusion, elation and sadness, making our hearts race, causing us to feel the tragic effects of drama), eliciting precisely the same disruption of the soul's faculties by "passionate speech" that provoked Hamlet's anxious wonder. Hamlet turns the mirror thrust upon Claudius and Gertrude to the audience in his final move. The "passionate speech" that disrupts the faculties of the soul is the playtext of *Hamlet* itself, which we have been reading all along.

The "wildness" of the soul provoked in the audience by Horatio's speech, and by the story of Hamlet itself, more accurately anticipates the seventeenth-century reception of Shakespeare's contemporaries than it does more modern interpretations that have obsessed over the protagonist's reflective self-consciousness. The majority of seventeenth-century responses to the play both parodied and puzzled over the "excited and violent motion" that marks the play's ending. As de Grazia mused in the epigraph to this chapter, "in the first decades of its performance, Hamlet's signature action may have been not paralyzing thought but frenzied motion."[67] However, the play's "frenzied motion" should not simply be characterized as the absurd "hyperactivity" of a "roustabout clown."[68] As I have claimed, the "frenzied motion" building to a crescendo by act 5 is part of the very point of the play. Hamlet's frenzy of the soul represents the culmination of a rhetorical strategy of provoking psychological turbulence, which Shakespeare adopts and revises from his schoolboy's education into a mode of tragic self-definition and ultimately, into the message that he transmits through the voice of Horatio to the audience as the prince's oratorical afterlife.

Chapter 3

✦

Sir John Davies and the Lyrical Psychology of the English Commonwealth

In moving from William Shakespeare in the previous chapter to Sir John Davies (1569–1626), the focus of the present chapter, we are shifting perhaps jarringly from the most famous author of the Renaissance world to one of the most "neglected" ones.[1] Davies represents something of an enigma, and it is fair to say that he possesses the most complicated reputation, at least in terms of biography, of all the authors in this literary history of the two souls. He is known among literary scholars as the author of *Nosce Teipsum* (Know Thyself), one of the most popular accounts of the soul in Elizabethan England, which was widely read and cited, and which had the particular honor of being "well relisht" by Queen Elizabeth in the course of her readings.[2] But he enjoys a second afterlife among legal historians and theorists as one of the foundational figures in the common law tradition, and has the dubious distinction of being the author of the "imperial formula" developed during his appointment as attorney general in Ireland, which would come to be applied to pernicious effect in the expansion of the British Empire decades after his death.[3] Reflecting upon these dissonant legacies, David Hadas has mused that "Sir John Davies touches us in two ways . . . his poems, particularly *Orchestra*, still give us pleasure, and the settlement of Protestants in Northern Ireland, for which he worked so hard, still gives us pain."[4] Scholars have rarely mingled the pleasure and the pain that Davies provokes. And so readers of his witty lyric poems lament his later turn to conservative legal principles, while scholars focused on his legal prose largely dismiss his poetry of the 1590s as underripe juvenilia.

This chapter reads Davies's lyrics and his legal prose as two faces of a single coin linked by an abiding concern with the specter of classical psychology haunting the definition of the Christian soul. Davies remains consistent throughout his life in the belief that the harmonious pleasure elicited by mellifluous poetry and rhetorical address can elevate the soul to a more sublime state. This lifelong obsession with the entrancements of beautiful language—what G. A. Wilkes has called the "aesthetic" tenor of his poetry—is for Davies a "universal principle of nature" that confers order and harmony on the soul's disparate faculties.[5] Part of this consistency across his career derives from the source materials he cites in his meticulous philological method, which draws in both the poetic and legal contexts extensively from classical texts. Particularly important for Davies in his definition of the soul is his recurring invocation of Orpheus as a poet whose language and accompanying song possessed the power to ravish and to transform the vegetative and animal faculties into a state of reason. In this Orphean fantasy of refining the soul, beautifully wrought language shaped by the meter and melody of lyric prosody contains the potency to lift the soul's faculties from a lower to a higher station on the chain of being.

This striving to lift oneself through aesthetic work upon the faculties comes to shape Davies's understanding of the soul as the locus of Christian devotion. He understands the spiritual substance of the soul to be, quite surprisingly, an emergent property of the "aesthetic" harmony resulting from lyrically arranged language inspired by the example of Orpheus. The soul of the Christian subject is something made and elevated through harmonious poetic and linguistic practices, and should not be understood a priori as a substance immanently implanted at the core of the self. The "aesthetic" principle of the soul that Davies formulates in his poetry of the 1590s becomes in his later legal prose a practical technique of colonial indoctrination to win the hearts and minds—or rather souls—of the Irish people. He is in some ways the most audaciously practical of the authors we are considering, since he takes the lessons learned from his literary experiments and almost literally attempts to implement them at a large political scale on the Irish population. If Davies initially used poetry as a medium to understand the puzzlements of the soul at the outset of his career, he later repurposes his literary strategies of the soul as a practical program to be applied in his colonialist legal policies. In mapping this peculiar application of a literary practice that becomes a political *techne*, I will read his lyric poetry as a space where Davies defines the parameters of his "aesthetic" model of the soul in order to set the stage for my reading of the soul's refinement in his legal prose.

The narrative of Davies's poetry as a template for his later politically charged prose is surprising because few scholars place the two bodies of work into contact in good faith; as a result, wildly differing appraisals of the author have emerged. For example, while E. M. W. Tillyard famously described Davies as an earnestly passionate and "authentic spokesman" of the Elizabethan worldview because of his poetry, Robert Krueger has dismissed the poems as his "best joke" and the idle work of a "schoolboy" who was simply going through the motions on "assigned themes."[6] Stanley Kunitz has called Davies's 1596 *Orchestra* a "neglected masterpiece," while G. A. Wilkes suggests that "there is no justification at present for calling attention to Sir John Davies as a neglected poet."[7] T. S. Eliot has called his poetry "highly original," while Sneath, Seemann, Bredvold, and Buckley have all gathered a considerable amount of evidence demonstrating that he was highly formulaic and followed Elizabethan conventions in a rote way.[8] Even evaluations of his legal legacy cannot agree on a single vision of the author: J. G. A. Pocock famously gave Davies the backhanded compliment of being "an ideal type of the 'common-law mind' rather than an authority in its making," while Hans Pawlisch disagrees entirely and suggests that Davies was highly influential in integrating Roman and Continental law sources into his theorizations of common law.[9]

The divide between the dueling faces of Davies's critical legacy can be encapsulated by Eliot's celebration of Davies the poet as "an independent mind" worthy of serious intellectual investigation, while Wilkes suggests that his poems were written "before he settled down to a serious career" and contends that "those who insist on the 'gravity' of Davies should attend rather" to his prose for serious study.[10] By contrast, I suggest that it is far more fruitful to consider the chiasmic relationship between the two phases of his career: his lyric verse possesses far more "gravity" than we have credited it, and his legal prose possesses glimmers of literary playfulness that have perhaps eluded us. By adopting this chiasmic reading strategy, this chapter identifies Davies's early poetry, and specifically the figure of the classical soul structured by "aesthetic" harmony developed in his verse, as an important influence on his later thinking on common law articulated during his tenure as a colonial administrator in Ireland. By breaking with the scholarly impasse that has defined Davies's career in terms of its incommensurate parts, I suggest that Davies's obsession with the soul allows us to trace a line through his writing, illuminating his later legal thinking's intrinsic debt to his earlier poetry.

Nosce Teipsum: An Elegy for Reason

Although John Davies's long poem *Nosce Teipsum* (1599) is not frequently recognized by readers today as a literary masterpiece on the topic of the soul, it was one of the best-loved poems in early modern England, with ten editions published from 1599 to 1700, garnering effusive praise from Elizabeth I and subsequently James I as an exemplar of classical philosophy versified into English. At first glance, *Nosce Teipsum* presents a straightforward description of the classical soul's faculties, reflecting concepts that could be extracted from Aristotle's *De Anima* almost verbatim. First, the vegetative or "quick'ning" faculty of the soul is described in terms of its domestic maintenance of the body:

> HER quick'ning Power in ev'ry living part,
> Doth as a Nurse, or as a Mother serve;
> And doth employ her Oeconomick Art,
> And buisy Care, her Houshold to preserve.

Here she attracts, and there she doth retain;
There she decocts, and doth the Food prepare;
There she distributes it to ev'ry Vein,
There she expels what she may fitly spare.

This Pow'r to Martha may compared be,
Who buisy was, the Houshold-things to do[11]

Davies compares the vegetative faculty to the function of a "Nurse" or "Mother" whose work preserves the vitality of the "Houshold." The labor of the vegetative faculty as an "Oeconomick Art" suggests at once the domestic labor of maintaining a home, *oikos*, and the economic vitality of the state.[12] In contrast to the domestic work of the vegetative faculty, Davies defines the sense faculty as the power of interacting with things "abroad":

THis Pow'r is Sense, which from abroad doth bring
The Colour, Taste, and Touch, and Scent, and Sound,
The Quantity and Shape of ev'ry thing
Within Earth's Centre, or Heav'n's Circle found.

This Pow'r, in Parts made fit, fit Objects takes;
Yet not the Things, but Forms of Things receives;
As when a Seal in Wax Impression makes,
The Print therein, but not it self, it leaves.

And though things sensible be numberless,
But only Five the Sense's Organs be;
And in those Five, all things their Forms express,
Which we can touch, taste, feel, or hear, or see.[13]

In his description of the soul's second faculty of sense, Davies again seems to profess an understanding that is straightforwardly Aristotelian in his adoption of sense perception as a "Seal in Wax Impression" which transmits the "Forms of Things" or "Print" of objects but not the materiality of the object itself.[14] What is markedly different from the standard account of the sensory faculty, however, is its expansive global reach. If the senses were conventionally defined as the soul's power to define its immediate local environment, Davies greatly expands the range of sense as a faculty that goes "abroad" beyond the immediate purview of the body, traveling vast distances to gather information of "ev'ry thing / Within Earth's Center, or Heav'n's Circle Found." Davies frames this expansive scope as a problem, however, and does not articulate this model of sensation in praise of global expansion.

The faculties of the soul are so obsessed with looking outward to "all things without" surrounding the body, that humans have become "Strangers" to our "selves," possessing no knowledge of "that whereby we reason, live, and be."

For why should we the busy Soul believe,
When boldly she concludes of that and this;
When of her self she can no Judgment give,
Nor how, nor whence, nor where, nor what she is?

All things without, which round about we see,
We seek to know, and have therewith to do:
But that whereby we reason, live and be,
Within our selves, we Strangers are thereto.

We seek to know the moving of each Sphere,
And the strange Cause o' th' Ebbs and Floods of Nile;
But of that Clock which in our Breasts we bear,
The subtile Motions we forget the while.

We that acquaint our selves with ev'ry Zone,
And pass the Tropicks, and behold each Pole;
When we come home, are to our selves unknown,
And unacquainted still with our own Soul.[15]

Davies compares this self-reflexive blindness to the constant exploratory strivings of empires, which search for the "strange causes" flooding the Nile, travel to foreign "zones," and explore the expanses of the "Tropicks" and the "Poles." The perpetual cycle of foreign exploration and colonization can only be self-defeating, since "when we come home, are to our selves unknown." Figuring the faculties of the Aristotelian soul as an empire with foreign territories does not lead to the internal strife of civil war, but rather causes the very different internal fissure of a self-reflexive alienation of the self from the self.

Apart from its apparent pessimism, Davies's definition of the faculty of reason enacts a subtle but significant shift in the language of the soul. He cleanly breaks from Aristotle, who set specific gender assignments to the body and soul. Consistently across a range of texts, Aristotle associates the soul and its powers with the male sex, and the body and its appetites with the female sex.[16] During the Reformation, part of Martin Luther's rejection of Aristotle involved a revision of this gendered psychology, with his figuration of the soul as a bride to Christ's bridegroom in a spiritual marriage of faith.[17] Davies moves even further away from Aristotle's gendered soul than Luther did, by making the soul as monarch a female ruler—"she"—who "boldly" makes conclusions, judges, and reasons in a manner that is emphatically male in the Aristotelian tradition, but becomes the attributes of a queen in *Nosce*

Teipsum. This is perhaps unsurprising to some extent because Davies eventually does come to identify Elizabeth I as the most successful incarnation of reason, but to enact this shift, he must initially scramble the gender roles defined by Aristotle and later Luther that had framed much of the gendered discourse of the soul in the Renaissance.

Davies's shift in reason's gendered identity comes with its own range of complications. Unlike most allegories of the soul's faculties found in the Renaissance, the faculty of reason does not control its lower faculties. In a jarring shift, the expansive geographical reach of the sense faculty could not be more different from the claustrophobic condition of the ruling faculty of reason.

> Yet in the Body's Prison so she [the rational soul] lies,
> As through the Body's Windows she must look,
> Her divers Powers of Sense to exercise,
> By gath'ring Notes out of the World's great Book.[18]

Describing the faculty of reason as locked inside the "Body's Prison" is entirely conventional, echoing the standard Christian dualist account of the body as the prison of the transcendent soul. What is surprising in Davies's formulation, however, is his insistent repetition of the sense faculty's global reach in striking contrast to the confined state of reason as an imprisoned monarch. The senses possess the physical freedom to span the globe and "gather Notes" from diverse regions of the "World's great book," in a way that is impossible for the imprisoned rational faculty. Davies creates a considerable spatial contrast between the confinement of reason—ostensibly the ruling monarch of the empire of man and yet one only able to peer through the narrow windows of the body—and the power of sense to traverse vast distances across the globe. For Davies, it is precisely the disjunction between the imprisoned faculty of reason ruling in confinement and the expansive global reach of the sense faculty that leads to fundamental problems in our understanding of man as a political state.

> Nor can her self discourse or judge of ought,
> But what the Sense collects, and home doth bring;
> And yet the Pow'rs of her discoursing Thought,
> From these Collections, is a diverse Thing.
> . . . .
> Kings their Affairs do by their Servants know,
> But order them by their own Royal Will.[19]

Reason cannot judge—her primary task—without the data from the Senses. In this unexpectedly skewed relationship, the isolated faculty of reason needs the wide-ranging sense faculty far more than the sense faculty needs to serve its ruler well. Although Davies asserts the priority of "Royal Will" to rule over the lower faculties, he creates in the poem an uncomfortable power relationship where the rational faculty relies on the sense faculties for her entire capacity to function.

> These Actions in her Closet, all alone,
> (Retir'd within her self) she doth fulfil;
> Use of her Body's Organs she hath none,
> When she doth use the Pow'rs of Wit and Will.[20]

Davies presents a pathetic vision of reason as a female monarch existing in a state of effective imprisonment, relying disproportionately on the vitiated senses. Confined in her Closet, "all alone" and "retir'd within her self," the rational faculty is so isolated that she is completely divorced from the function of the organs underpinning the function of the soul: "Use of her Body's Organs she hath none." The rational faculty's lack of direct influence over the "Body's Organs" leads more often than not to a state of utter confusion. The "tenderness" of the soul's organs "blots" the data of the senses, distorting potentially correct information into falsehoods. Reason must "build fond conclusions on . . . idle grounds," and can create no "true relation" between the facts upon which the monarch must base her decisions.

Davies's popular poem defines the human soul as an ember of the fire that is life. His critique of faculty psychology as it is conventionally understood argues that popular Renaissance allegories of the human soul as actively engulfed in a perpetual state of civil war, with the senses and passions rising up in arms against the iron fist of reason, fail to grasp the more fundamental problems plaguing human life.[21] In *Nosce Teipsum*, Davies articulates a passionate elegy for a human soul that is barely holding on to life.[22]

Emergent Properties of the Soul

In the opening stanzas of *Nosce Teipsum*, which I have considered to this point, Davies's definition of the soul draws almost exclusively from classical faculty psychology. *Nosce Teipsum* is, however, a decidedly Christian poem, but it expresses its devotional nature in a peculiar way. In the later moves of the poem, Davies recovers from the dysfunction of the soul's faculties a way to transform the soul as the basic foundation of the Christian faith. In doing so, he rethinks the nature of the Christian soul's original sin and its promise of immortality, two major theological issues that triggered the crisis of two souls in the early sixteenth century. Davies challenges the popular Protestant account of the bound soul, but in a manner different from Shakespeare, as we have seen in the previous chapter on *Hamlet*. Davies rather prompts us to revise our understanding of Christian doctrine by renegotiating the central terms of immortality, original sin, and the promise of salvation as emergent properties of the soul arising from the lyrical harmony of the soul's constituent parts properly placed into alignment, and not as concepts that are incontrovertibly fixed by the edict of God.[23]

The idea of lyrical harmony to which Davies gravitates takes on a decidedly political edge. Particularly important is a renegotiation of the scar of original sin in terms of a vocabulary that begins to take on the characteristics of political contract. In the standard Protestant account, original sin was the scar of the fall burned deeply into the faculties of the Aristotelian soul. The original sin is so deep that an individual human cannot change the nature of the faculties and instead becomes locked in a state of simultaneous freedom and slavery. Davies contests this ubiquitous narrative that turns the soul's faculties into the substrate of original sin, arguing that the fall has little to do with the fate of the soul. Rather, he suggests quite surprisingly that original sin could be seen as a positive triggering event serving as the original motivation for uniting all Christian souls into a corporate entity, mimicking something like a political state:

> For as that easie Law was giv'n to all,
> To Ancestor and Heir, to First and Last;
> So was the first Transgression general;
> And all did pluck the Fruit, and all did taste.
>
> Of this we find some Foot-steps in our Law,
> Which doth her Root from God and Nature take;
> Ten thousand Men she doth together draw,
> And of them all, one Corporation make:
>
> Yet these, and their Successors, are but one;
> And if they gain, or lose their Liberties,
> They harm, or profit not themselves alone,
> But such as in succeeding Times shall rise.[24]

The "easie Law" forbidding eating the apple was not only given to Adam and Eve, but "was given to all, To Ancestor and Heir, to First and Last." The breaking of God's law did not happen once in a mythical prelapsarian past; for Davies, the transgression itself recurs continually. "We all did taste" of the apple and break the law. The fall has the unexpected consequence of binding all human souls into a universal shared experience—we are "drawn together" by the unifying power of transgression into "one Corporation" that coalesces all individual subjects into one corporate body across successive generations: "these, and their Successors, are but one." Therefore, the original act of breaking God's law unifies humans into a "Corporation" of the fallen. In this bizarre conception of the soul, the "Corporation" of fallen

Christian subjects suffers "harm" or gains "profit" as one conjoined entity, and not as individuated persons.

Davies's notion of a corporate soul here should not be understood as a proleptic anticipation of Hobbes's Leviathan. It can more accurately be placed into context as a revision of the "infamous" Averroist concept of the "material intellect," which he defines as a "single, eternal" substance that "serves the entire human species."[25] For Averroes, the material intellect is the plane of ideation that allows the human soul to understand universals beyond the human body. All possible universal forms cannot be contained or understood within any particular person; therefore, each individual soul has a receptive capacity to take in all potential intelligible ideas that become actualized within the soul as particular thoughts. Averroes's material intellect functions like the potentiality of Aristotle's wax tablet, and particular thoughts at any given moment are the inscriptions upon it. The complexity and uncanniness of Averroes's definition of a shared universal power of intellect have been called a "bizarre book of metaphysical science-fiction" that raises the question of "what is the point of an individual self?"[26]

Unlike the Averroist material intellect, however, Davies's conception of the universal soul in *Nosce Teipsum* is not a shared substance or a receptivity to universal forms. Davies defines the binding of the soul into one corporate entity as an act of "assent," an action and not a passive openness to potentiality. Actively forming a corporate entity uses the act of original sin as a catalyst. By redefining the original transgression of breaking God's law as a form of contract joining all Christian souls into a political union of the fallen, Davies rejects the widely accepted story of the fall as a decisive moment of rupture alienating humans from God's love and dividing humans within their own souls—in the fissure between the sinful condition of the Aristotelian soul and the redeemable state of the Christian soul. In Davies's revised story of the fall, original sin was not a foundational act of rupture splitting the soul in two, but rather a decisive moment of unification incorporating all Christian souls bound by law-breaking into a communion of commonwealth-making. Similarly, Davies understands the soul to be immortal as promised in Scripture only to the extent that all humans "assent" to this promise beyond life.

> Doubtless, all Souls have a surviving Thought,
> Therefore of Death we think with quiet Mind;
> But if we think of being turn'd to nought,
> A trembling Horrour in our Souls we find.
>
> . . . .
>
> If then all Souls, both good and bad, do teach,
> With gen'ral Voice, That Souls can never die;
> 'Tis not Man's flatt'ring Gloss, but Nature's Speech,
> Which, like GOD's Oracles, can never lye.

Hence springs that universal strong Desire,
Which all Men have of Immortality:
Not some few Spirits unto this Thought aspire,
But all Men's Minds in this united be.

Then this Desire of Nature is not vain,
She covets not Impossibilities;
Fond Thoughts may fall into some idle Brain,
But one Assent of all, is ever wise.[27]

Davies argues that all souls are by their very nature driven by the instinct of self-preservation. The Christian soul is so powerfully motivated by "survival" and so terrified by the horror of negation that all souls come together in one voice to declare their desire for immortality. Just as in the "Corporation" binding all fallen Christian souls into a united commonwealth that suffers and profits as a single unit, Davies argues that the universal desire for immortality constitutes "one Assent for all," binding all Christian souls into a corresponding corporation of the immortal.

In these surprising moves, Davies transforms the soul in its relationship with God into an emergent property of harmonious incorporation and "assent." The elegiac voice that systematically dismantled classical faculty psychology in the opening phase of the poem gives way to a sublime prophetic voice ambitiously redefining in its verses the very idea of immortality as an emergent form of truth that gains form and definition through a harmony of the soul's faculties, and indeed all living souls, coalescing into a psychological "Corporation" bound by "one Assent." For Davies, the soul is not a substance or an individuating property defining the idea of the self. In his account, the soul itself is a collective. It comes into being through the knitting together of the soul's faculties within the Christian subject at the microscopic level, and through the incorporation of all souls at the macroscopic scale. *Nosce Teipsum* thus modifies the Protestant narrative of the conditions binding the fate of the Christian soul—its original state of sin and its promise of immortality—from fixed truths dictated by the law of God into concepts that are emergent properties of a soul harmoniously arranged.

Significantly, these harmonious arrangements are for Davies only made possible through lyric poetry, the textual medium in which he is writing and the solution to the psychological dissonance that consumes much of the poem. I am using the term "lyric" purposefully to classify the theme of Davies's poetry descriptively and not in a restrictive generic sense, since he frequently returns to his favorite trope of invoking lyres, lutes, and the "instruments" of classical poetic song as a way to figure the idea of harmony in physical terms. This is important for Davies, since he suggests that the lyric produced by these instruments regulates the binding of the soul's faculties into a psychological harmony. The key for Davies is refiguring the ruling faculty of reason as a poet or bard playing the body's organs as if they were instruments producing the harmony of a lyric song.

> Her Harmonies are sweet, and full of Skill,
> When on the Body's Instruments she plays;
> But the Proportions of the Wit and Will,
> Those sweet Accords are even th' Angels Lays.
>
> These Tunes of Reason are Amphion's Lyre,
> Wherewith he did the Thebane City found.
> . . . .
> Thus the Soul tunes the Body's Instruments,
> These Harmonies she makes with Life and Sense;
> The Organs fit are by the Body lent,
> But th' Actions flow from the Soul's Influence.[28]

Nosce Teipsum's transformation of the Aristotelian soul into the very different framework of a "city," one based on "accord" and "proportion" rather than the internal division and dissonance besieging the poem's initial global model of empire, therefore culminates in the lyric harmony created by "tuning" the faculties and organs like an instrument. As we shall see, it is Davies's understanding of the lyric's power to transform the soul's faculties that shapes the logic of much of his poetry and prose written across a seemingly unrelated series of contexts.

Orchestra: Orpheus and the Political Science of the Soul

Orchestra (1596), Davies's other popular poem of the 1590s, has conventionally been read as a playful frivolity that clashes in style with the philosophical import of *Nosce Teipsum*. Some scholars have taken the shift in tone quite literally in his biographical context as a movement from his rowdy youth to a stage of soul-searching redemption.[29] However, I suggest that *Nosce Teipsum* and *Orchestra* should be read as two facets of Davies's larger project of redefining the relationship of the two souls. In *Orchestra*, lyric poetry itself embodies a transformative force that is capable of triggering the harmony of the soul's faculties, which is proposed in *Nosce Teipsum*. In Davies's estimation, the power of lyric lies in its capacity to bridge the chasm between the different faculties of the soul into a musical harmony in a way that is powerful enough to refine lower animal faculties such as sensation into the higher faculty of reason. *Orchestra* illustrates how lyric, and specifically lyric dance, transforms the internal harmony of the Aristotelian soul's faculties into a model for civil order.

In *Orchestra*, Davies argues that the "harmony" and "proportion" of the faculties are a form of dancing structured by the meter and harmony of lyric.[30] The "dance" of the Aristotelian soul's faculties enables an evolution from the lower faculties to reason, leading animals to become rational humans, and eventually leading humans to coalesce into social arrangements based on "consent."[31]

> For what did he who with his ten-tong'd Lute
> Gaue Beasts and blocks an vnderstanding eare?
> Or rather into bestiall minds and brute
> Shed and infus'd the beames of reason cleare?
> Doubtlesse for men that rude and sauage were
> A ciuill forme of dauncing he deuis'd,
> VVherewith vnto their Gods they sacrific'd.
>
> So did Musaeus, so Amphion did,
> And Linus with his sweet enchanting song
> . . . .
> And Theseus to his wood-borne slaues among
> Vs'd dauncing as the finest pollicie
> To plant religion and societie.
> . . . .
> Loe this is Dauncings true nobilitie.
> Dauncing the child of Musick and of Loue,
> Dauncing it selfe both loue and harmony,
> VVhere all agree, and all in order moue;
> Dauncing the Art that all Arts doe approue:
> The faire Caracter of the worlds consent,
> The heau'ns true figure, and th'earths ornament.
> . . . .
> For that true Loue which dauncing did inuent,
> Is he that tun'd the worlds whole harmony,
> And linkt all men in sweet societie.[32]

In *Orchestra*, Davies uses Orpheus as an example of a bard who, through the power of his "ten-tong'd Lute," could not only create a harmony between the faculties, but could also imbue the lower faculties with the power to evolve into the higher faculty of reason. The conversion of lower faculties to higher, more rational ones involves an ascension up the taxonomy of creatures, from animals to humans. Orpheus's powerful mode of song was capable of transforming "Beasts" possessing only the faculties of nutrition and sense, without the power of reason, and "rude and savage" men, into rational humans. Orpheus's song enabled the sense organs, and specifically the "ear" limited to the sense of hearing, to evolve into an "understanding eare," or a sense made more powerful by the capacity for reason. The lyric mode Davies describes in *Orchestra* encompasses the transformative power to sublimate "bestial" and "brute" creatures dominated by the lower faculty of sense into the higher state of the rational faculty's "understanding."

The evolution of mere sensory "beasts" into rational humans that Davies describes serves as his primary account of how humans move from the state of animals to social beings. According to Davies, humans do not enter into social arrangements such as the political commonwealth through war or legal contract, as is conventionally claimed. Davies surprisingly locates the origins of society in the power of lyric to refine the Aristotelian faculties into a condition where reason, and not the lower faculties of sense or nutrition, guide human decision-making. In the narrative of social formation that Davies recounts, the harmony and eventual refinement of the soul's faculties through the transformative power of song are the basis of civil society. The refinement and evolution of the faculties provoked by song lead to the creation of society because the harmony of lyric stimulates humans to "dance." The rhythm and melody of song motivate a "civil form of dancing" that is the foundation of the political state, in Davies's mind. Davies draws from both Greek poets (Orpheus, Musaeus, and Linus) and heroic rulers of cities (Amphion and Theseus) to demonstrate that poetry and song should be considered potent instruments in the establishment of political rule and the creation of city-states, not simply aesthetic ornaments divorced from questions of power. For Davies, "dauncing" is an important matter of "pollicie" and the most effective means of uniting rational humans into the political arrangements necessary for civil society. The "dance" provoked by lyric is an aesthetically charged mechanism of transforming "brute" humans into rational political subjects.

Defining the soul as a "harmony" is a fairly conventional early modern vernacular topos that was often attributed to Aristotle. For example, we can find the trope in John Dickenson's widely read translation of the *Politics*:

> It seemeth that there is affinity betweene harmonies and rimes. Therfore many wise men affirme that the soule is an harmony, or that there is harmony in it. . . . Therefore if the soule be a certaine harmonie . . . Socrates answering hereunto, doth by many goodly reasons confute that opinion of them who supposed the soule to bee a harmony and mixture of humours, comparing the bodie to a Harpe, and the soule to a harmonie.[33]

Davies's innovation in this historical context lies in shifting our frame of reference from the music produced by the "Harpe" as a way to figure the soul, defined by Aristotle, to the subtly intricate logic of musical harmony as the steady cadence conferring structure on the motions of the soul's faculties, and ultimately refining the soul's lower animal faculties into the nobler, more refined plane of reason.[34] Davies deploys the movement of dance as a surprising way to recount the story of the soul's evolution from a mode of being governed by the lower faculties of raw sense and the brute urges of the vegetative faculty to a mode of rational being uniting humans into the harmony of "societie." Such a refinement of the Aristotelian faculties leading to social harmony is precipitated by the harmony of lyric song and the power of the "dauncing" provoked by that song, leading humans into the coordinated set of movements in space that Davies defines as "consent." For Davies, dancing in harmony is the master trope of political unity, serving as the template or "faire Caracter" of the "worlds consent." The "worlds whole harmony" and the ability of humans to be "linkt" into "sweet societie" rely on the power of dancing to turn scattered and isolated individuals living in a state of brute sensation and visceral urges, into rational subjects refining their souls to a higher state so as to coalesce into an enormous collective dance that *Orchestra* imagines to be the fabric of civil society.

The genesis of political consent in Davies's account is not rooted in a legal tradition, which one might fairly assume given the fame he garnered as a common law jurist. Rather, Davies identifies the origin of society in the classical power of lyric to reshape the soul from a brute state dominated by the lower plant and animal faculties to a state of human subjectivity governed by the decisions of the rational faculty. Davies's imagination of the political is thus at its heart a psychology; a transformation of the classical soul's faculties from animalistic sense to political reason, inflected by the aesthetic power of lyric to create harmonious arrangements within the soul and between individuals in society. *Orchestra* therefore construes political harmony as a harmony of the soul enabled by lyric and not necessarily a legal contract understood in the terms of Hugo Grotius or Thomas Hobbes. Davies imagines in his poetry that the topic of political consent which dominates his later legal prose is grounded in a psychology of lyric.

I have been consistently using the term "lyric" to refer to the "song" identified by Davies as the means to harmonize the previously discordant faculties of the Aristotelian soul and to convert the lesser faculties into the higher faculty of political reason. This is because *Orchestra* specifies that the music in question is literally produced by a lyre, but more importantly because poetic language and meter, and not just instrumental melody, structure the "civill forme of dauncing" that unites humans into society. Note that in the previously cited passage, Davies describes Orpheus's lute as a "ten-tong'd," and not a ten-stringed, instrument. The "enchanting song" compelling humans to dance in ordered social arrangements is produced by the "tongue," and is composed of the metrically organized language of lyric, and not just musical melody. Davies frequently reminds his readers that he privileges the power of dancing because it is an evocative way to incarnate the metrical organization of poetic language, turning words on the page into living, leaping bodies:

What shall I name those currant trauases
That on a triple Dactyle foote doe run
Close by the ground with slyding passages,
VVherein that Dauncer greatest prayse hath won
. . . .
Yet is ther one the most delightfull kind,
A lofty iumping, or a leaping round,
VVhere arme in arme, two Dauncers are entwind,
And whirle themselues with strict embracements bound,
And still their feet an Anapest do sound:
An Anapest is all theyr musicks song,
VVhose first two feet are short, & third is long.[35]

Davies figures the various metrical feet governing the organization of versified language as different dance moves. So, the "triple" stressed syllables of the "Dactyle foote" correspond to the dancer's foot sliding across the ground as the metrical pulse "slydes" across the language of the passage, and the galloping rhythm of the "Anapest" or the antidactylus in which the "first two feet are short, and the third is long," approximates "two Dauncers" locked "arme in arme" joyfully "jumping" and "leaping round." In both metrical arrangements, the dancers are "bound" in a "strict embracement" following the rules of poetic meter. Davies himself insists that among all disciplines involved in the "teaching" of dancing, poetry is the preeminent discourse in explicating how language structures the metrical organization of motion:

And those great Maisters of the liberall Arts
In all their seuerall Schooles doe Dauncing teach:
For humble Grammer first doth set the parts
Of congruent and well-according speach:
Which Rhetorick whose state ye clouds doth reach,
And heau'nly Poetry doe forward lead,
And diuers Measures, diuersly doe tread.[36]

Several "Schooles" are capable of "teaching" dancing among the "liberall Arts." At the most basic level, "humble Grammer" sets the fundamental structure of "speach," and "Rhetorick" attempts to raise language to the lofty heights of the "clouds." However, the path to understanding the mechanics of dancing as it relates to the formation of political consent is "lead" by "heav'nly Poetry," whose "Measures" step forward, "treading" as feet dancing across the ground and as syllables sliding across the page. Davies gives a tremendous amount of power to the poet as the unique conductor of the metrical rhythm of language and song that governs the harmony of the soul's faculties and unites humans into the political dance of consent.

For Davies, then, the commonwealth of fallen souls described in his account of original sin by consent that he articulates most fully in *Nosce Teipsum*, is ultimately a commonwealth governed by its subjects dancing in "measure." The dystopian vision of the faculties to which we are introduced at the outset of *Nosce Teipsum* evolves across his poetic corpus into an alternative utopian account of a harmonious commonwealth as the massive dance of its subjects joining together in a unified state of consent in *Orchestra*.

In arguing that England has "retained" the "rules" established in the mythical origin of the political dance, Davies also applies this model of the fallen commonwealth to the specific recent history of England. Davies recounts the genealogy of the English commonwealth that he will later serve in his capacity as James I's attorney general in Ireland. He argues that the political harmony enjoyed by the late Tudor commonwealth is a rare moment of peace forged by the exemplary clarity of Elizabeth's faculties. The "Musick" that most clearly indicates the commonwealth's harmony during Elizabeth's reign is the prolific volume of poetry produced by England's authors:

> Our glorious English Courts diuine Image
> As it should be in this our golden age.
> . . . .
> O that I could old Gefferies Muse awake,
> Or borrow Colins fayre heroike stile,
> Or smooth my rimes with Delias seruants file.
>
> Yet Astrophell might one for all suffize,
> VVhose supple Muse Camelion-like doth change
> Into all formes of excellent deuise:
> So might the Swallow, whose swift Muse doth range
> Through rare Ideas, and inuentions strange,
> And euer doth enioy her ioyfull spring,
> And sweeter then the Nightingale doth sing.[37]

Invoking Geoffrey Chaucer as an English "Muse," and citing Spenser's Colin Clout, Samuel Daniel's Delia, Sir Philip Sidney's *Astrophil and Stella*, and Michael Drayton's *Idea*, Davies concludes *Orchestra* by demonstrating that the English poetic tradition represents the symphony reflecting the stable harmony of the commonwealth. For Davies, the national harmony produced by its flowering lyric tradition serves as the standard for the "Golden Age" in the final years of Elizabethan rule. He unabashedly admits that he hopes to join the ranks of this pantheon by "borrowing" Spenser's "heroike stile" and "smoothing" his rhymes with Daniel's "file." Unfortunately, despite the popular success of Davies's poetry in the 1590s and early 1600s, his stamp on English history has largely been dictated by his conservative imperialist legal prose, to which we shall now turn as the final inflection in his thinking on the problem of two souls.

Davies's Irish Impasse: From the "Good Conversion" to the "Heart of the Beast"

Legal scholars have long been drawn to the minutiae of Davies's biography in order to understand the striking change in style and content from his early poetry to the conservative sternness of his common law prose. It is not my purpose here to retread these biographical speculations. Suffice it to say that scholars interested in Davies's impact on legal history have minimized the influence of his earlier poetry upon his later prose, with Robert Krueger famously dismissing his literary efforts as a massive "joke" which Davies could not have taken seriously, to the more tempered appraisal of Hans Pawlisch, who suggests that surely "literary efforts alone would have been scarcely sufficient to secure the attention" of serious and prominent members of the court.[38]

But even in the markedly different context of Davies's prose, we can find throughout his later work precisely the same logic of lyric harmony as the basis of political concord. Indeed, the introductory address "To the Reader" in the *Perfect Abridgement of the Eleven Books of Reports of the Reverend and Learned Edward Cook* describes Davies' writing as a feat of lyricism itself by invoking the power of Orpheus as we have seen in *Orchestra*—"a miracle next the Harpe of Orpheus" for the manner in which Davies "smoothed and softened the hardnesse" of his rather prosaic subject matter.

Apart from third-party descriptions of the smoothness of Davies's prose style, Davies himself consistently returns to the metaphor of lyric and song in the content of his legal prose. He displays this logic most consistently in his *Discoverie of the True Causes of Why Ireland Was Never Entire Subdued*, which he wrote in 1612, thirteen years after *Nosce Teipsum*. The *Discoverie of the True Causes* serves as a narrative of the manifold errors performed by English monarchs over several centuries of conflict and insurrection in the Irish colonies.[39] In a pointed example, he diagnoses the political mismanagement in the late fifteenth-century legislation of Sir Edward Poinings, the lord deputy of Ireland under Henry VIII, as a music lesson gone awry:

> These Lawes, and others as important as these, for the making of a commonwealth in Ireland, were made in the Gouernment of Sir Edward Poynings. But these Lawes did not spread their Vertue beyonde the English Pale, though they were made generally for the whole Kingdome. For the Prouinces without the Pale, which during the warre of Yorke and Lancaster, had wholly cast off the English Gouernement, were not apt to receyue this seed of reformation, because they were

> not first broken and maistered againe with the sword. Besides, the Irish Countreyes, which contained two third parts of the Kingdome, were not reduced to Shire-Ground, so as in the Lawes of England could not possibly be put in execution. Therefore, these good Laws & prouisions made by Sir Edward Poynings, were like good Lessons set for a Lute, that is broken and out of tune; of which Lessons, little vse can be made, till the Lute bee made fit to be plaid vpon.[40]

The best "lessons" to teach how to play a lute are of little utility if the musical instrument itself is "broken and out of tune." The work of crafting law, then, should not be understood as the performance of music, but rather as the tuning of the lute to "bee made fit to be plaid upon" for the purpose of good instruction.

By contrast, when the teacher properly calibrates the instrument, the political harmony promised in *Orchestra* can occur, manifested in the case of Davies's legal prose as a psychological transformation from rage into peace:

> Briefly, the clock of the ciuil Gouernment, is now well set, and all the wheeles thereof doemoue in Order; The strings of this Irish Harpe, which the Ciuill Magistrate doth finger, are all in tune . . . and make a good Harmony in this Commonweale: So as we may well conceiue a hope, that Ireland (which heertofore might properly be called the Land of Ire, because the Irascible power was predominant there, for the space of 400. yeares together) will from henceforth prooue a Land of Peace and Concorde.[41]

Significantly, it is precisely the same power of lyric that Davies identifies in *Orchestra* as the most effective way of thinking about English government and the exemplarity of its monarchs, that we see in his later legal tracts on Ireland. Notably, in this moment Davies argues that the harmonizing power of lyric and poetic meter can serve as a mechanism to promote social harmony in the previously discordant Irish colonies. In this crucial moment from Davies's *Discoverie of the True Causes*, he refigures the "civil Government" of Ireland as a clock whose wheels move in "Order" like the harmoniously patterned dance of political consent regulated by lyric "measure" and meter first presented in *Orchestra*. Thus, Davies's experience in Ireland confirms his intuition of the political possibility of lyric harmony that he first developed in the 1590s as a poet. The incorporation of Ireland into the commonwealth is possible only if its population derives pleasure from the experience of joining together into harmonious political arrangements, just like dancers who enjoy the synchronous movements governed by the metrical harmony of lyric and song.[42]

Davies's reimagination of Irish government as the playing of a harp emphasizes the power of aesthetic harmony in stimulating the faculties responsible for affective pleasure to counteract the irascible appetite's predilection for rage and despair that had defined Ireland for centuries. The tuning and teaching of the musical instrument to calm the "ire" of the rebellious Irish soul functions as a potent metaphor in these instances, but at other moments in his legal prose, Davies shifts to a more literal register in thinking about the power of teaching song. Drawing from classical precedent, Davies cites Tacitus's account of the Roman conquest of the "ancient Brittaines."[43] The mythical British race was "rude, and dispersed, and therefore prone upon every occasion to make warre." Much like the agitated state of the inhabitants of the "Land of Ire," the Roman conquerors "induced them by pleasure to quietnesse and rest." Rhetorical eloquence, and not military force, was the Roman instrument of conquest. The Roman general Julius Agricola accomplished this conversion of the "rude" British ancestors through pedagogy: "he tooke and instructed in the Liberall Sciences" those who were "now curious to attaine the Eloquence of the Romaine Language." The Romans could bring the previously "rude" Britons to the "heighth of Civility" through lessons in mellifluous "Eloquence" conducted in the language of the conqueror, which could induce "pleasure" just as the "rhetorike" of *Orchestra* had the power to incite harmonious sensations of beauty.

The pedagogy and experience of eloquent pleasure in the Irish context differ from *Orchestra* in two subtle ways. First, where "rhetorike" in the earlier poem is decidedly lyric in nature and rooted in the act of dancing, the "Eloquence" described in *Discoverie of the True Causes* hews much more literally to the Latin arts of rhetorical eloquence we have considered as a part of the humanist education of the English Renaissance. As Rebecca Rush has suggested, the idea of "rhetoric" itself in Davies's work possesses this slippery double valence that gestures at once to lyric and to the arts of persuasion, and we see him oscillating between both usages in his prose.[44] Second, the target audience of the examples deployed in the Irish prose is not English subjects unified into a political harmony. In the case of the *Reports*, the teaching of musical eloquence aims to hasten the subjugation of an "alien" population.[45] Through the pleasing strains of rhetoric, "they were thereby brought to an absolute subjection."

In general, throughout his legal prose, Davies considers the literary instruction, whether poetic or rhetorical, in the language of the invader to be the most effective means of indoctrinating a colonized people. Speaking as a poet adopting the guise of a colonial administrator, he declares quite earnestly that the Irish, for all the "desolation and barbarism" of their land, could be civilized because they possessed two intrinsic redeeming qualities: "they had received the Christian faith, above 1200 yeares since, and were Lovers of Musicke, Poetry," which are "all things necessary for the Civill life of man."[46] Besides the more obvious criterion of Christianity, the love of music and poetry in particular marks the Irish, to Davies's mind, as a people capable of being refined. This regime of linguistic and rhetorical education "reclaiming the Irish from their wildnesse" takes on its most insidious spin in his proposed educational reform for children:

> Moreouer, these ciuil assemblies at Assises and Sessions, haue reclaymed the Irish from their wildenesse, caused them to cut off their Glibs and long Haire; to conuert their Mantles into Cloaks; to conform themselues to the maner of England in al their behauiour and outward formes. And because they find a great inconuenience in mouing their suites by an Interpreter; they do for the most part send their Children to Schools, especially to learne the English language: so as we may conceiue an hope, that the next generation, will in tongue & heart, and euery way else, becom English; so as there will bee no difference or distinction, but the Irish Sea betwixt vs. And thus we see a good conuersion, & the Irish Game turned againe.[47]

Ultimately, the "good conversion" of the intransigent Irish into English subjects will take hold in the "next generation" of children. Davies conjectures that the motivation for this conversion is rhetorical, since the Irish will grow increasingly frustrated that they must use an "Interpreter" to translate their words in civil assemblies and before courts of law. It is difficult to "move" an audience using persuasive rhetoric if they cannot understand the words you are speaking. If in *Orchestra* the rhetorical harmony of lyric underwrites political unity, Davies observes in the Irish context that the *disharmony* between the Irish and English languages is the greatest barrier to the obtainment of such a peaceful political consensus. To remedy this language difference, he suggests that the Irish will be driven to "send their Children to Schools" in order to "learne the English language" much in the same way that their British ancestors sought to acquire the art of eloquence from their Roman conquerors.

This system of schooling comes to occupy an important place in Davies's account of Ireland's future, since adopting the English language takes root and comes to define the Irish children whose "behavior," along with the "form" and organs of their souls, is transformed to such a profound extent that in "every way" they "become English; so as there will bee no difference or distinction" between the two races. In Davies's imagination of the "good conversion," the lyrical harmony that he developed in his poetry expands in his political prose into a far more ambitious program of a vernacular English ideology in which the dissolution of linguistic differences can shape the organs and faculties of Irish children at an ontological level—by speaking English mellifluously and in a persuasive manner, they can "become English." Here we can see the darker side of the vernacular English system of rhetorical instruction we considered in Shakespeare's education applied, in Davies's case, to more insidious ends as an instrument of colonial indoctrination.

The most surprising consequence of Davies's model of English language education is his conclusion that the difference between the English and Irish people—rooted in "race" and not simply culture—is not merely based upon bodily difference, but rather is a feature of the gap between their two languages. Davies specifies that teaching the aesthetically harmonious strains of English becomes important since the Irish language, in his estimation, is phonetically unpleasant but not necessarily semantically inaccurate. The Irish tongue has "a whining tone or Accent in their speech, as if they did still smart or suffer some oppression."[48] Much like the case of Orpheus in *Orchestra*, the aesthetic dimension of language has the power to refine the substance of the soul from "Ire" to peace and from "whyning" noise to persuasive rhetoric so as to "become English" in a fundamental way.

Davies's unexpected articulation of the idea of the English race as an emergent property of language, an identity built upon the malleability of linguistic education and not the fixity of biology, reflects what Hans Pawlisch has called the "anthropological" bent of his legal prose, in which he focuses his attention on the linguistic, psychological, and racial dimension of law beyond the strictly formal parameters of legal precedent.[49] In shifting from the deterministic conception of being "English of bloud" to being "English of birth," as opposed to becoming English through proper language training, Davies opens the idea of the English race to the possibility of hybridity, which he praises as the most exquisite "maisterpiece" attainable by the English in Ireland. In an extended plant metaphor, he argues that a "mixt plantation of British and Irish" represents the best way to ensure that both "might grow up togither in one Nation."[50] Here Davies literally refers to the development of plantation estates as a practical unit of colonial administration, but he subsequently veers into a broader discussion of a "mixed" people. The Irish people, figured "like wild fruit trees," were "transplanted" from the rugged terrain of the forests and mountains into the plains and "open countries" of organized plantations. "When this plantation hath taken root," both literally and figuratively, "it will secure the peace," since both their crops and the "wild" Irish themselves "might grow the milder, and beare the better and sweeter fruit."[51]

As naively utopian as this may sound, Davies does acknowledge that the transplantation and "mixture" of the English and Irish will not only allow the latter to "become English," but indeed the reverse is also true: he has opened up the prospect of the English becoming Irish. Davies never fully resolves his observation in the legal tracts that the racial metamorphosis triggered by his proposed model of linguistic harmony paves the way for racial hybridity. This issue comes to haunt him in the final years of his life. He frequently cites but never develops a coherent response to the existing cases of English subjects who "married and fostered" in Ireland so that "in one age . . . the English became degenerate and meer Irish in their language . . . and all other customes of life whatsoever."[52] This reversed conversion of the English into the condition of being Irish manifests itself first as a descent into the adoption of the Irish language, which subsequently spreads to every aspect of their lives, in a type of perverse inversion of the positive poetic transformation incited by Orpheus in *Orchestra*.

> These were the Irish Customes, which the English Colonies did embrace and vse, after they had reiected the Ciuill and Honorable Lawes and Customes of England, whereby they became degenerate and metamorphosed like Nabuchadnezzar: who although he had the face of a man, had the heart of a Beast; or like those who had drunke of Circes Cuppe, and were turned into very Beasts; and yet tooke such pleasure in their beastly manner of life, as they would not returne to their shape of men againe: Insomuch as within lesse time then the Age of a man, they had no markes or differences left amongst them of that Noble nation, from which they were discended. For, as they did not only forget the English Language, & scorne the vse thereof, but grew to bee ashamed of their very English Names, though they were Noble and of great Antiquity; and tooke Irish Surnames and Nicke-names.

These bad converts forgot the "English language" and began to "scorne the use thereof" by growing to be "ashamed of their very English names." Ultimately, they adopted the Irish language and new names. The linguistic degeneration that Davies describes here from English to Irish precipitates in his reading a corresponding decay in their souls, from being a human into the state of a beast, much as in the classical example of Odysseus's sailors who "had drunke of Circe's cuppe." His second example referring to Nebuchadnezzar is also illustrative, since the biblical king depicted in the book of Daniel was interpreted by a long exegetical tradition including Tertullian, Origen, and later Jean Bodin as slipping from a human soul defined by the rational faculty into an animal state dominated by the pre-rational impulses of the sensory faculty.[53] Davies cites both examples, one classical and one biblical, to bolster his case; to depict in vivid terms the "metamorphosis" of the soul from the height of human reason to the animal psychology of "beastly sense."

The linguistic renunciation of English that Davies decries follows precisely the same logic as in the rhetorical indoctrination of Irish schoolchildren, but in the other direction. "Within lesse time then the Age of a man" the distinguishing racial characteristics marking the English versus the Irish dissolved—"they had no markes or differences left amongst them of that Noble nation, from which they were discended." Davies acknowledges that the plasticity of the soul to be altered by the language one chooses to speak cuts both ways, and can perform a transformation of the soul to good or bad ends, depending on one's perspective. In the case of Orpheus in *Orchestra*, and for the Irish children trained in English, the adoption of harmonious and aesthetically pleasing linguistic practices has the potency to refine the faculties of the soul. Davies does recognize, however, that precisely the same metamorphosis can occur by employing the strains of the Irish that he found so aesthetically displeasing and politically intransigent. This possibility is significant because it threatens to subvert the primary stated goal of his political prose, which is nothing less than the complete subjection of the hearts and souls of the Irish people. The mechanism for creating psychological harmony first worked out in his poetry on the soul in the 1590s serves as the basis for his idealistic linguistic solution for securing colonial hegemony in Ireland. And yet, by his own admission, it is the same pliability of the soul's faculties that undermines the stability of his own exercise, since the English share the same psychological susceptibility.

Davies's Irish prose tracts therefore contain nothing so stable or fixed as a rote "formula" for imperial conquest that came to be "fundamental in the creation of the British empire," as Hans Pawlisch has suggested in his description of how Davies was appropriated and applied by subsequent generations of colonial administrators.[54] Ultimately, the instability of the soul that can be reconfigured by language to either politically harmonious or disharmonious ends is where Davies ends his career, with an unfinished program for maintaining colonial stability. We see how this impasse shapes the final moves of his career most clearly in the 1622 edition of *Nosce Teipsum* and *Orchestra*, in which Davies makes substantial revisions to both poems four years before his death.[55] These modifications prompt him to rethink his own understanding of the power of lyric language to refine the soul's faculties to a nobler state, as he promised in the first edition of the poems. Most notably, Davies adds a prefatory poem to *Nosce Teipsum*, designating its address to the "Faire Soule" as an offering of "some sparkling of that fire, whereby wee reason, live, and be, / These sparkes by Nature evermore aspire." The second major change involves a substantial rewriting of *Orchestra*, to which he now appends the subtitle "Not finished," and which removes the laudatory verses at the conclusion extolling the achievements of English poets found in the 1596 edition. He replaces the pantheon of English poets with a far more somber and fragmented vision, which fails by the end of *Orchestra* to fulfill the promise of igniting the "sparkes" of the soul's faculties to which we "aspire," as suggested in the introductory poem.

Shifting away from the triumphant song celebrating England's literary glory in the 1596 edition of *Orchestra*, Davies describes in its place a "solemne melody" whose form and measure provoke a "subtile" and "curious," rather than harmonious, affective response in the reader. The final moves capture the surprisingly "solemne," "subtile," and "curious" tone of the poem in the classical allusion to Penelope's weaving in the *Odyssey*—the same source from which Davies drew the example of Odysseus's sailors degenerating into beasts by drinking from Circe's cup.

> So subtile and so curious was the measure,
> With such unlookt for chaunge in every straine;
> As that *Penelope* rapt with sweet pleasure,
> Weend shee beheld the true proportion plaine
> Of her owne webb, weavd and unweavd againe (*Orchestra*, stanza 129)

Here he has revised his understanding of the purpose of lyric harmony. In this instance, pleasure and unity are not the ultimate ends of poetry. When Penelope is "rapt with sweet pleasure" upon gazing at the "true proportion plaine / Of her own webb," she immediately destroys the beautiful object she has created—she "weavd and unweavd againe." In this revision of the poem performed at the end of his life, Davies "unweaves" the poem he has made by rewriting it in fragmented form, precisely as Penelope unravels the beautiful proportion she has wrought.

In the place of the harmonious lyric concord of the English poets that he praised in the 1596 edition, Davies concludes the 1622 edition of *Orchestra* with a self-reflexive account of his own lyric work "here" as akin to the "silkewormes industry," whose "beauty it selfe out of its selfe did weave":

> For here, like to the Silkewormes industry,
> Beauty it selfe out of it selfe did weave
> So rare a worke and of such subtilty,
> As did all eyes entangle and deceive,
> And in all mindes a strange impression leave:
> In this sweet Laborinth did Cupid stray,
> And never had the power to passe away. (Stanza 130)

In an ironic about-face from *Nosce Teipsum*'s titular injunction to "know thyself," the logic of self-reflexivity in the final version of *Orchestra* takes a decidedly negative turn, with the work of the silkworm's beauty creating proportion and harmony in a solipsistic labor upon itself, creating itself by weaving from itself. The aesthetic effect emerging from this work is so "subtile" in its tangled recursive logic that the result can only be confusion, leading Penelope to "unweave" what she has woven, "entangling and deceiving" the sense organs, and ultimately etching a "strange impression" upon the mind's reasoning power.

The promise of "nosce teipsum," translated literally as "knowing thyself," has tangled Davies after his political career in Ireland into a "sweet Laborinth" from which he never fully emerges. The final two fragmentary stanzas of *Orchestra* replace the glorious English tradition of poetry with a jarringly different image of "Indians" greeting the rising sun. This move is perhaps a fitting coda to Davies's career, however, since the "swarmes" of Asians and Africans he laments in his 1609 poem "Reason's Moane" become by the end of his career his chosen self-reflexive mode of identifying his own life's work.[56] He declaims in the prefatory epistle of "Jus imponendi vectigana" that his own meticulous textual work of gathering "records" and quotes to build the case for legal precedent in the common law tradition, which legal scholars have trumpeted as his great innovation in legal history, is a form of labor mimicking the "Indian" who digs "up the Oare of Mine."[57] Unlike the prefatory address to the reader in the *Perfect Abridgment of the of Dauncing.*

131

As when the Indians, Neighbours of the morning,
In honour of the Cheerefull riſing Sunne,
With Pearle and painted plumes themſelues ador-
A ſolemne ſtately meaſure haue begun. (ning,
The God well pleaſd with that faire honour done
Sheds foorth his Beames and doth their faces kis
With that immortall glorious face of his.

132

So &c. &c. * * *

Figure 1. Final stanza from the 1622 edition of *Orchestra.* (By permission of the Folger Shakespeare Library)

Eleven Bookes of Reports, which describes Davies's scholarly legal textuality as an echo of Orpheus's lyricism, Davies prefers instead to liken his linguistic labors to the workmanlike digging of the "Indian." In this sense, the invocation of the "Indians" greeting the rising sun at the end of *Orchestra* is a fitting acknowledgment of how Davies came to define the legacy of his own legal work. If English settlers in Ireland can, by adopting Irish linguistic and naming practices, degenerate into the state of animal souls, so too can Davies himself recursively define his own career in its complexity as an "Indian" while rejecting the triumphant purity of the English race he so confidently extolled in the 1596 *Orchestra*. Davies never moves beyond this impasse, with the final stanza of the 1622 edition concluding with the fragmented lines "So &c &c." revoking the emphatic unity of the original ending. (See figure 1.)

Davies's theory of linguistic harmony as a means to refine and lift the animal faculty of sensation to the higher plane of reason that he developed in his early lyric efforts gave him a practical model of psychology to apply in his deployment of English vernacular rhetorical pedagogy in Ireland. But by the end of his career, Davies revises his understanding of its transformative power based on his growing acknowledgment that Orpheus's ability to purify animal souls is haunted by the possibility of falling into the condition of Nebuchadnezzar or Circe, who degenerated rational souls into the psychological state of animals. The mutability of the soul's powers as inherited from the classical tradition of faculty psychology is a two-way street, and its plasticity bespeaks both its capacity to be perfected to a better state and its potential instability. Davies registers his own dissatisfaction with the accomplishments of his career by characterizing his scrupulous methodology of common law philology, long identified as his lasting contribution to the history of law, as the manual drudgery of digging in an Indian mine rather than the sublime lyric produced by Orpheus, to which he once aspired.

At Davies's funeral in 1626, John Donne, by this point serving in his role as dean of St. Paul's Cathedral, delivered his funeral oration in an uncanny intersection of biographies.[58] This chance convergence of life histories is perhaps apt, however, since both men began their careers as witty lyric poets in the 1590s, suffered disappointments in their political aspirations, and subsequently remade their legacies by fashioning a career writing in prose—in legal tracts in the case of Davies, and in celebrated sermons in the case of Donne. Both of these poets-turned-prose stylists share a link in the story I am telling about the two souls in early modern culture because they represent the two vernacular English authors who lingered upon, and anguished over, the intrinsic instability and tension that the plasticity of the classical organic soul implanted at the core of the idea of a Christian self. Where Davies ends his life on a tempered note, lost in a recursive "laborinth" of the soul, Donne takes the unstable mutability of the soul and struggles in his own lyric verse and prose over the course of his life to define a positive vision of the two-souls dilemma as the basis of the English devotional subject, which was not disruptive, as in the case of Shakespeare's *Hamlet*, nor solipsistically bound in recursive knots, as Davies came to conclude. Through this struggle, Donne builds from the confusion of the two-souls dilemma the first generative account of a Christian subject constructed from the fragments of the classical organic soul. This transition from Davies's irresolution to Donne's new model of the soul sets the stage for the final two chapters of the present story.

Chapter 4

✦

"Be Thou *Verbum*": John Donne's Printerly *Techne* of the Soul

> He that desires to Print a book, should much more desire, to be a book; to do some such exemplar things, as men might read, and relate, and profit by.
>
> —John Donne

Scholars of John Donne (1572–1631) have frequently turned to his complex biography as a way to understand how he established his "uncompromising and antagonistic" voice across an impressively diverse range of poetic and prose genres. Born into a prominent Catholic family in an Anglican setting, Donne experienced persecution and paranoia from an early age, and his political aspirations were crushed after his ill-fated marriage to Ann More, the daughter of a wealthy landowner, which led to a thirteen year period of depression, isolation, and poverty. He is best known for the witty and experimental edge of his early lyrics, which are perhaps his most distinctive poetic creations. By contrast, his rise to become one of the most famous preachers of the Anglican Church and the dean of St. Paul's Cathedral at the end of his life marks a puzzling turn, in what John Carey has called a "disconcerting" shift to a conservatism of "the most splenetic and authoritarian stamp."[1] Like Sir John Davies, the poetic creativity of Donne's youth seems at first glance to give way to a dismaying about-face. But unlike Davies, Donne retains in his later theological prose the "imaginative commitment to instability" that drives the energy of his poems.[2] Unlike Davies, Donne harnesses this preoccupation with instability, particularly as it concerns the soul, as the "defining bond of his life."[3]

The paradox of two souls haunted John Donne throughout his life. From his early poetry to his final sermons, Donne translated this paradox into a question of textuality, shifting the problem of the psyche into the linguistic medium of the poet and preacher. His efforts to remedy the tension between the organic and Christian souls led him to a new model of Christian subjectivity figuring the soul as a textual medium that is subject to tracing, writing, and ultimately printing. During his final sermons, Donne went so far as to redefine ontology not in anticipation of the Cartesian cogito as some have suggested, but rather as the declaration of *imprimo ergo sum*: to have a life of consequence, one must "be a book." This materialist statement represents Donne's greatest innovation by demonstrating how technologies such as printing and engraving offer an alternative material vocabulary to think about the two souls in a way that was not irreducibly paradoxical.

A survey of Donne's writings across his career reveals the evolving nature of his thought about the paradox of the two souls. The *Songs and Sonnets* that circulated in manuscript early in the poet's career play with the idea of the two souls as a way to define the relationship of two lovers. The poems use the vocabulary of graphical traces—etchings, carvings, and circles—to figure this erotic "interanimation." In the *Anniversary* poems (1611–12), Donne shifts his tone considerably as he recognizes in the years before his ordination that the presence of two souls in one body is a paradox at the heart of Christian soteriology. The *Anniversaries* represent a point of transition in Donne's understanding of faculty psychology. He turns to the figure of the manuscript as a textual medium allowing him to rethink the relationship between the two souls in a way that is not paradoxical, as the complementary dual faces of a reversible inscribed sheet. Yet he hesitates, by admitting in his poems that he is not yet capable of articulating a specifically printerly *techne* of the two souls. In his sermons (1615–31), Donne confidently adopts the printing press—emblematic for him of repetition and reprinting—as a model for the relationship of the two souls. Donne posits that a lifetime of etching and detail, undertaken upon the flesh-bound organic faculties of the classical soul, will imprint the Christian soul with the fiat of immortality at the moment of one's death. By reconfiguring the textuality of the two souls into the mechanics of print technology late in his life, Donne expresses the view that Christian salvation is a mode of printerly textuality—a second printing of our souls—and should not exclusively be understood as a promise of eternal life or a redemption by grace. Print technology offers to Donne a way to rethink the substance of the soul as something intrinsically malleable, capable of being edited with reset type, or reengraved, by the individual over the course of his or her life. The metaphor of print opens the possibility of a psychological agency to rewrite the soul as a mode of publication.

The printing press, which was invented in the mid-fifteenth century, proliferated widely in Donne's lifetime. Donne's ultimate choice of it as a model for the two-souls problem is surprising, given the common assumption among scholars that he distrusted the print medium and preferred to circulate his works in manuscript among a coterie of poets. It is not simply Donne's rejection of the medium that is at stake here, since Richard Wollman has suggested that Donne's textual choices affected his sense of self: "his emphasis is not on print, but on the damage print inflicts on his identity . . . [which] cannot be controlled" once the texts "reach print."[4] The lack of "control" that defines the printed text for Donne frames a larger debate in early modern scholarship, with Elizabeth L. Eisenstein arguing that the printing press introduced a level of epistemological and material "stability" and "fixity" to the ephemeral nature of manuscript culture, and with Adrian Johns arguing exactly the opposite—that print served to destabilize language and to introduce "inconstancy" and "difference" into discourse.[5] Alvin Kernan frames the lack of consensus on this issue as a "tension, if not downright contradiction, between the two primary energies of print logic, multiplicity and fixity."[6] Donne has been squarely placed in the camp of those who are suspicious of the "fixity" of print.

Donne's extended exploration of the printing press as a technological metaphor to understand the nature of the two souls in one body unexpectedly reverses his positions on textual fixity versus freedom. Donne suggests that the soul, figured as a printed text or engraving, is fundamentally unstable, but this instability is a positive attribute since it introduces a form of malleability immanent to the human psyche and is open to multiple iterations of editing, revising, and reprinting. Donne sees the press as a model for the soul, understanding the printed text in terms of its instability and internal difference. But he does not view this as a pernicious effect, and instead he harnesses the free play of revision and reprinting as the basis of a new form of psychological agency defined by a soul composed of a malleable substance that we have the power to rewrite.

Donne attempts from his earliest poems to recuperate a positive vision of the two souls as a productive occasion to redefine psychology in literary terms. In his poetry and later prose, he clears a space for a new mode of Christian agency by rewriting how the two souls define the subject in the malleable rhetoric of literary language and by asserting that the contents of the soul are not fixed but can be rewritten by the devotional subject. Ultimately, by the end of his life, Donne articulates a rhetoric of the two souls in terms of a printerly textuality that rethinks the psychological dilemma of the sixteenth century as the basis of a novel vision of spiritual plasticity, which gives to the Christian subject the power to edit the soul's substance precisely as a text's type can be reset or as an image can be recast and engraved anew.

Fantasies of "Interanimation" and the Problem of the Two Souls

Donne's earliest efforts to comprehend the two-souls dilemma appear in the *Songs and Sonnets*, which draw on the image of two lovers. In these early works, Donne lays out a method based upon metaphor, analogy, and the rhetoric of figural language more generally, as the terrain on which he attempts to work through the presence of two souls in one body. His poem

"Extasie" describes the lovers' relationship as an intersubjective link that "interanimates two souls."[7] Donne defines the lovers' relationship as necessarily mediated by the living functions of the classical organic soul: "Pure lovers' souls" cannot remain on a disembodied plane of ideation and must "descend / t'affections, and to faculties, / which sense may reach and apprehend" (ll. 65–67). "Extasie's" assignment of the organic soul's faculties as the material, affective, and sensory bond between two lovers is a common trope in Donne's early lyrics, and he explores a range of metaphors to understand the soul's fusing power:

> On man heaven's influence works not so,
> But that it first imprints the air,
> So soul into the soul may flow,
> Though it to body first repair.
>
> As our blood labors to beget
> Spirits, as like souls it can,
> Because such fingers need to knit
> That subtle knot, which makes us man:
>
> So must pure lovers' souls descend
> T'affections, and to faculties,
> Which sense may reach and apprehend,
> Else a great prince in prison lies. (ll. 57–68)

At first glance, these lines seem to endorse the sensuous body over the purity of the soul. However, the poem turns to the body only to the extent that the spirits, faculties, and affections of the Aristotelian soul can be "knit" with the purity of the "heavenly" soul. Lines 61–64 use the Galenic system of humors to establish a series of analogies between the two souls.[8] The blood "labors" to create humoral spirits, which strive to link the body's organs to the higher-order operations of the soul. The bond between the spirit and the soul is only partial, since the spirits are "as *like* souls it can" (my emphasis), and can only imitate the souls in a figural comparison. However, such a figural movement from blood, to spirit, to soul, is vitally important since it defines the "subtle knot, which makes us man." The "knot" defining us as human is not the chemical conversion of blood, to spirit, to soul, but rather a figural effort to create a string of analogies between them.

The "as . . . so" structure of the final two cited quatrains binds the two stanzas into a cause and effect logic. Just as the blood and spirits of Galenic physiology use figures to move upward to the operations of the soul, so too must the "heavenly" soul descend to the Aristotelian soul. The "pure" soul of lovers must be placed into relation with the "affections," "faculties," and "sense" of the Aristotelian soul. To the extent that the poem defines the "subtle knot" of man as an upward chain of analogies between blood, spirit, and soul, the poem argues forcefully that we "must" create a downward, reversed "knot" binding the pure soul to the Aristotelian faculties, passions, and sense. Just as the blood and spirits strive upward to figure the soul, so too must the "pure" soul reach downward to the domain of sense and the function of the Aristotelian faculties. The sequence taken as a whole asserts that "heaven's influence" does not work separately on the material body or on the soul, but requires a more "subtle knot" intertwining the blood and spirits of the Galenic humoral system, the Aristotelian faculties, and the "pure" lover's soul. The "subtle knot, which makes us man," therefore does not describe the dualism of the body and the soul. The "Extasie" defines the human as the concatenation of the Galenic humors and spirits, the Aristotelian soul's faculties, passions, and senses, and the "purity" of the heavenly soul.

Although the "Extasie" proposes the figure of the "knot" interweaving the Galenic humors, the Aristotelian faculties, and the Christian soul into a constitutive relation, Donne's early poetry in general demonstrates great confusion as to how such a knot might be tied. Take, for example, the "Valediction: Forbidding Mourning," which embodies the confusion attending the two souls, signified by "ourselves know not what it is," by openly displaying Donne's struggle to work through different figures to find the proper way to understand the two souls, and how they might be unified into the "subtle knot, which makes us man" proposed by the "Extasie."

> Dull sublunary lovers' love
> (Whose soul is sense) cannot admit
> Absence, because it doth remove
> Those things which elemented it.
>
> But we by a love, so much refined,
> That ourselves know not what it is,
> Inter-assured of the mind,
> Care less, eyes, lips, and hands to miss.
>
> Our two souls therefore, which are one,
> Though I must go, endure not yet
> A breach, but an expansion,
> Like gold to airy thinness beat. (ll. 13–24)

The poem divides the two souls in terms of the quality of one's love: "Dull sublunary" love corresponds to the faculty of sense ("Whose soul is sense") since it requires the physical presence of perceptible objects: it "cannot admit / Absence." By contrast, the "refined" soul of the lover works on an immaterial plane of intellection ("Inter-assured of the mind"), and does not need the organs of sense, such as the "eyes, lips, and hands." As attractive as such a refusal of any debt to the sense organs may seem, the poem admits that it has no idea how to create such a distinction between the two different types of soul: "ourselves know not what it is." The following quatrain, far from resolving such confusion, compounds the problem. The poem proposes to unify the "two souls" into one by hammering "gold to airy thinness" so as to bridge the distance between separated souls. It is not entirely clear, however, what "two souls" might signify here.

The final lines of the poem state that the figure of beaten gold is not a firm conclusion, but rather one of two possible ways to figure the difference between two souls:

> If they be two, they are two so
> as stiff twin compasses are two,
> Thy soul the fixed foot, makes no show
> To move, but doth, if th'other do.
> . . . .
> Such wilt thou be to me, who must
> Like th'other foot, obliquely run;
> Thy firmness makes my circle just,
> And makes me end, where I begun. (ll. 25–36)

The suppositional term "If" marks the transition from the figure of gold beaten to "airy thinness," to the alternative figure of the compass. "If" the figure of hammered gold cannot bridge the gap between the two souls, then the poem admits that "they be two," but divided in two only insofar as they can be figured as the two arms of a compass. The "If" indicates Donne's struggle to find the correct metaphor to describe the problem of two souls. By creating two parallel figural tracks in the poem, Donne literalizes the uncertainty of the preceding admission that the lovers "know not what" the difference of the two kinds of soul might be and how such a difference might be bridged.

The "Valediction: Forbidding Mourning" tentatively concludes by moving from the image of gold hammered into a sheet extending between separated souls, to the figure of the twin-armed compass in which the two souls are joined at a fulcrum. The figure of the twin-armed compass transforms the dilemma of two different souls, initially marked by uncertainty ("ourselves know not what it is"), into a functional codependence.[9] Without a difference of souls the compass could not work: "Thy soul the fixed foot, makes no show / To move, but doth, if th'other do." The souls of the two lovers are not so much "knit" together (as suggested in the "Extasie"), as they are mechanically joined together as two interlocked arms enabling the graphical trace of "just" circles.

Thus, by the end of the "Valediction: Forbidding Mourning," the relation of two souls is best figured in terms of a tracing instrument. The two souls are not "knit" into the perplexing loops of a constitutive knot, but are more accurately figured as the recursive writing of a compass folding in upon itself, in a pattern of inscription that "makes me end, where I begun." If the poem begins with "virtuous men" whispering to their souls in a muted verbal address, then the poem's conclusion moves to the specific mechanics of "oblique" writing joining the two souls into a reflexive circle.

The "Valediction: Of My Name in the Window" turns the figure of tracing crucial to the recursive logic of the compass into a mechanism to "interanimate" souls between the self and other. This poem, which Donne wrote upon departing from his wife, depicts a name carved in glass:

> Or think this ragged bony name to be
> My ruinous anatomy.
>
> Then, as all my souls be
> Emparadised in you, (in whom alone
> I understand, and grow and see) (ll. 23–27)

Critics have recently read the "ruinous anatomy" sequence as proof of Donne's obsession with anatomy and the scientific study of the body.[10] It is the written name, however, and not the poet's physical body that possesses a "bony" structure, and the anatomy being performed is one of the soul.[11] The "ruinous anatomy" enabled by the "ragged bony name" involves the anatomization of the Aristotelian soul into its three faculties of reason, nutrition, and sensation: "I understand, and grow, and see."

The "Valediction's" anatomy of the soul, however, does not follow the procedure of a scientific dissection, insofar as the anatomy precipitated by the engraved name becomes a transplantation of the poet's three Aristotelian faculties into the lover. Where a scientific anatomy would conclude with a taxonomy of the body's parts, the poet's "ruinous anatomy" goes much further, by excising the anatomized faculties of the soul and transposing them into the lover reading the name. The poem describes a prosthesis of the soul, which implants the Aristotelian faculties into the reader of the name but permits the anatomized poet to use the displaced powers of ratiocination, growth, and sensation by proxy. The transferral of the Aristotelian faculties to the reading lover is absolute, and the poet retains none of his soul: "*all* my souls" are transplanted into the other "in whom *alone*" (my emphasis in both) the poet can perform the living functions of his soul. The anatomized poet can be called living only insofar as he experiences the three faculties of his soul functioning within someone else reading his name. The anatomy of the poet's soul is "ruinous" to the extent that it displaces the faculties marking him as an individuated living being into another person, thus obliterating the boundaries between souls and between selves.

If the *Songs and Sonnets* in general are obsessed with the possibility of "interanimating" the souls of two lovers, the "Valediction: Of My Name in the Window" goes to great lengths to accomplish this enmeshing of souls. The "Valediction" suggests that the "interanimation" of two lovers can only occur through an anatomy of the soul that literally excises the poet's faculties of reason, sensation, and nutrition, and implants them in the other. The impetus of the poet's "ruinous anatomy" and the prosthesis of his Aristotelian faculties is the writing of the "ragged bony name" upon the window. In both the figure of the compass and the name written in glass, the mechanics of the graphical trace become vitally important in unifying the two lovers' souls. In the compass, the two souls are joined at a fulcrum to draw reflexive circles. In the "ruinous anatomy," two souls can "flow" into one another by "imprinting" to the extent that the poet's inscribed name anatomizes the faculties of his Aristotelian soul and transplants them into the reader.[12] In both cases, the graphical trace serves as both the material bond between the two lovers' souls, which can only draw a circle in the functional interrelation of two legs of a compass, and the anatomical transplantation of the organic soul's faculties of reason ("I understand"), nutrition ("grow"), and sensation ("see") from the poet into his lover.

"Both Sides Written Rolls": Writing the Two-Sided Soul in the *Anniversaries*

Donne's two *Anniversary* poems (1611–12) nominally mourn Elizabeth Drury, the daughter of Sir Robert Drury of Suffolk, who died in December 1610 at the age of fourteen. But despite the poems' stated purpose of commemorating Drury, Donne did not know her personally, and the more likely motivation for writing the poems was "to attract Sir Robert's patronage."[13] The emotional charge of the poems, however, is not simply exaggerated, since both poems lament the decay of the soul as their primary subject matter, for which Elizabeth Drury serves as a type of allegorical, and fictive, inspiration. The *Anniversaries* stand as Donne's elegy for the soul prompted by the death of young Elizabeth.

Donne's early fantasies of "interanimation" in the *Songs and Sonnets*, which used the faculties of the organic soul as a tissue between lovers, serve as the basis of the dilemma that motivates Donne's elegy to Elizabeth Drury in the *Anniversary* poems.[14] The "subtle knot, which makes us man" takes on a new life as a perplexing problem, since the existence of two souls in one body rather than in the distance between two people leads to a logical paradox that makes Christian self-knowledge impossible. The presence of two souls confuses any effort to obey the command to "know thyself," provoking a "wretched" condition of ignorance and paralysis. The *Second Anniversary* lays out a somewhat dismaying state of affairs for the human soul: the soul knows so little about itself as to be "Oppress'd with ignorance" (line 253). Elizabeth Drury's passing is significant since, as the poem states hyperbolically, she was the "electrum" that seamlessly resolved any contradictions between body and soul and between the two souls. Critics have long sought to find a coherent theory of the soul in the *Anniversary* poems and have identified the enigmatic assertion that Drury's "body thought" (line 246) as Donne's formulation of a mature psychology.[15] The sequence following the statement of "her body thought," however, is primarily concerned with a conflict between different models of soul and not the amalgamation of body and soul or a consistent theory of mind:

> Poor soul, in this thy flesh what dost thou know?
> Thou know'st thyself so little, as thou know'st not,
> How thou didst die, nor how thou was begot.
> Thou neither know'st how thou at first cam'st in,
> Nor how thou took'st the poison of man's sin.
> Nor dost thou (though thou know'st, that thou art so)
> By what way thou art made immortal, know. (ll. 254–60)

The seventy-five lines following the statement of "her body thought" carefully describe the problems besieging the soul after Drury's death. The dilemma emerging after her death is not a dualist schism of body and soul, but rather a conflict between two warring souls. We are "Oppress'd with ignorance" since there are too many different types of soul existing simultaneously within us, resulting in a psychological cacophony. The poem articulates, in sequence, a contradiction between the Christian soul defined by immortality and original sin on the one hand, and the organic soul defined by the Aristotelian faculties on the other. The speaker first addresses the "poor" soul who knows nothing about its existence in the terms of the Christian mysteries: its own birth or death ("How thou didst die, nor how thou was begot"), its implantation into the body prior to birth ("how thou at first cam'st in"), the infection of original sin ("how thou took'st the poison of man's sin"), and its immortality ("what way thou art made immortal"). If the Christian soul is indeed immortal, it has no way to confirm it. By contrast, locating the origins of life in the faculties of the organic soul leads to an apriori state of "infirmity":

> Think further on thy self, my soul, and think
> How thou at first was made in but a sink;
> Think that it argued some infirmity,
> That those two souls, which then thou found'st in me,
> Thou fed'st upon, and drew'st into thee, both
> My second soul of sense, and first of growth. (ll. 157–62)

The organic soul "made in but a sink" is trapped in a state of impasse in which the faculties of "sense" and "growth" represent an original "infirmity."

The diseased condition of the soul leads to a claustrophobic psychology that ruins any attempt to "comprehend" one's own nature:

> Thou art too narrow, wretch, to comprehend
> Even thyself: yea though thou wouldst but bend
> To know thy body. Have not all souls thought
> For many ages, that our body is wrought
> Of air, and fire, and other elements?
> And now they think of new ingredients.
> And one soul thinks one, and another way
> Another thinks, and 'tis an even lay.
> Know'st thou but how the stone doth enter in
> The bladder's cave, and never break the skin?
> Know'st thou how blood, which to the heart doth flow,
> Doth from one ventricle to th'other go?
> And for the putrid stuff, which thou dost spit,
> Know'st thou how thy lungs have attracted it?
> . . . .
> And of those many opinions which men raise
> Of nails and hairs, dost thou know which to praise? (ll. 261–78)

The lines following the ambiguities of the Christian mysteries address a soul "too narrow . . . to comprehend / Even thyself," defined not by Christian ontology but by its bias to the body: "thou wouldst but bend / To know thy body." Unfortunately, the body's structure is "too narrow" to encompass both souls. The second model of the soul differs fundamentally from the Christian soul—it is defined by the elements ("our body is wrought / Of air, and fire, and other elements"), humors and spirits, and the faculties of nutrition and sense. Historians of science have long read this sequence as displaying Donne's enthusiasm for recent scientific and anatomical discoveries.[16] However, the passage does not reference its array of scientific facts as being revelatory or useful. Precisely the opposite occurs—the "new philosophy" of the time can only introduce a jumble of contravening theories of the soul's faculties and organs, which amplify rather than resolve the soul's confusion.

The classical soul differs from the Christian soul to the extent that it is physically rooted in the function of the body's organs. However, the organic soul knows nothing about the workings of the organs in which its faculties are embedded. It does not "comprehend" the vegetative faculty's living processes, such as excretion ("know'st thou but how the stone doth enter in / The bladder's cave"), circulation ("know'st thou how blood, which to the heart doth flow, / Doth from one ventricle to th'other go?"), and the imperceptible growth of nails and hair (line 278).[17] Beyond the autonomic processes of the vegetative faculty, the poem argues that the faculty of sense offers no insight into human nature, since it is confounded by errors of perspective:

When wilt thou shake off this pedantery,
Of being taught by sense, and fantasy?
Thou look'st through spectacles; small things seem great
Below; but up unto the watch-tower get,
And see all things despoiled of fallacies:
Thou shalt not peep through lattices of eyes
Nor hear through labyrinths of ears, nor learn
By circuit, or collections to discern. (ll. 291–98)

The speaker urges us to abandon the empirical "pedantery" of the faculty of sense, which is subject to constant distortion by "spectacles" and distance. The sense organs ("lattices of eyes" and "labyrinths of ears") and the rational faculty's power of memory ("nor learn / By circuit") are utterly confused, and therefore we cannot use the higher faculties of the soul to "discern" our own nature. Taken together, the organic soul's faculties of nutrition, sensation, and memory are characterized by error and ignorance. The *Second Anniversary* presents two souls locked in paralysis: "one soul thinks one, and another way / Another thinks, and 'tis an even lay." The soul knows nothing about its mystical nature. Nor does it know how its faculties are embedded in the body's organs. The confusion of both souls leads to a paradoxical impasse: " 'tis an even lay."

This psychological dilemma within each body prompts us to revise our vision of the macrocosm, whose organs now constitute the body politic in a "decrepit" fashion, as Donne muses in "A Funeral Elegy" (1610), the poem dedicated to Drury before he wrote the *Anniversaries*:

The world contains
Princes for arms, and counsellors for brains,
Lawyers for tongues, divines for hearts, and more,
The rich for stomachs, and for backs the poor ;
The officers for hands, merchants for feet,
By which remote and distant countries meet ;
But those fine spirits, which do tune and set
This organ, are those pieces which beget
Wonder and love ; and these were she ; and she
Being spent, the world must needs decrepit be. (ll. 21–30)

The conventional enumeration of the organs corresponding to the political and social offices that compose the "world" suffers from the loss of the humoral substance of the "fine spirits," which "tune and set / This organ." Drury functioned in a macrocosmic sense as the humors and spirits that linked the disparate organs of the body ("arms," "brains," "tongues," "hearts," "stomachs," and "hands") into the coherent faculties of the living soul. Without these "spirits," the organs of the soul's faculties are out of "tune" and are knocked out of harmony. Extending the macrocosmic analogy, we must conclude that "she / Being spent, the world must needs decrepit be."

The confusion of two souls out of "tune" represents the central problem of the poem. Donne defines the human in terms of two souls confused about themselves and about their relation to each other, with little prospect of harmonious synthesis. Thus, the problem identified by Donne is not one of a conventional dualism of body versus soul, nor is it a coherent theory of mind. The poem rather voices confusion about two diseased and contradictory souls, one defined by Christian mystery and the other by the Aristotelian organic faculties. Without the fantasy of Drury's lost "body thought," the poet is left to reconcile two warring souls, with no hope of psychological harmony or illuminating self-knowledge.

The solution that Donne proposes is a mode of double writing that only Drury was capable of performing. If the early lyrics sought to bridge the divide between two lovers' souls through figures of the graphical trace, here Donne transforms the rhetoric of the trace into the different scribal metaphor of the two-sided manuscript:

> She, who left such a body, as even she
> Only in heaven could learn, how it can be
> Made better; for she was rather two souls,
> Or like to full, on both sides written rolls,
> Where eyes might read upon the outward skin,
> As strong records for God, as minds within;
> She, who by making full perfection grow,
> Pieces a circle, and still keeps it so (*Second Anniversary*, ll. 501–8)

In stating that "she was rather two souls," the poem moves away from the body and transforms the paralyzing confusion of the two souls evinced in the preceding section into a new figuration of death and redemption. The poem uses the figure of the "written roll" as the figural structure of the two souls: "two souls . . . on both sides written rolls."[18] By writing the two souls on "both sides" of a sheet of text, the poem shifts away from the body and the traditional metaphors describing the body/soul relation. Drury was not defined by the conventional tropes of an interior soul housed within the physical shell of the body, nor does her soul rise to heaven, leaving her body at the moment of death.[19] The conventional dualism of body and soul can be "made better" by shifting to the alternative tropology of the two souls defined in terms of their textual nature, "written" on "both sides" of the text. The poem reconceives the soul in terms of a sheet existing in three dimensions, which requires the reader to rotate the "written roll" in space so as to read the reverse, hidden surface of text. In writing the two souls on the obverse and reverse surfaces of the dual-sided sheet, the poem circumvents the traditional Christian metaphysics of the soul's interiority. The Christian soul's "strong records for God" are invisible to the reader not because they are nested in the body, but rather because we have failed to "roll" over the sheet in space, revealing a reverse surface. For Donne, the three-dimensional conception of the two-sided textual soul represents a "fuller" understanding of Drury's existence than does the dualism of body and soul.[20]

The poem's conclusion attempts to resolve the conflict and paralysis of the organic and Christian souls marking earlier passages. The inscription of the two-sided soul permits a new understanding of the organic faculties as existing cohesively with the invisible mysteries of the Christian soul. The organic soul is the legible surface of the text facing the reader, the "outward skin" visible to the "eyes": we can "read" the soul insofar as the eyes can visually perceive the language composing it. Donne therefore defines the act of reading the soul's textual substance as a function of the faculty of sense. The sensible soul is the "outward skin" of the two-sided soul to the extent that it can be read by the organs of the visual faculty. The poem subsequently defines the second, Christian soul imperceptible to the sense organs as "strong records" partially obscured or facing away from the reader. The faculty of sense can "read" the language etched upon the "outward skin" of the Aristotelian soul, whereas the words making up the "strong records for God" function in terms of the rational faculty: "as *minds* within." The "strong records for God" defining the Christian soul are written in a different textual medium that can be most accurately grasped by the rational faculty of the "mind" beyond the sense faculty's visual perception of language. Donne defines the Christian soul in terms of its spiritual textuality: it is "records" written for God in a language encoded in the mind. In the "Funeral Elegy," Donne works through precisely this difficulty of describing the "paper wrapp'd" mind as a "through-light scarf her mind to enroll, / or exhalation breathed out from her soul" (ll. 60–61). In this earlier poem addressing the same topic, Donne figures a similar mechanism in which Drury's "mind" is a diaphanous tissue, "a through-light scarf"— that partially obscures our field of vision by "enrolling" the mind within its folds. This "enrolling" of the rational faculty is significant not only because it parallels the "written roll" that Donne ultimately uses to describe Drury's two-sided soul, but also because it begins to approximate the classical idea of *pneuma* animating the psyche or soul: the "exhalation breathed out from her soul." The inscription of the "two souls" as the dual faces of the "written roll" amounts to a state of psychological perfection corresponding to the vegetative faculty's principles of growth: "She, by making full perfection *grow*." Inscribing the dual surfaces of the "written roll" creates a soul that "grows" as the body's organs would. The two-sided soul inscribed upon the "written roll" becomes by the end of the passage a growing, seeing, and thinking textual entity that describes Drury's irrecoverable psychology.

The description of the reversible "written roll" specifically appropriates the manuscript medium as a way to define the dual faces of Drury's soul. This move would seem to confirm the interpretation of Donne's career that has studied his preference for manuscript and the circulation of his poetry as "loose sheets" among his coterie of literary associates.[21] According to this reading of Donne's participation in Renaissance manuscript culture, his decision to publish the *Anniversaries* in printed form constituted a shameful "descent."[22] But although Donne expresses a wariness about printed texts in his letters, the language of this poem is not as decisive in its rejection of the medium. *The Second Anniversary* could have stopped with the triumph of script in the form of the two-sided sheet of the soul, but it does not. Rather, the poem describes the exemplary textuality of Drury's soul in two competing idioms of textuality: the "written roll" of the soul and, alternatively, as a printed book:

> She, who in th'art of knowing heaven, was grown
> Here upon earth, to such perfection,
> That she hath, ever since to heaven she came,
> (In a far fairer print), but read the same:
> She, she, not satisfied with all this weight
> (For so much knowledge, as would over-freight
> Another, did but ballast her) is gone,
> . . . .
> (Taking herself) our best, and worthiest book.
> Return not, my soul, from this ecstasy,
> And meditation of what thou shalt be,
> To earthly thoughts, till it to thee appear,
> With whom thy conversation must be there.
> With whom wilt thou converse? (ll. 311–25)

Drury's exemplary soul representing a state of "perfection" is composed in a "far fairer print," and her death stands as the loss of "our best, and worthiest book." This initial move defining Drury's psychological perfection in the "print" medium of the bound "book" and not the script of the "written roll" is not so much a critique of the press as it is a translation of print into the substance of elegiac loss. The description of her soul as a printed book measures the extent to which she is irrecoverably "gone." She has departed to "heaven" and has "taken herself" away from the earthbound poetic speaker and his audience. The "Funeral Elegy" preceding the *Anniversaries* frames the project of the two poems in precisely these terms, describing her death as a textual rupture: her loss amounts to "leaves . . . torn out of the book" (line 90). The poet therefore casts his gaze upon a world where the integrity of the print medium has been lost in something like a textual fall. With Drury's passing, she has taken with her the possibility of the "far fairer print" of her own exemplary book-bound soul.

The extent of this loss is evident in the description of "earthly thoughts" after her death. With her "printed" soul departed to heaven, humans on earth must understand the substance of their souls differently. In the reflexive address to "my soul," the speaker suggests that living in the wake of her death requires a verbal address to define the soul—"conversation"—since we no longer have unmediated access to the "print" composing Drury's exemplary "book": "To earthly thoughts, till it to thee appear, / With whom thy conversation must be there. / With whom wilt thou converse?" Scholars of the circulation of Donne's work among his coterie of poets have argued that manuscript represented for him a medium that opened a "dialogue" between the poet and his audience, embodying a form of "living presence" in script.[23] The language of the *Second Anniversary*, however, shifts this view by proposing that "conversation" is what *remains* after we have lost Drury's printed soul-as-book. "Conversation" and dialogue constitute an elegiac remainder of psychological loss and absence, and not a yearning for the lyric immediacy of presence. The *Second Anniversary* therefore concludes with the two-sided "written roll" to describe the soul not because of an unqualified preference for manuscript, but rather because we have lost the better psychological medium of Drury's "print." In light of the emphasis placed on Drury's lost "printed" soul as an exemplary mode of psychology, it is perhaps unsurprising that the *Anniversaries* published in 1611–12 were Donne's first poems to appear in print. Despite the hesitation expressed in his letters, the language of the *Anniversaries* suggests a shift in his attitude toward the printed text. And indeed, he began to publish his works in prose, including his sermons and the *Devotions upon Emergent Occasions*, after this point.

The *Anniversaries* thus embody a point of transition in Donne's rhetoric of the two-souls dilemma. In the *Anniversary* poems, however, Donne is not ready to commit fully to the print medium as the rhetorical medium of the soul, since the goal of the poems is to describe the extent to which we no longer have recourse to it. Print in the *Anniversaries* functions as the substance of elegy and loss and as such cannot serve as a stable rhetoric of the two souls. Donne must articulate a positive and not elegiac definition of print as the rhetorical tissue of the soul in another place, his later sermons, where he presents his final vision of the textuality of the two-souls dilemma.

"Be Thou *Verbum*": Printing the Image of God in Donne's Sermons

The two-souls paradox as presented in the *Anniversaries* is never resolved in the poems. After all, the stated goal of the *Anniversaries* is to describe the "world's general sickness" (*An Anatomy of the World*, line 240) after the passing of Drury. The issue of classical faculty psychology as a basis for Christian theology reemerges most prominently in the final phase of Donne's career as royal chaplain to the household of James I and Charles I and as dean of St. Paul's Cathedral. In his sermons, Donne uses the rhetorical media of prose and oratory as a space to work out the puzzling role of the classical organic soul in Christian salvation.

The two-souls problem links Donne's poetry and prose in an unexpected way. Critics since Izaak Walton in his 1640 *Life of John Donne* have read Donne's sermons as a body of mature theological thought in contradistinction to the juvenilia of his earlier "metaphysical" poetic conceits fixated on eroticism and love. This popular critical stance, most famously expressed by John Carey, has argued that Donne's ordination by the Church of England represented a clean break from his earlier poetic career and has expressed dismay at Donne's alarmingly conservative positions as a priest in contrast to the radical ideas of the poet.[24] The critical assumption that Donne abandoned the radical ideas and figures of his poetry in his later "mature" conservative sermons does not take the intellectual import of his poetry seriously enough and fails to acknowledge that Donne constantly returned to earlier poetic preoccupations in his sermons. It is this continuity of thought that makes Donne's obsession with the problem of two souls in his poetry a dominant theme in his sermons: 79 of his 160 sermons refer to the paradoxical relationship of the organic and Christian souls first introduced in the *Songs and Sonnets*. The sermons function as a rhetorical space permitting Donne to work out the psychological problems posed in his lyric poems by shifting from an erotic fantasy of "interanimation" or a frustrated quest for self-knowledge to a new textuality of the soul opened up by print technology.

Donne's rethinking of the two-souls problem in his sermons as a productive basis for theology, rather than a paralyzing contradiction, involves a different definition of the organic soul and its faculties as a material substrate for the impression of God's image in man. No longer does he attempt to understand the workings of the soul through scribal metaphors of a name etched in glass, a circle traced by a compass, or a two-sided manuscript. Donne shifts in his sermons to the alternative model of a physical impression of an engraved image as the basis of Christian grace implanted within the organic soul. Donne accomplishes this change across the sermons by engaging in a sustained project revising the traditional doctrine of the "image of God" in man.[25] Donne engages in his most systematic treatment of this concept in his 1629 sermon preached to King Charles upon Genesis 1:26, in which he evinces the radical position that God places his image within the "natural faculties" of the Aristotelian soul and not upon the immortal substance of the Christian soul:

> And there remaines onely now, the operation thereof, how this Image of God in the soule of man works. The Sphear then of this intelligence, the Gallery for this Picture, the Arch for this Statue, the Table, and frame and shrine for this Image of God, is inwardly and immediately the soule of man . . . But this Image is in our soule, as our soule is the wax, and this Image is the seale. . . .

> Let us consider the having of this Image: in what respect, in what operation, this Image is in our soule. For, whether this Image, bee in those faculties, which we have in Nature; or in those qualifications, which we may have in Grace; or in those super-illustrations, which the blessed shall have in Glory; hath exercised the contemplation of many. Properly this Image is in Nature; in the natural reason, and the other faculties of the Soule of man . . . For it is radically, primarily, in the very soule it selfe. . . .
>
> For the steppes, which we consider are four; First, *Esse*, Beeing; for some things have onely a beeing, and no life, as stones: Secondly, *Vivere*, Living; for some things have life, and no sense, as Plants: and then, thirdly, *Sentire*, Sense; for some things have sense, and no understanding. Which understanding and reason, man hath with his Beeing, and Life, and Sense; and so is in a nearer station to God, then any other creature, and a livelier Image of him, who is the root of Beeing . . . Now in all these respects man, the meer naturall man, hath the Image of the King of Kings. And therefore respect that Image in thy selfe, and exalt thy natural faculties.[26]

By considering the "operation" of the "Image of God in the soule of man" in great detail, Donne begins to shift the relationship of the two souls. He works through several metaphors describing the relation of God's image and the human soul: "The Sphear then of this intelligence, the Gallery for this picture, the Arch for this Statue" all figurally approximate how the soul serves as the "table and frame" of the image of God. Ultimately, however, Donne selects the figure of the seal impressed into wax to describe how God's image is imprinted in the human soul.

Donne's final choice of the wax seal is startling, since it adopts the privileged metaphor used in Aristotle's *De Anima* to characterize the hylomorphic interaction of form and matter. Aristotle writes: "The soul may therefore be defined as the first actuality of a natural body potentially possessing life, and such will be any body which possesses organs. . . . So one need no more ask whether body and soul are one than whether the wax and the impression it receives are one," and "the wax receives the impression of the signet-ring without the iron or the gold."[27] By appropriating Aristotle's figure of the "impression" of a seal in wax, Donne surprisingly turns the paradigmatic metaphor of the Aristotelian organic soul into the basis of his explication of the specifically Christian concept of the image of God. In Donne's modification of the Aristotelian metaphor, the "Image of God" is the "seale" imprinted into the wax substrate of the soul. Donne not only cites Aristotle's organic soul, but goes so far as to mobilize Aristotle's exact metaphors to describe a vitally important Christian concept. Donne uses Aristotle's metaphor of the soul as a wax impression as the primary way to describe the Christian process of the soul imprinted by God's image. This passage is startling precisely because it argues that the best way to explicate the impression of God's image on the Christian soul is by turning to figures conventionally associated with the organic soul.

Donne's reading of the "image of God" continues in an unexpected direction in his assertion that God "impresses" his image in the "natural faculties" of the organic soul and not in the "grace" of the Christian soul. Donne acknowledges that generations of thinkers have struggled to ascertain whether the image of God rests in "those faculties, which we have in Nature," or in "those qualifications, which we may have in Grace," or finally in "those super-illustrations, which the blessed shall have in Glory." One might expect that as a Christian thinker preaching to the king, Donne would advocate the primacy of "Grace" or "Glory." He does not, and instead guides his audience to the faculties of the organic soul: "Properly this Image is in Nature; in the natural reason, and the other faculties of the Soule of man." The image of God is "properly" located in the "faculties" of the "natural" soul, and not in the Christian soul more obviously marked by "Grace" and "Glory."

Donne specifically cites the "steppes" of the ascending faculties of the Aristotelian soul to emphasize his point. Donne's natural "steppes" directly cite Aristotle's hierarchy of the faculties in *De Anima*.[28] The first "step" of nature is bare being without life, as in the case of stones; the second is life without sense, as in the case of plants; the third is sense without understanding, found in animals; and the final "steppe" is the human soul that combines "understanding and reason" with being, life, and sense. Donne's taxonomy is a direct citation of Aristotle's hierarchy of the faculties, which organizes living beings according to the ascending faculties of nutrition, sensation, and reason. Humans possess the "liveliest" image of God to the extent that we have all of Aristotle's faculties, separating us from animals, plants, and stones: we are in a "nearer station to God" inasmuch as we have the faculty of "understanding and reason" combined with "Beeing, and Life, and Sense." According to the sermon's logic, the "image of God" is impressed upon the "natural faculties" of the organic soul, and since humans possess the greatest number of faculties, we have the fullest image of God in our souls. In this additive logic composing the "image of God," humans are a "livelier image" since we have all four of the "natural faculties," while perhaps animals only have three-quarters of his image since they are defined by three faculties, without reason, and plants only have two-quarters of his image, since they lack the higher faculties of sensation and reason.

After repeatedly emphasizing the primacy of the organic soul's "natural faculties" in the impression of the "image of God," Donne culminates his reading with the assertion that all humans, every "meer naturall man" and not exclusively the elect, possess the "Image of the King of Kings." More "radically," as he puts it, the effect of the image of God on the "natural faculties" of the organic soul is "the very soule it selfe," positioning humans "in a nearer station to God." The "soule it selfe" that Donne invokes to link humans to God is not a conventional understanding of the immortal, immaterial Christian soul trapped in a flesh-ridden, sinful body. Donne reconceives the Christian soul as an emergent property resulting from the fusion of God's image impressed upon the "natural faculties" and sustained by the act of "exalting" those organic powers as the substance of Christian grace. Since the "image of God" is contained in the organic soul's faculties, Donne exhorts his audience to alter their strategy of worship: devotion requires one to "respect that Image in thy selfe" by "exalting thy natural faculties." In placing God's image in the organic soul, Donne shifts the locus of proper worship to the "exaltation" of the "natural faculties."

This 1629 sermon demonstrates that late in his life, Donne's fascination with the relation of the classical and Christian souls has not diminished, and if anything, his position has become more confident. In his use of Aristotle's figure of stamped wax as a way to define the image of God in the Christian subject, in his assertion that God implants his image in the "natural faculties" of the organic soul and not in the "grace" of the Christian soul, and in his insistence to the king to direct the act of "exaltation" not toward the Christian soul but toward the faculties of the organic soul, Donne shows that even late in his career as an ostensibly Christian thinker, he does not abandon the problem of two souls that lay at the heart of much of his earlier poetry. Even as a priest, Donne continues to understand the organic soul's faculties as the most important way to define fundamental Christian concepts such as the "image of God."

Surely Donne's account of the organic soul as the matter of the Christian "soule it selfe" would have struck his audience, composed of Charles and his court, as a strange brand of doctrine. Donne's model of the soul did not conform to the tenets of any major sect, Anglican or otherwise. Many critics have identified the tenor of Donne's sermons to be distinctly Augustinian, at least as far as the question of the soul goes; however, Donne's position differs markedly from the doctrine of both Saint Augustine and Thomas Aquinas. Aquinas's position from the *Summa Theologiae* was largely regarded as a philosophical justification of the immortal soul as intrinsically rational.[29] Aquinas responds to the question of "whether besides the intellectual soul there are in man other souls essentially different from one another?" in emphatic terms, concluding that "there is no other substantial form in man besides the intellectual soul." The faculties of the classical soul—"sensitive," "intellectual," and "nutritive"—are in fact "numerically one soul" subsumed under the intellectual soul. If Aquinas places a heavy emphasis on the primacy of the intellect, Augustine in the *Confessions* famously defines the power that "animates" the body and which "fills its whole frame with life" as memory. For Augustine, memory is a "spacious palace" storing sensory perceptions for future thought: within memory "there is stored up, whatsoever besides we think, either by enlarging or diminishing."[30] Both doctrinal explanations of the Christian soul in terms of faculty psychology reify higher cognitive functions—either the intellect for Aquinas, or memory as the "space" of thinking for Augustine.[31]

Donne's sermons revise these received traditions by reversing their logic. The foundation of immortality, grace, and salvation does not inhere in the noble cognitive powers of the intellect or memory, but rather arises from the "natural faculties" composed of the body's organs, which Augustine and Aquinas were seeking to transcend. For Donne, all of the soul's faculties—"the very soule it selfe"—are "impressed" with God's image and, as a composite, draw humans into a relationship with God. If Pomponazzi's critique of Augustine and Aquinas turned the immanent relationship of the immortal Christian soul and the organic faculties into the flash point of a theological crisis, Donne performs exactly the opposite maneuver, by viewing the necessary role of the "natural" faculties in defining Christian spirituality as a glorious thing, an occasion to "exalt" those faculties as a mode of transcendence immanent to the materiality of the body's organs.

Donne can exhort us to "exalt" the organic faculties in a way that Pomponazzi could not in contesting Augustine and Aquinas because he understands the materiality of the organic soul differently. Pomponazzi envisions the necessary link between the immortal and mortal parts of the soul in a vocabulary of decaying, flesh-bound sin, much like Donne paints a gloomy picture of a diseased dualism in the *Anniversary* poems. By moving away from the idiom of flesh, disease, and decay, as well as from the methods of anatomical dissection and medical diagnosis, Donne finds a productive and indeed creative alternative strategy of figuring the materiality of the soul in the mechanics of print technology. To accomplish this, he turns from the impression of wax appropriated from Aristotle's *De Anima* and begins to rethink the physical impression of the soul as a text. Take, for example, Donne's figuration of the skin as a written sheet in his definition of the image of God "imprinted" upon the soul: "These be the Records of velim, these be the parchmins, the endictments, and the evidences that shall condemn many of us, at the last day, our *own skins*; we have the book of God, the Law, written in our own hearts; we have the image of God imprinted in our own souls; wee have the character, and seal of God stamped in us . . . and, all this is bound up in this velim, in this parchmin, in this skin."[32] In this sermon performing a reading of Job 19:26, Donne uses the figure of "parchmins" and "velim" that record the "image of God imprinted in our own souls" upon "our *own skins*." The stamp, imprint, character, and seal describe a method of printing upon vellum and parchment precisely as God's image is impressed "in our own souls" upon the material substrate of "our *own skins*." This transformation graphically corporealizes the impression and "exaltation" of the organic faculties seen in the previous sermon by specifically rendering the body's skin into the vellum, and not simply the paper, upon which the soul is imprinted.

Donne illuminates a new form of Christian agency, whereby the "exalting" of the natural faculties performs the "publication" of oneself as an embodied type of devotion. In a 1627 sermon, he instructs his listeners: "Be thou *Verbum* too, A Word, as God was, A Speaking, and a Doing Word, to his glory, and the edification of others. . . . Let thy mouth, let thy hand, let all the Organs of thy body, all the faculties of thy soule, concurre in the performance of this duty, intimated here. . . . That they speak, utter, declare, publish the glory of God."[33] Donne instructs his audience to "be thou *Verbum*" or "A Speaking, and a Doing Word." His version of ontology culminates in an act of printerly dissemination: "publish the glory of God." This publication of the self occurs through the actions of the organic soul: "let all the Organs of thy body, all the faculties of thy soule, concurre in the performance of this duty." The "organs" and "faculties" of the active soul align to perform a mode of "publication" that transforms the self into "*Verbum*" or the "Doing Word." Donne's injunction to "exalt" the organic soul takes on a new spin in this sermon, with the work of the faculties constituting a publication of the self as the word incarnate.

For Donne, this publication through the soul's "organs" and "faculties" is not a form of original creation but is a continuing action, repeated throughout one's life. The possibility that the organic soul can serve as a material substrate for "imprinting" and "publishing" Christian devotion suggests to Donne that our souls can be revised and reprinted, precisely like successive editions of a book. It is in the vocabulary of reprinting that Donne articulates a radically different account of God's relationship to the human soul and of Christian salvation. In his 1623 sermon on All Saints' Day, Donne meditates upon how the reprinting of God's image shines a new light on the possibility of Christian salvation:

> Both Angels and we have the Image of God imprinted in us. . . . They have it not in the highest degree, (for so Christ onely is the Image of the invisible God) but they have it in a deep impression, so as they can neither lose it, nor deface it. We have this Image of God so as that we cannot lose it, but we may, and doe deface it; *Vri potest, non exuri*; The Devil hath this Image in him, and it cannot be burnt out in hell; for it is imprinted in the very naturall faculties of the soule . . . which though God have a purpose, *Resculpere imaginem*, to re-engrave, to refresh, to polish this Image in us.[34]

Donne's sermon again uses the Aristotelian figure of the soul as an impressed medium as a way to figure the difference between God's image in angels, devils, and humans. The image of God has been "imprinted" in the "natural faculties of the soule" of all three creations, but the nature of the image varies based on specific differences occurring during the engraving process. Angels have a "deep impression" that cannot be altered: "they can neither lose it, nor deface it," while even the Devil has a permanent impression that cannot be "burnt out in hell." Humans, on the other hand, possess an impression deep enough so that "we cannot lose it," but superficial to the extent that we can "deface" it through sin. Donne insists that since the image of God is imprinted in the "natural faculties" of the organic soul marking us as living beings, we can never lose the image as long as we are alive and can grow, sense, and think.

By defining the taxonomy of angels, devils, and humans as a difference of how deeply the image of God is imprinted upon the natural faculties, Donne refigures the promise of Christian salvation into God's act of reengraving his image in our soul. Humans can attain a status closer to angels not by cultivating the virtue of the Christian soul, but by allowing God to work upon the organic soul, where he will "re-engrave" his image on the natural faculties. Donne defines God's ultimate "purpose" as a labor of printing and "re-engraving" our natural faculties, and he claims that if we are to be saved, then the path to salvation traces an arc through the classical soul's capacity to be imprinted and reengraved by God. The force of Donne's argument in this moment is surprising: the promise of salvation does not lie in the Christian soul's immortality, but rather in the possibility that the faculties of the organic soul can be imprinted and reprinted by God, restoring the original depth and quality of his image in our souls. For Donne, the possibility of Christian immortality and salvation lies in the soul's capacity to serve as a medium of repeated printing, and not in the grace or virtue of the Christian soul. In heaven, we will not have a second life but, rather, will experience our second printing.

Donne's vision of printing as a reengraving and repetition differs from the conventional early modern understanding of the printing press as a fixing or stabilizing instrument, expressed here by Walter Ong:

> Print encourages a sense of closure, a sense that what is found in a text has been finalized, has reached a state of completion. . . . The printed text is supposed to represent the words of an author in definitive or "final" form. For print is comfortable only with finality. Once a letterpress is closed, locked up, or a photolithographic plate is made, and the sheet printed, the text does not accommodate changes (erasures, insertions) so readily as do written texts. By contrast, manuscripts, with their glosses or marginal comments . . . were in dialogue with the world outside their own borders. They remained closer to the give-and-take of oral expression.[35]

Printing performs the "closure" and "completion" of linguistic meaning, and the press produces a "final form" that is "locked up" from future changes. Manuscript, by contrast, should be open to the "give-and-take" of discussion, revision, and editing. Donne's printerly technology of the soul reverses this common-sense logic by proposing that the possibility of repetition and revisiting the cast—"to re-engrave" and "to refresh"—allows us to imagine a soul open to revision in the medium of print. The "re-engraving" process, however, does not suggest the "chronic instability" or the "destabilizing and threatening" effect of the press that Adrian Johns has articulated.[36] Nor do we find in these sermons the haunting possibility of misinterpretation that Donne voiced earlier in his career when circulating his poetry in manuscript. It is the variable "deepness" of the impression on our soul's faculties that mediates our relationship to God. The human soul has a stable but malleable "impression," which can be defaced and altered but not completely effaced. These modulations of the depth of the soul's imprint allow God to rework and reprint the soul, and we would assume that some souls will require more "refreshing" and reprinting than others. For Donne, the partial instability of the print medium is a decidedly good characteristic, since it permits alterations to the quality and meaning of the soul's "impression," and thus opens a form of psychological malleability through repetition, editing, and reprinting that we did not see in his earlier works preoccupied with classical faculty psychology.

The specificity of Donne's diction in his reading of Christian salvation as a reprinting of the organic soul is important here. Donne argues that the image of God etched upon the natural faculties can be reprinted only insofar as God "re-engraves" his image. By selecting the word "engrave," Donne indicates that what will be "refreshed" and "polished" is not so much an image imprinted in ink, but rather the engraved metallic plate that serves as the template for the printed image. Donne goes into great detail in his February 29, 1627, sermon on Acts 7:60, describing how such a process of engraving a plate defines human life, culminating with the printed image created at the moment of one's death.

> Wee give you a Picture too. There is not a minute left to do it; not a minutes sand; Is there a minutes patience? Bee pleased to remember that those Pictures which are deliver'd in a minute, from a print upon paper, had many dayes, weeks, Moneths time for the graving of those Pictures in the Copper; So this Picture of that dying Man, that dies in Christ, that dies the death of the Righteous, that embraces Death as a Sleepe, was graving all his life; All his publique actions were the lights, and all his private the shadowes of this Picture. And when this Picture comes to the Presse, this Man to the streights and agonies of Death, thus he lies, thus he looks, this he is. His understanding and his will is all one faculty; He understands Gods purpose upon him, and he would not have God's purpose turned any other way; hee sees God will dissolve him, and he would faine be dissolved, to be with Christ; His understanding and his will is all one faculty; His memory and fore-sight are fixt, and concentred upon one object.[37]

Donne previously defined "God's purpose" as a return to "re-engrave" the image imprinted upon the natural faculties. In this passage, Donne specifically demonstrates how "God's purpose" becomes actualized at the moment of death: "He understands Gods purpose upon him, and he would not have God's purpose turned any other way." Donne initially adopts an urgent tone, underlining the lack of time one has to successfully print one's image at the moment of death: "There is not a minute left to do it; not a minutes sand." However, the dying individual can be comforted by the fact that an image "deliver'd in a minute, from a print upon paper," has required a long process of graving an image in a "copper" plate for months before the moment of printing. For Donne, the printing of the dying person represents the culmination of a lifetime of "graving" the copper template, in which the "publique actions" compose the lights and the "private" moments compose the shadows of his final image. If, in the previous sermon, Donne argued that God will return to the image imprinted in the organic faculties so as to "re-engrave" the soul at the end of one's life, then in this passage he asserts that human life itself is a long process of "graving" a copper plate in preparation for this final printing. In this radical move, Donne redefines human life itself in terms of the mechanics of copper engraving and printing, arguing that each moment of an individual's life coalesces into a slow process of constructing the copper plate that will be used at the instant of our death, "when this Picture comes to the Presse." Donne's enunciation of the two souls moves away from intellect and memory as the basis of Christian transcendence, as Augustine and Aquinas had argued, to a model that bases salvation in our malleable textuality and ability to be reprinted at the moment of our reunion with God.

In the final analysis, Donne views the organic soul's faculties as the locus of Christian agency mediated through a publication of the self. Donne's model of one's life as a continued process of "graving" the soul on a copper plate, in which the "public actions" as well as the "private" give substance and tone to its image, opens a space for a new definition of Christian agency. This vision of "action" in life as a mode of printerly self-work hearkens back to Donne's exhortation to "be thou *Verbum*," where the "performance" and work of the "organs" and "faculties of thy soule" transform the devotional subject into a "Speaking, and a Doing Word." The organic soul's faculties function as the instruments of "performing" and "Doing," and these "public actions" come together in the process of continuously engraving the image of one's soul in copper in anticipation of our final printing. In Donne's final understanding of the relationship between the two souls, the organic faculties are not simply a material substrate of the image of God in man. The faculties and organs of the soul serve an even more vitally important purpose as the medium of Christian agency—the "performance" and "action" of the self as a "Doing Word"—that mediates the process of "graving" our image and informs our final reprinting by God. Donne's struggle with the two-souls problem has come full circle. No longer does the presence of two souls in one body mire the self in the psychological and spiritual paralysis of the *Anniversary* poems, which appealed to the methods of anatomy and medicine. By turning to the techniques and vocabulary of printing and engraving, Donne's late sermons recuperate a form of devotional agency that redefines the substance of the soul in malleable terms—the Christian subject can revise and recast the content of his soul by changing his "actions" and their manner of "performance." The command to "be thou *Verbum*" confers on the subject the power to "do," to "perform," and to "publish" the self through the actions of the organic soul's faculties in a way that mediates his final reunion with God as a second printing.

This resolution of the psychological contradiction unifies the soul in a way that was not previously possible. Printing the image upon one's death "dissolves" the internal divisions of the soul, transforming the higher-order cognitive powers of the understanding, will, and memory into "one faculty."[38] The printing of the final image "dissolves" the schism between the powers of the organic soul and the Christian soul's single-minded desire to "be with Christ." The unity of the cognitive faculties at the moment of death represents an enormous contrast to the divided, warring state of the two souls described in the *Anniversary* poems. For Donne, if in life our two souls are divided, such divisions are "dissolved" into "one faculty" upon our death by God's act of reprinting our soul. In the sermons, the mechanics of "imprinting" and "graving" God's image upon the "natural faculties" give Donne a powerful array of metaphors to think about God's return to the human soul at the moment of death and how Christian salvation might be refigured in terms of the soul's textuality and ability to be printed. Ultimately, the extent of Donne's fascination with how the soul "comes to Presse" in a final image can be clearly seen in his own final portrait, in which he famously poses in his shroud (see figure 2). For Donne "embraces Death as a Sleepe," with closed eyes, lying in a death pose for a final "graved" image: "thus he lies, thus he looks, this he is." Donne abides by the sermon's articulation of the soul's final printing, in his own memento mori, printed months before his death.

The afterlife of Donne's soul in print, if anything, respects the message of his late sermons. John Marriott, printer of the first edition of Donne's poetry in 1633 and of his sermons, invokes Donne's model of printing-as-salvation in his prefatory verse to the 1635 edition of Donne's *Poems*. Citing the frontispiece to *Deaths Duell*—"his picture in a sheete" contained in "his last preach'd and printed booke"—Marriott creates a link between the "sheetes" of Donne's shroud, which "present him dead," and his own book: "these if you buy, / You have him living to Eternity."[39] As David Scott Kastan has cogently observed, Marriott's clever move revolves around "Donne's corpse" and the "corpus of his poetry," which are both "wrapped" in sheets.[40] There is more to Marriott's pun, though, since his description of the "printed booke" matches Donne's very precisely articulated understanding in the sermons of the reunification with God upon one's death as a second printing. Marriott's

Figure 2. John Donne in his shroud, frontispiece to *Deaths Duell* (London, 1632). (By permission of the Folger Shakespeare Library)

book materializes Donne's soul in literal form as "printed" sheets that contain within them the author "living to Eternity." It is not so much, however, that Donne "lives on in print," as Kastan suggests, as the text "publishes" his soul as the printerly salvation in death that is detailed in the sermons contained within the book itself. Marriott follows Donne's rulebook of the "published" soul and goes so far as to draw the reader of the sermons into this economy of a textual afterlife: "Print but his Sermons, and if those we buy, / Hee, Wee, and Thou shall live t'Eternity" (*Poems by J.D.*, A^{v}). Donne's urgent command to "be thou *Verbum*" takes on a new meaning, with Marriott's poem defining the relationship between Donne's printed text and the reader as performing the publication of the soul to "Eternity," precisely as Donne had imagined. In reading Donne's sermons, as we have in this chapter, the reader "publishes" Donne's soul in its immortal state, in effect eternalizing his soul as the printed text before us.

In this chapter, I have argued that Donne's sustained attention to the problem of two souls extends throughout his career, from the early lyrics to his final sermons in the years before his death. For Donne, the problem of two souls could only be resolved by redefining the psychological conflict in terms of textuality: the capacity to be written and imprinted in life and reengraved upon one's death. Ultimately, Donne redefines the immortality of the Christian soul and the promise of salvation in his sermons as God's reprinting of the faculties of the organic soul in "a far fairer print." The initial paradox of two souls leads Donne to reconceive the nature of the Christian soul in terms of the organic soul's textuality. This arresting vision of Christian immortality as a reprinting informs Donne's preparation for death in his late sermons and in his final portrait, where he anticipates his own return to God's "Presse."

Chapter 5

✦

From Animal to *Anima*: Milton's "Living Soul" and the Promise of Discursive Reason

By the time that John Milton approached the problem of the two souls in the mid-seventeenth century, much had changed in the English political landscape. Writing during the Civil War and interregnum, at a time of increased restrictions on the press and the theater, Milton did not have recourse to the same set of metaphors and discursive resources as his predecessors. In contrast with Donne, who viewed the print medium as a material basis of the soul, Milton was driven by his political context to find an alternative vocabulary for understanding the legacy of the classical soul in Christian doctrine.[1] *Areopagitica* (1644) is the most obvious example of how Milton was circumscribed by restrictions on the press in a way that his sixteenth-century predecessors were not, and it shows how Milton shifted to the register of "discourse" as his way to imagine the workings of the soul.

Milton's famous metaphor of the living book in *Areopagitica* establishes this strong tie between reason and discourse. Books "contain a potency of life in them to be as active as that soul whose progeny they are . . . they do preserve as in a vial the purest efficacy and extraction of that living intellect that bred them."[2] Writing encapsulates the "potency" of the soul's "life" within the book, which represents the material "extraction" of the "living intellect" and indeed the "reason itself" of the author in textual form. We can see evidence of the work performed by human discursive reason across a wide range of texts in Milton's corpus. In *Areopagitica*, Milton uses the metaphor of a city "besieged and blocked about" as a call to "discourse" vigorously and not necessarily to man the barricades. People in times of crisis "should be disputing, reasoning, reading, inventing, discoursing . . . things not before discoursed or written of."[3] When challenged by trying circumstances, and even military confrontation, the public should engage in the exercise of "reasoning" in a discursive medium of reading and writing. This active public work of rational linguistic discourse evinces the robustness of the soul's faculties. Engagement in reasoned discourse reflects the "good plight and constitution" of "not only . . . vital, but to rational faculties."[4] In Milton's later prose and epic verse, the emphasis on the print medium of books that is so distinctive in *Areopagitica* diminishes, but the primacy of "discourse" as a way to understand the vitality of the soul persists.

Apart from a political context that changed the viability of the press as a medium of psychological freedom, Milton also differs from his sixteenth-century antecedents because he does not view the two-souls problem as a constitutive *difference* defining the Christian subject that needs to be addressed or remedied. For Shakespeare, Donne, and Davies, the difference between the two souls opened up by their paradoxical coexistence represented a unique literary space to reimagine what the soul was, and how it composed the human as at once God's favored creation and something distinct from other animals on the chain of being. The linguistic, rhetorical, and material figures used by these authors to imagine the soul as the basis of a writerly psychological agency nonetheless assumed that the two-souls paradox was a problem or psychological knot that needed to be remedied to productive literary ends. Milton asserts in *Paradise Lost* and *De Doctrina Christiana*, by contrast, that the classical organic soul *is* the Christian soul described in Scripture, but it is one that needs to be patiently refined and converted to a more spiritual form capable of attaining salvation over the course of one's life—what the angel Raphael in *Paradise Lost* calls a "tract of time." For Milton, language—or what he terms "discourse"—and not simply the presence of reason, is central to this process. Milton shifts the assumptions framing the two-souls problem, by moving from a vocabulary of paradox or internal difference so common in the sixteenth century, into the idiom of refinement over time and patient translation through the rational operations of language.

Milton shares Donne's belief that the faculties of the organic soul can be worked upon and converted into a more spiritual form over one's embodied life. He differs from Donne, and the writers of the Elizabethan era previously considered, to the extent that he literalizes their strategy of deploying figures and extended systems of metaphor of the press and of writing as a literary means to conceptualize and redefine the nature of the two souls. Milton argues, by contrast, that the substance of the soul *is* language and that man is defined by the soul's unique capacity to reason in "discourse," in a manner quite different from other animals. In his poetry and prose, language as the matter of reason literally enables the conversion of the soul's organic faculties into a purer, more spiritual form. Man is not simply placed in a station superior to animals or plants because he possesses a faculty of reason (as suggested by Aquinas and humanists like Ficino in chapter 1), but rather must continually exercise his powers of reason within language in order to refine the soul to a higher plane closer to the state of angels.

Milton's linguistic solution to the two-souls dilemma allows us to see how he attempted to reconcile his rationalist Aristotelian commitments with the tenets of Christian doctrine. The *soul* is the place where he accomplishes this most fully. By focusing on Milton's reimagination of the Christian soul and soteriology in terms of classical, and specifically Aristotelian, faculty psychology, I am aligning myself with those critics who interpret Milton as a rationalist, including Richard Strier, Marshall Grossman, Mary Ann Radzinowicz, and Paul Cefalu. These rationalist scholars view reason as Milton's way of attempting to understand God's word. As Tobias Gregory suggests, "Milton was an exceptionally rationalist religious thinker. Not only did he believe that individuals, through hard study, could reason their way to right understanding of God's word, but he also believed it was one's Christian duty to do so."[5] Paul Cefalu has also proposed that this commitment to a reasoned "understanding of God's word" pervaded Milton's project—and that *De Doctrina Christiana* in particular "recommends the employment of deliberative rationalism under all conditions."[6] Similarly, Richard Strier points to a pair of paradigmatic moments from *De Doctrina Christiana* that insist on the power of reason, in which Milton rhetorically answers his own question: "I ask you, what can reason do here?"—"everything," concluding with the confident tautology that "the product of reason must be reason."[7] However, not all rationalist readings of Milton see his negotiation of reason and faith as one between Aristotle and Christian doctrine. Rationalist critics largely interested in the topics of theodicy and God's justice have not focused adequately on Aristotle's role in Milton's rationalist definition of the soul.[8]

Among Milton's contemporaries, the Cambridge Platonists, whose "rationalist emphasis" has been the focus of recent scholarship, stand out in their attempt to use reason as a way to answer a more fundamental question: the existence of God.[9] Ralph Cudworth, for example, insisted that by "the Truth of our Understanding Faculties . . . we are assured of the Existence of a God Essentially Good, who therefore cannot deceive."[10] He stated elsewhere even more bluntly, "if our faculty be True . . . then there is a God."[11] Cudworth's proof of God relies on a foundational assumption that "our humane faculties be true," and that "God hath here purposely left Free to use of their own faculties" in order to "find out Truth by them."[12] Cudworth and the Cambridge Platonists thus identified the *faculties of the soul* as the locus and instrument of a rationalist understanding of God.

Freely using the soul's faculties was, for seventeenth-century rationalists, a form of mathematical reasoning. Thomas Hobbes famously defines reason, the power distinguishing humans from animals, as "reckoning" or arithmetic.[13] As Philip Pettit has suggested, Hobbes viewed the invention of language as the medium of thought, but ultimately turned the linguistic nature of reason into a mathematical process based upon the "consequences" of words: "When a man 'reasoneth,' he does nothing else but conceive a sum total . . . which, if it be done by words, is conceiving of the consequence of the names of all the parts, to the name of the whole . . . In sum, in what matter soever there is a place for 'addition' and 'subtraction' there is also a place for 'reason,' and where these have no place, there 'reason' has nothing at all to do."[14] Similarly, Henry More uses addition and subtraction as the basic principle defining the faculties of the organic soul, since as "Aristotle has somewhere noted, the Essences of things are like Numbers, whose Species are changed by adding or taking away an Unite; adde therefore another Intrinsecall power to this of Vegetation, viz. Sensation, and it becomes the Soule of a Beast."[15] Like Hobbes, the addition and subtraction of the soul's faculties differentiate "vegetation" from "brutes" and humans, as if the hierarchy of living beings shaped by their soul's defining faculties was organized like a math problem. Even further, More suggests that math and geometry are immanent to the soul's reasoning power itself:

> The Ideas of Equall and Unequall, Double and Sub-double, Like and vnlike, with the rest, are no externall Impresses upon the Senses, but the Souls own active manner of conceiving those things which are discovered by the outward Senses . . . the Soul hath actuall knowledge in her self, in that sense which I have explained . . . the nature of the Soul is such, that shee will certainly and fully assent to some conclusions, how ever shee came to the knowledge of them, unlesse shee doe manifest violence to her own Faculties. Which truths must therefore be concluded not fortuitous or arbitrarious but Natural to the Soul: such as I have already named, as that every Finite number is either even or odde. If you adde equal to equal, the wholes are equal; and such as are not so simple as these, but yet stick close to the Soul once apprehended, as that The three angles in a Triangle are equal to the two right ones.[16]

To More, mathematical proofs themselves are immanent to the soul, and any lack of "assent" to the soul's own mathematical substance constitutes a form of "manifest violence to her own Faculties." Cudworth, Hobbes, and More all stressed the Aristotelian faculty psychology underlying the rationalist attempt to understand God, defining the faculty of reason as "naturally" mathematical. These rationalist appropriations of Aristotle's hierarchy of the soul's faculties as a way to define reason largely neglect language and rhetoric in favor of a quantitative model of the mind's ratiocinative power. For Hobbes and the Cambridge Platonists, the quantitative soul is fixed by "intrinsicall" forms and "essences" determined by mathematical law. By contrast, Milton, as a humanist and Protestant invested in the power of rhetoric and poetics, saw the centrality of the word/Word in making sense of the classical Aristotelian soul in a Christian context.[17]

Milton's innovation lies in his reconciliation of rationalist Aristotelianism with Christian doctrine by defining the reasoning soul through language and rhetoric. Milton, in contrast to his contemporaries, seeks to open up a capacity to reason in discourse and rhetoric that allows the soul unmoored from essences to change and to evolve to a more spiritual, purely intuitive state. It is the stress on the importance of language, to his mind, that enables the conversion of and translation between the two models of soul. In focusing on language as the bridge that allows him to move between the boundaries of the classical and Christian souls, Milton breaks from his humanist and Protestant peers: he claims that the rational faculty structured by language, and not simply the presence of a rational capability in general, marks the human as different from animals, plants, and angels in the Aristotelian chain of being.[18]

The plasticity of language unconstrained by mathematical law or the fixity of "intrinsicall" rational forms or "essences" gives Milton the power to imagine a spectrum or continuum of souls, where the use of "discursive reason," or reason in language, gives to humans a medium to refine the substance of their souls and convert it into the more spiritual, rarefied matter of angelic souls characterized by an intuitive form of reason. As we shall see, Raphael's "one first matter all" speech in book 5 of *Paradise Lost* offers one of the clearest articulations of discursive reason, but the logic of discursive reason defining the human soul recurs throughout Milton's work. So too, does the logic of the shift of the human soul to a more heavenly, angelic form, a transformation of reason as something structured by discourse and language into the immediate and intuitive intellection of angels. In this sense, Milton views the promise of salvation in terms of the classical organic soul's intrinsic plasticity and dynamic capacity to be converted into a better substance. Unlike Cudworth, who requires that the "humane faculties" of the soul be true and "essentially good" in order to stand in relation to God, Milton abolishes such a fixed criterion. For Milton, it is the classical organic soul's intrinsic instability and malleability, and not its stable essence or truth, that ultimately draws us closer to the state of angels.

Aristotelian Rationalism and *De Doctrina Christiana* on the Soul

De Doctrina Christiana, or *Christian Doctrine*, is a good place to begin to understand how Milton used the two-souls dilemma as a way to synthesize his rationalism with his theology. As Richard Strier has suggested, *De Doctrina Christiana* "helps us understand Renaissance theological rationalism" in general. Strier argues that the treatise should be classified with the "rationalist and Biblicist critics of Reformation theology."[19] At first glance, Milton's revision of the Aristotelian hierarchy of souls in terms of language might not be apparent, since his definition of the soul in *De Doctrina Christiana* seems to be a direct appropriation of Aristotle's terminology in *De Anima*. Milton assumes that the soul is composed of the Aristotelian fusion of form and matter: "It is acknowledged by the common consent of almost all philosophers, that every *form*, to which class the human soul must be considered as belonging, is produced by the power of matter."[20] For Milton, laying out the basic parameters of the soul in itself is not a controversial exercise. Philosophers agree that "form" defines the human soul, which is "produced by the power of matter." This general definition of the human soul corresponds directly to Aristotle's hylomorphism, a belief that form and matter conjoin to compose the soul. As Aristotle explains: "Now matter is potentiality, form actuality . . . the body cannot be soul; the body is the subject or matter, not what is attributed to it. Hence the soul must be a substance in the sense of the form of a natural body having life potentially in it."[21] Milton co-opts this understanding and interpretation of the soul when he offers an account of creation in *De Doctrina Christiana*. He describes the genesis of matter and form into the substance of the human soul in causal terms that rely on Aristotle's logic:

> Therefore the material cause must be either God, or nothing. Now nothing is no cause at all . . . But matter and form, considered as internal causes, constitute the thing itself; so that either all things must have had two causes only, and those external, or God will not have been the perfect and absolute cause of every thing. Secondly, it is an argument of supreme power and goodness, that such diversified, multiform, and inexhaustible virtue should exist and be substantially inherent in God (for that virtue cannot be accidental which admits of degrees, and of augmentation and remission, according to his pleasure) . . . For the original matter of which we speak, is not to be looked upon as an evil or trivial thing, but as an intrinsically good, and the chief productive stock of every subsequent good.[22]

The "material cause" is God, the "internal causes," or form and matter, "constitute the thing itself," and the created substance must be distinguished from accidental characteristics. This explanation of God's creation of form and matter as a mode of causation directly borrows from Aristotle's distinction between material and formal causes and between essential and accidental characteristics in the *Physics* (2.3.194b24ff.).[23] Milton's hylomorphic definition of the soul's substance as composed of both matter and form appropriates Aristotle's vocabulary and seems to be straightforwardly Aristotelian.

Yet Milton's vision of the soul becomes decidedly more complicated when he attempts to integrate the Christian concept of spirit into the amalgam of form and matter outlined above:

> For spirit being the more excellent substance, virtually and essentially contains within itself the inferior one; as the spiritual and rational faculty contains the corporeal, that is, the sentient and vegetative faculty. For not even divine virtue and efficiency could produce bodies out of nothing, according to the commonly received opinion, unless there had been some bodily power in the substance of God; since no one can give to another what he does not himself possess.[24]

Milton rejects the hierarchy of faculties traditionally used to describe the different powers of the soul, in favor of a model where all of the soul's faculties are subsumed within each another, like a Russian matryoshka doll. Christian spirit is the "more excellent substance," but one that is not removed from, or superior to, the organic substance of Aristotle's soul. Spirit "virtually and essentially contains within itself" the inferior substance of the organic soul defined by form and matter. The "spiritual and rational faculty contains" the lower powers of the "sentient and vegetative faculty" as part of its essence. Spirit is not divorced from form and matter, and the faculties defining the soul share this hybrid nature; the "spiritual and rational faculty" is enmeshed with the lower, organic sensory and vegetative faculties. The more refined substance of spirit and the "rational faculty" are not removed from the organic workings of the body, but indeed they circumscribe and "contain" the lesser faculties of sense and nutrition. The organic soul, defined in an Aristotelian vocabulary of form and matter, and the faculties of nutrition, sense, and reason, are not substantially distinct from the soul created in Genesis, nor do these two models of the soul need to be reconciled. For Milton, the organic soul is immanent to—it is contained within—Christian "spirit." They are from the moment of creation conjoined as extensions of a single form of Christian substance. This is surprising in contrast to the familiar logic of psychological stratification or the hierarchy of faculties described by Pomponazzi, Ficino, and Aquinas that we have seen before in chapter 1.

At other moments in *De Doctrina Christiana*, Milton is willing to extend his revision of the idea of Christian "spirit" by turning the problem of the two souls into the basis of his most direct positive definition of the soul: "Nor has the word *spirit* any other meaning in the sacred writings, but that breath of life which we inspire, or the vital, or sensitive, or rational faculty, or some action or affection belonging to those faculties."[25] Here Milton attempts to perform a synthesis of the classical pagan and Christian modes of psychology by implanting the classical faculties of the organic soul at the core of his clearest enunciation of spirit composing the soul. In effect, the organic powers of the "vital, sensitive, or rational faculty" compose the very substance of spirit marking humans as God's creation in Genesis. The Christian spirit that confers life on man at the moment of creation can *only* be understood in the fusion of God's divine inspiration animating the tripartite faculty psychology drawn from Aristotle's classical texts.

In the introduction, we have previously examined how Francis Bacon viewed the "two emanations of soul"—one "springing from the breath of God" and the other an animal soul composed of physical "elements." For Bacon, the two sources of the soul led to a fundamental "maze-like" confusion about how to accurately define the soul.[26] By contrast, these two origins of the soul—God's "breath of life" and the faculties of the organic soul—offer to Milton the clarity to perform the linguistic work of defining the word "spirit," which to his mind cannot have any other meaning than the mixture of Christian and classical substances of the soul. The result of this recasting of spirit involved in man's creation is a new understanding of the soul itself: "Man having been created after this manner, it is said, as a consequence, that *man became a living soul*; whence it may be inferred . . . that man is a living being, intrinsically and properly one and individual."[27] This passage is crucial to an understanding of Milton's treatment of the human soul because it links the logic of consequences with the power of inference in order to map out the chain reaction of spirit, to soul, to the living human. The assumption that consequences can be inferred by the human mind is a rationalist claim, since as Hobbes suggests in *Leviathan*, the very idea of "consequence" can be defined as the "train of thoughts" composing the reason.[28] The direct consequence of the cross-pollination between God's spirit and the organic faculties is a transformation from man as a creation of God—"man having been created after this manner"—to man as an autonomous living being—"man became a living soul." In the cause and effect structure of the sequence, the main consequence after being created as a blend of classical and Christian psychologies is the human living soul. The soul is therefore not simply generated by an act of divine inspiration, but rather requires a process of "becoming," where the Aristotelian "vital," "sensitive," and "rational faculties" play a central role in giving shape to the Christian spirit that transmutes matter into the living soul marking man as God's creation. In Milton's account of creation, God's spirit and the living soul it suffuses require the faculties of the Aristotelian soul to gain a sense of being.

The process of "becoming" a soul is decidedly linguistic in nature, with God creating the soul through a speech act: "The whole man, when finally created, is called in express terms *a living soul*. Hence the word used in Genesis to signify *soul*, is interpreted by the Apostle, 1 Cor.XV.45, 'animal.'"[29] Milton's exegesis here presents a hyper-linguistic shaping of the soul. God's creation is not so much an act as it is a naming or hailing in language. Man is finally created only when he is "*called* in express terms a living soul." The soul's coming into being is mediated by a moment of verbal articulation or calling.[30] Another passage in *De Doctrina Christiana* stresses the necessary performance of naming in the creation of the soul: "Man being formed after the image of God" is "given names to the whole animal creation."[31] This constitutive naming of the living soul stands as the culmination of Milton's rationalist reading of Genesis. The "soul must be *understood* as *signifying* either the spirit, or . . . the vital or sensitive faculty" (emphasis mine). To understand the soul requires us to grasp how it signifies as the faculties of the classical soul bound up in God's creative linguistic utterance. Milton's philological work here aims to decipher what specific words constitute the naming of the soul. He concludes that the "word used in Genesis" to perform the creation of the living soul is not "man," but "animal." This exegesis is important because for Milton, the soul does not compose man as man, but man as animal, binding the human soul into the hierarchy of the faculties of other animals and living beings outlined by Raphael above, and asserted by Aristotle in *De Anima* (413a23ff.). Milton's interpretation of the animal also gestures to the Latin root of *anima* or "soul": "For the word *soul* is also applied to every kind of living being; Gen. i. 30. 'to every beast of the earth,' &c 'wherein there is life' (*anima vivens*)."[32] Identifying animal as the word "signifying" and "calling" the human soul into being thus denotes at once *anima* as soul and "animal" as animated life in the chain of being, binding man into a psychological affiliation with "every beast of the earth" that also shares a living soul, much like Raphael communicates to Adam in book 5 of *Paradise Lost*.

We have previously considered Royal Society figures like Thomas Willis, and Cambridge Platonists like More and Cudworth, who followed their antecedents like Marsilio Ficino and Thomas Aquinas in attempting to dissociate the human faculty of reason from the nonhuman "soul of a brute."[33] Milton, by contrast, goes to great lengths to insist that the human soul is intimately related to the souls of lower beings. He sees "no reason, why the soul of man should be made an exception to the general law of creation . . . God breathed the breath of life into other living beings, and blended it so intimately with matter, that the propagation and production of the human were analogous to those of other forms . . . for the word soul is also applied to every kind of living being."[34] The linguistic act of naming the living soul as the word signifying "animal" applies to all beings, and the "soul of man" does not serve as an exception, but is indeed analogous to the form and matter of all types of life. As we have already seen, the two-souls dilemma in the sixteenth and seventeenth centuries provoked anxiety in a diverse range of thinkers and writers precisely because the mingling of Christian and classical psychologies brought the human soul into an uncomfortable contact with the "soule of brutes." Milton's exegesis in *De Doctrina Christiana* specifically identifies the word "animal" as the word signifying God's creation as a living soul and purposefully plays with the term's two valences as *anima*/animal—our animation with a soul constitutes us in an "intimate" and "analogous" relationship with "beasts."

By selecting the term "animal" as the word enunciated by God in his generative act of naming, Milton abolishes the difference between the two souls by, in effect, rewriting the creation of man in Genesis. The inspiration of the soul does not mark man as God's favored creation, set apart from animals and plants in the chain of being. The human soul signified as "animal" and Milton's intricate logic of *anima*/animation/animal binds humans into a constitutive relationship with the "soule of brutes," which was created by God in the same act of naming. By turning God's creation into a linguistic act centered on the word "animal," Milton can play with the sliding register of signification between *anima* (soul), animation (ensoulment), and animal (the soul of beasts). The blurred linguistic boundaries within the very concept of the "animal" allow Milton to dissolve the difference between the two souls at the very moment of the soul's creation in Genesis. There is no paradox or contradiction between the two souls, because the soul of man was created by the same act of naming as the "soul of brutes," and they share the same substance, matter, and analogous forms. The two souls, in Milton's reading of Genesis, have become one.

These passages from *De Doctrina Christiana* have been cited as a confirmation of Milton's monist materialism, or a belief that man is defined by a single substance of a material nature rather than by a dualism of body and soul. The "living being" of the human is certainly monist here, but it is not specifically materialist in flavor. Rather, the account of the living soul's creation here suggests a psychological monism:

> Man is a living being . . . not, according to the common opinion, made up and framed of two distinct and different natures, as of soul and body—but that the whole man is soul, and the soul man, that is to say, a body, or substance individual, animated, sensitive, and rational; and that the breath of life was neither a part of the divine essence, nor the soul itself, but as it were an inspiration of some divine virtue fitted for the exercise of life and reason, and infused into the organic body.[35]

De Doctrina Christiana therefore does not present a dualism of body and soul. In Milton's chiasmic formulation of "the whole man is soul, and the soul man," the soul in question is characterized by an Aristotelian faculty psychology—a "substance individual, animated, sensitive, and rational." The monism of his treatise involves a psychological monism of the soul's three faculties, which exclusively compose the substance of God's creation. This model of faculty psychology also defines the divine spirit animating the soul. The breath of life is not an incorporeal "divine essence," but is "infused into the organic body." God's generative breath of life initiates an embodied process, triggering the infusion of "divine virtue" and "spirit" into the "organic" faculties. Or, as Milton interprets Job 32:8, it was not sufficient for God to "merely breathe that spirit into man," but indeed the infusion requires a work upon the faculties, with God "moulding" spirit in "each individual, and infusing it throughout, enduing and embellishing it with its proper faculties."[36]

In essence, the creation of the soul in Genesis, as Milton interprets it in *De Doctrina Christiana*, defines the very infusion of the organic soul's faculties. God's creation performs the molding and "enduing" of the organic soul that comes together to give coherence to the "whole man." Milton dismisses the possibility that the soul could be derived from any other type of immaterial or incorporeal "divine essence" apart from this infusing of the organic soul. Milton's text effectively suggests that no intractable difference or paradox exists between the two souls that compose man because the Christian soul inspired by God's spirit in Genesis is, in its entirety, defined by the "infusion" and molding of the organic faculties making up, quite surprisingly, an Aristotelian faculty psychology.[37] The Christian soul *is* the classical organic soul.

Milton's "Discursive" Reason

For Milton, the unexpected equivalence between the Christian soul created by God and the organic faculties of the classical soul as its substance, is just the beginning of the story of how he comes to understand the soul. *Paradise Lost* develops a more expansive view of the fusion of the two souls by specifying the role of language in this psychological process. In book 5, the angel Raphael tells Adam of the chain of being that links man to angels and to God:

> O Adam, one Almightie is, from whom
> All things proceed, and up to him return,
> If not deprav'd from good, created all
> Such to perfection, one first matter all,
> Indu'd with various forms, various degrees
> Of substance, and in things that live, of life;
> But more refin'd, more spiritous, and pure,
> As neerer to him plac't or neerer tending
> Each in thir several active Spheare assignd,
> Till body up to spirit work, in bounds
> Proportiond to each kind. So from the root
> Springs lighter the green stalk, from thence the leaves
> More aerie, last the bright consummate floure
> Spirits odorous breathes: flours and thir fruit
> Mans nourishment, by gradual scale sublim'd
> To vital Spirits aspire, to animal,
> To intellectual, give both life and sense,
> Fansie and understanding, whence the Soule
> Reason receives, and reason is her being,
> Discursive, or Intuitive; discourse
> Is oftest yours, the latter most is ours,
> Differing but in degree, of kind the same.
> Wonder not then, what God for you saw good
> If I refuse not, but convert, as you,
> To proper substance; time may come when men
> With Angels may participate, and find
> No inconvenient Diet, nor too light Fare:
> And from these corporal nutriments perhaps
> Your bodies may at last turn all to Spirit,
> Improv'd by tract of time, and wingd ascend

Ethereal, as wee, or may at choice
Here or in Heav'nly Paradises dwell;
If ye be found obedient, and retain
Unalterably firm his love entire
Whose progenie you are. Mean while enjoy
Your fill what happiness this happie state
Can comprehend, incapable of more. (*Paradise Lost* 5.468–505)

Much like the previously considered passages from Milton's prose, Raphael's extended meditation on the chain of being hinges on the nature of the creation. The living universe "proceeds" from and "returns" to the Almighty, who created all. The account of creation here also shares the same vocabulary as *De Doctrina Christiana*: "One first matter all, / Indu'd with various forms, various degrees / Of substance." Precisely as in Milton's interpretation of Genesis in *De Doctrina Christiana*, here Raphael integrates *De Anima*'s language of "matter," "form," and "substance" in framing God's creation of life. He also employs the same verb as in the prose text—"indu'd"—as the primary action that God performs in molding matter, form, and substance into the living soul. This "indu'd" fusion of form and matter results in the tripartite faculties of the Aristotelian model of the soul: "vital" or vegetative faculties that confer life, "sense" faculties that define the "animal," and "fansie and understanding" that mark humans as "intellectual" or rational beings.[38]

Raphael adds a wrinkle to this conventional faculty psychology in his articulation of the "gradual scale sublim'd." By suggesting that movement or progress along the scale entails an active form of "work," the speech's logic introduces the possibility that the soul's faculties framing one's position or sphere on the continuum of life are not fixed substances, but rather they possess a malleable quality—they can be "refin'd" and "sublim'd," much like the chemical conversion of solids, to liquids, to gases. Indeed, Milton's primary usage of the term "sublime" in *Paradise Lost* is not in the aesthetic sense of the term later deployed by Addison or Burke (in reference to Milton), but rather the chemical one, the abrupt phase transition of a substance converting physical states from a solid to a gas. The slippery distinction between the "sublime" as a chemical process and as an aesthetic category was exploited for rhetorical effect most frequently in the seventeenth century within the domain of natural philosophy, and specifically, within the writings of the early Royal Society.[39] Raphael in his speech engages with the sublime's dual valences by using the term to describe in productive—and for Adam's benefit, pedagogically illuminating—terms, the patient "work" that the human soul must undertake in order to be refined into higher forms, but in far less hyperbolic terms: "vital spirits aspire, to animal, to intellectual."

But to what do human souls in Paradise, which is ostensibly at the apex of this scale of souls, aspire? Raphael's rationalist presentation of the human soul defines "reason" as "her being," much as we saw previously in *De Doctrina Christiana*. Here, however, Raphael expands upon our previous reading of Milton's rationalist faculty psychology by proposing that humans aspire to reach the state of angels, and this can only occur through the refinement of reason. If reason functions as the sole means of attaining the more spiritual state of angels in this rational psychology, it also serves as the bridge that links us to them. Both humans and angels possess reason, "differing but in degree, of kind the same." Human reason is "discursive," whereas angelic reason is more "intuitive." The work of human reason allows us to progress up the "gradual scale sublim'd" to a more angelic soul by "converting" the substance of reason to proper substance, from a reason structured by discourse, to one that intuits.

Monist readings of this passage have largely underemphasized the key place of *language* in shaping this rationalist account of the soul's malleability.[40] In Raphael's rationalist lesson on the soul to Adam, the refinement of human reason to attain a place among the angels *requires* the work of reason in discourse. If man is to be virtuous and faithful to God's word, this must occur through the discursive operations of the rational faculty. The choice of the word "discursive" to characterize human reason's mediation in language is apt, since, as the *Oxford English Dictionary* defines "discourse," the term gestures in the seventeenth century both to reasoning in an abstract sense and to the linguistic dimension of thought: it signifies at once the "process or faculty of reasoning" and the "process of communicating thought by means of words."[41] The linguistic axis of the definition is etymologically influenced by the Middle French *discors*, seen today in the contemporary *discours*, which describes a "treatment of a subject, either written or oral," or even conversation. By contrast, the older etymological root of the classical Latin *discursus* evinces a much more process-oriented definition of the terms, signifying the "action of running off in different directions . . . bustling activity." If the French root is firmly linguistic, the Latin etymology suggests rational work and the processes of the active mind.

Raphael's attribution of "discursive" reason as the faculty of the soul that sets humans apart from plants and other animals, and that also marks the difference between humans and the "intuitive" reason of angels, is important since it sets the stage for much of the content of *Paradise Lost*'s plot. Raphael's extended pedagogy to Adam from books 5 through 8 unfolds in such a protracted and meticulous fashion precisely because he must bridge the gap between angelic intuition and Adam's discursive comprehension. The angel's model of linguistic accommodation struggles to "relate / To human sense th'invisible exploits" of heaven, and he attempts to "delineate" that which "surmounts the reach / Of human sense . . . By lik'ning spiritual to corporal forms" (*Paradise Lost* 5.564–72). The work of teaching across the different planes of the soul, from "spiritual to corporal *forms*," represents a work of linguistic translation. Raphael's accommodation attempts to "relate" through narrative means and to "express" in human language the existence of spiritual forms functioning beyond human discursive reason in the chain of being. Because Adam cannot learn by immediate intuition, Raphael must express in language and story his teachings to his human pupil. It is precisely the organic soul's malleable capacity to be "converted" that enables humans to strive for the purer spiritual state of angels through the continual work of reason. For Raphael, the possibility of sublime transcendence beyond one's position or sphere in the chain of being is mediated by discourse.[42] The result is, of course, the extended discourse of books 5 through 8, which composes 2,750 lines, or 26 percent of the poem—indeed, a considerable amount of discourse dedicated to pedagogy moving Adam to a place of understanding.

Of course, however, it is not exclusively language and discourse that define the human soul in *Paradise Lost*. The main condition that Raphael places on the possibility of converting discursive reason to intuition is not linguistic, but temporal: the malleability of the soul's faculties depends on a "tract of time." As Raphael explains to Adam, the "time may come when men / With Angels may participate" by "converting . . . to proper substance." But the human soul defined by discursive reason can only be "improv'd by tract of time" so as to "ascend ethereal" (5.498–99). In Raphael's temporality of psychological refinement, *time* dictates how discourse can be "converted" into intuition in defining the transformation of the soul to the state of angels. The scope of what human reason can comprehend constitutes a period of patience—a "mean while"—during which obedience and rational work can slowly move humans up the "scale" of souls.[43]

The temporality of discursive reason also informs the poem's recounting of creation. Book 7 of the poem complicates Milton's previous exegesis of the creation narrative in *De Doctrina Christiana* by stressing the multiple temporalities involved in understanding the generative act:

> So spake th' Almightie, and to what he spake
> His Word, the Filial Godhead, gave effect.
> Immediate are the Acts of God, more swift
> Then time or motion, but to human ears
> Cannot without process of speech be told,
> So told as earthly notion can receave. (7.174–79)

In this speech act, God's word "gave effect" with instantaneous consequences—"immediate are the Acts of God, more swift / Then time or motion." The performance of God's word is immediate and its temporality is so swift that it paradoxically exceeds time itself. Humans, by contrast, cannot conceive of this swiftness beyond time, since we require a "process of speech" to be told of what creation entails. Our reason can only grasp notions by being told what they signify in language. In this uneven temporality of language, God's "Word" is immediate and more swift than any unit measuring time, while the human mind needs words—a slow "process of speech"—in order to understand earthly notions. According to *Paradise Lost*'s account of God's speech act, the difference between heavenly language and human "speech" is the time required for the Word/word to take effect. This occurs immediately for God, but it takes a slow "process" for human reason to comprehend what God has accomplished.

"Paradise Within"

The presence of "discourse" as the defining characteristic marking the human soul's rational faculty also drives the main drama of the poem in book 9, with Satan's temptation of Eve. Eve finds the serpent's account of eating the apple from the tree of knowledge plausible in the first place because the serpent has gained language and the rational capability that comes with it, which moves it closer to the state of humans:

> Though at the voice much marveling; at length
> Not unamaz'd she thus in answer spake.
> What may this mean? Language of Man pronounc't
> By Tongue of Brute, and human sense exprest?
> The first at lest of these I thought deni'd
> To Beasts, whom God on thir Creation-Day
> Created mute to all articulat sound;
> The latter I demurre, for in thir looks
> Much reason, and in thir actions oft appeers.
> Thee, Serpent, suttlest beast of all the field
> I knew, but not with human voice endu'd;
> Redouble then this miracle, and say,
> How cam'st thou speakable of mute (9.551–63)

Eve "marvels" and is "not unamaz'd" at the "language of Man pronounc't / By Tongue of Brute" and the serpent's consequent ability to exhibit the reasoning capacity of "human sense exprest." Indeed, Eve's doubts begin by questioning God's creative link between language and reason. Although beasts were "created mute to all articulat sound," Eve starts to believe that the serpent's human voice expresses "much reason," blurring the boundaries between the different types of soul in the hierarchy of being described by Raphael. If, in the case of Raphael's pedagogy, the need for an extended narrative explanation marks the gap between Adam's discursive reason and angelic intuition, in the case of Eve's temptation, language as the substance of reason signifies an unsanctioned leap from the beast to the human voice, and this leads her to begin to question Raphael's account of the hierarchy of living beings structured by the faculties of the soul, and correspondingly, her place in it.

Both cases hinge on the assumption that the linguistic basis of human reason as "discursive" measures the difference between the animal soul (in the case of the serpent), the human soul, and the angel (in the case of Raphael), on the "gradual scale sublim'd." But reading the two episodes together shows in stark relief that the discursive understanding of the soul can be used badly or well. In each encounter, for better or worse, "discourse" and the "language of Man pronounc't" mediate the human soul's relationship to animals and angels. This linguistic assumption also leads Adam and Eve to test the boundaries of their rational capabilities and their place in God's hierarchy of living souls, in conversation with the angels (leading Raphael to admonish Adam to "be lowly wise" [8.173]), and in confrontation with the serpent.

Book 9's depiction of the fall does not only hinge on the logic of the "Beast" rising to the state of reason by gaining a human voice, thereby tempting Eve with the possibility that humans might analogously rise to a more heavenly state by eating from the tree of knowledge. Temporality and the necessity of time form a central problem that precipitates the fall, in contrast with Raphael's continuum of souls distributed along the "gradual scale" mediated by the "tract of time." Eve does not follow the rules of the "tract of time" required for souls to be refined. In her decision-making process before eating the apple, she lingers on the uncanny language acquisition of the brute, inarticulate serpent as clear evidence of his leap up the hierarchy of souls to the rational state of humans: "hee hath eat'n and lives, / And knows, and speaks, and reasons . . . Irrational till then" (9.764–66). The ability to speak gives to the previously irrational animal the power to "reason" and to "know." What leads to the fall, then, is a desire to replicate the serpent's quick rise from mute irrationality to reason by language, or as Satan frames the "proportion meet" as a series of dissonant hybrids—"I of brute human, ye of human Gods." Eve's final words before plucking the apple reflect this over-hasty will to rise beyond the bounds of human reason to the state of gods, in what amounts to an impulse to "feed *at once* both Bodie and Mind" (9.779). "At once" suggests an immediacy of refining "bodie and mind" that Raphael already described as impossible for humans. In essence, the fall is motivated by an attempt to perform Raphael's refinement and conversion of the soul's faculties—an enrichment of "bodie and mind" to the station of angels—without respecting the key proviso that the malleability be regulated by the steady metronome of the "tract of time," which requires the patient work of reason. The time markers of the moment of the fall—"her *rash* hand in evil *hour*" (9.780)—all suggest a hastiness of thought and action that goes against Raphael's insistence on the "tract of time" and the slow "process of speech" necessary for human reason to unfold. Importantly, Milton's major revision to the story of the fall from Genesis 3 is his incorporation of Eve's meditative puzzling over the serpent's linguistic capability that signals his so-called rise up the chain of souls—the subject matter of Raphael's teachings to Adam in book 5—and also the impatient rashness of Eve's act.

> But of the fruit of the tree which is in the midst of the garden, God hath said, Ye shall not eat of it, neither shall ye touch it, lest ye die.
>
> And the serpent said unto the woman, Ye shall not surely die:
>
> For God doth know that in the day ye eat thereof, then your eyes shall be opened, and ye shall be as gods, knowing good and evil.
>
> And when the woman saw that the tree was good for food, and that it was pleasant to the eyes, and a tree to be desired to make one wise, she took of the fruit thereof, and did eat, and gave also unto her husband with her; and he did eat.[44]

Milton's staging of the fall certainly emphasizes the transgression of God's command, but it also integrates the serpent's acquisition of language as the uncanny rationale for his temptation, along with the description of the over-hasty temporality marking Eve's act.

In a jarring shift from the rapidity of the fall, *Paradise Lost* ends by reasserting the slow temporality or "process" of speech. The angel Michael recounts for Adam the future history of mankind in a long and laborious narrative session that does indeed consume almost the entirety of the final two books. Notably, Michael uses the same verb as Raphael—to "relate"—as his means of telling this protracted story (12.11). In both cases, Adam cannot instantaneously *see* what he needs to grasp intellectually because the ideas and events the angelic messengers perceive are "invisible" to the human senses. As a result, both angels must "relate" extended narratives to teach Adam by engaging the "discursive" and linguistic medium of his reasoning capability. The difference in rational faculties, between angelic "intuition" and human "discourse," is persistently on display in these scenes of instruction, and it requires both teachers to translate one mode of understanding into the other. One result of the fall is the reassertion of human reason as a mode of slow discourse. Michael's narrativization of humanity's future in book 12 addresses Adam not as a seer of a prophetic vision, since "objects divine / must needs impaire and wearie human sense" (12.9–10), but rather as the participant in a verbal discourse "related" to him by the angels, with Adam "giving due audience" and "attending" (12.11–12). Michael's imperative "to attend" as an "audience" for the telling of his story signifies presence and attention, but also patience and waiting, as in the French verb *attendre*.[45] Michael's discourse of future time requires patient "audience" members, who must grasp his message slowly, by "attending." The slow unfolding of Michael's narrative certainly justifies his admonishment to "attend," since it requires two entire books and 1,550 lines of the poem to recount.

Indeed, the final moments of the epic poem insist upon lingering on the slow "tract of time" shaping human reason, particularly in the postlapsarian world. Adam and Eve face their fallen future with "wandring steps and slow" (12.648), as if to inaugurate the epoch of fallen time with "slow" and faltering progress into an uncertain period to come. Part of the tentative "wandring" slowness of the final lines derives from an overwhelming presentation of choice to them—"the World was all before them, / where to *choose* their place of rest" (12.646–47). Their destination, however, is a place of rest, anticipating pause and the cessation of motion, rather than further progress or advancement. In a peculiar form of halting, stuttering agency, Adam and Eve are given the power to "choose" so as to eventually stop. Richard Strier has claimed that Milton conceives of "freedom as entirely a matter of deliberation and choice."[46] The opening of a future shaped by choice and not a single constitutive prohibition or indeed its transgression as represented within the text of *Paradise Lost*, gives to Adam and Eve a path forward defined by rationalist "deliberation." But Adam and Eve's future of rational choice is one of a difficult freedom involving "deliberation," and one that reasserts the primacy of a "slow" temporality to their operations of reason that they struggled to accept in Paradise.

A new model of the soul guides their choices and the operations of their reason after the fall. The ultimate goal of Michael's extended lesson tracing a human history to come is the declaration to Adam that they have lost Paradise, but have gained "paradise within thee, happier far" (12.587), consisting of faith, virtue, patience, temperance, love, and charity, which the angel calls "the soul" that will come to define human life after the fall. The point of Michael's teaching is that with Paradise lost, Adam and Eve are now defined by a "soul" shaped by attributes that lie at the core of the Christian faith. Drawing attention to the "paradise within" the soul echoes the logic of the soul's interiority in *De Doctrina Christiana*, in which God "infused" his spirit into man during the creation. "Infusion" certainly describes an implantation of the spirit into the core of the soul, but the word also describes a peculiar process of steeping or rendering a substance soluble in a liquid medium, much like tea leaves infuse water in a slow process from which the substance cannot be distilled or extracted. *De Doctrina Christiana* delineated in great detail the process by which God integrated the spirit into the very fabric of the soul's faculties to such an extent that spirit itself became "infused" within the organic faculties. By the end of *Paradise Lost*, Adam and Eve emerge from the slow process of animating and infusing their souls over the course of the poem. Where Raphael in book 5 explicates a classical understanding of the soul situated on the "gradual scale sublim'd" that echoes Aristotle's chain of being, Michael's parting message to Adam and Eve instead speaks to a soul infused by faith, love, and charity, which more closely matches the tenets of Scripture and Christian doctrine. The fall in book 9 and the conclusion of *Paradise Lost* in book 12 are therefore informed by Raphael's earlier speech on the importance of slow psychological refinement, but with the important addition of the "paradise within" reflecting the teachings of the New Testament, which now defines their souls. Raphael's account of Aristotelian faculty psychology as the basis of the human soul's "gradual scale sublim'd" comes together with the "paradise within" evinced by Michael to define Adam and Eve's peculiar agency after the fall. Their ability to choose begins with slow steps into the "tract of time" patiently returning the human soul to its promised station closer to angels and to God.

By the final lines of *Paradise Lost*, we have reached a vantage point to fully grasp the understanding of the soul that Milton developed through a meticulous exegesis of scriptural texts in *De Doctrina Christiana*, and which he embodies and to which he gives life as Adam and Eve in his epic poem. *Paradise Lost* performs the psychology sketched in *De Doctrina Christiana* by representing the creation of the human soul in Genesis as less of a single act by which God breathed "spirit into man" and more prominently as a steady labor of "moulding it in each individual, and infusing it throughout, enduing and embellishing it with its proper faculties."[47] God's creation of the soul consists of a patient work described in *De Doctrina Christiana* and staged in detail through the course of *Paradise Lost*. The poem culminates in the implantation of the "paradise within happier far," by which the form and matter of Adam and Eve's souls have been molded and infused in a way that makes them recognizably human, but distinctly fallen.

Milton's synthesis of the classical organic soul with the scriptural architecture of the soul's creation and fall in Genesis stands as the most ambitious and indeed audacious fusion of pagan and Christian psychologies in the early modern world. In reaffirming the tenets of Christian doctrine in this unorthodox manner, Milton acknowledges that his theological position serves as a "confirmation of . . . Aristotle's argument" that "every *form* to which the human soul must be considered as belonging, is produced by the power of matter."[48] In Milton's clever reversal, the language of Genesis resoundingly confirms Aristotle's logic from *De Anima* in a mutually reinforcing way, and does not imply a contradiction or conflict between incompatible models of soul. This positive relationship between Aristotle and scriptural authority represents Milton's unique basis of Christian thought. More specifically, Milton's linkage of classical and Christian modes of psychology constitutes the poorly recognized crux of his rationalism. The fate of the soul assumes a central place in both *De Doctrina Christiana* and *Paradise Lost* because Milton states that the "original subject of sin" in Eden is "namely, the rational soul."[49] The faculty of reason is for Milton not just the locus of original sin, but also that which holds the promise of improving and perfecting man's station in the chain of being. Milton's identification of the fall and original sin, but also the possibility of redemption, with the faculty of discursive reasoning reveals the complexity of his rationalism in stark relief as it joins together Aristotelian and Christian lines of thought.

And so at the end of *Paradise Lost*, Milton leaves us at the beginning of a fallen time in which the rational faculty pulls us two ways: it defines man's "original subject of sin" upon the expulsion from Paradise, but it holds the distinctly human potential to engage in the medium of "discourse" as a way to reclaim the promise of salvation that will one day draw us closer to God.

Milton implants this tension immanent to the soul into the story of Genesis itself at the origin of biblical time. In this way, he imagines the contact of the two souls as the space of the "gradual scale sublim'd" along which humans strive in a state of potentiality to gain the "choice" to "here or in Heav'nly Paradises dwell" (5.499–500) at the end of time.

Coda

✦

"Incompletely Human" before Descartes

Donne and Milton are fitting capstones to the literary history of the two-souls dilemma I have traced, because they transformed the crisis-provoking theological problem of the Reformation into a positive redefinition of the Christian subject that rejected the dogma of the soul espoused by Protestant doctrine. Both poets use the presence of two souls in one body as a way to rewrite the origin and ending of the Christian doctrine of life, by discovering in the remnants of the classical organic soul a way to reimagine the foundational tenets of the creation and the fall in Genesis, in Milton's case, and our death and the promise of salvation and reunion with God, in the case of Donne.

These ambitious literary efforts to remake the soul come to an abrupt end, at least according to the standard story, with the philosophical paradigm shift precipitated by René Descartes. In his 1637 *Discourse on the Method*, Descartes initiates a dualist philosophy that decisively splits the body and mind (or more precisely, what he calls "l'âme" or soul in the text) by first acknowledging, as his debt to the Aristotelian tradition of the classical organic soul, the margin of difference between "reason and sense, inasmuch as it is the only thing that constitutes us men and distinguishes us from brutes."[1] This debt is quickly obliterated, however, as Descartes subsequently undertakes a method of radical skepticism that leads him to imagine himself created as a body composed of pure matter, without any of the soul's faculties.

> From a description of inanimate bodies and plants I passed on to that of animals, and particularly to that of men . . . I contented myself with supposing that God formed the body of man altogether like one of ours, in the outward figure of its members as well as in the interior conformation of its organs, without making use of any matter other than that which I had described, and without at first placing in it a rational soul, or any other thing which might serve as a vegetative or as a sensitive soul.[2]

According to this line of reasoning, even if Descartes did not possess rational, vegetative, or sensitive faculties, the very fact that he can think about not having a soul demonstrates the existence of the soul independent of the body:

> From that I knew that I was a substance the whole essence or nature of which is to think, and that for its existence there is no need of any place, nor does it depend on any material thing; so that this "me," that is to say, the soul by which I am what I am, is entirely distinct from body . . . and even if the body were not, the soul would not cease to be what it is.[3]

In Descartes's proof of dualism, his "whole essence or nature . . . is to think," and this power of thought does not depend in any way "on any material thing." In cleaving the body from the soul, Descartes ultimately defines that soul as the recursive definition of the "I": "the soul by which I am what I am" ("l'âme, par laquelle je suis ce que je suis").

As Garrett Sullivan has suggested, Descartes's use of classical faculty psychology in his skepticist thought experiment as a lever to pry the mind apart from the body in the articulation of his dualism is almost a more historically profound rupture than the declaration of "*I think, therefore I am*": "Descartes transforms the way in which plant, animal and human life were conceptualized—a transformation arguably more profound than the better-known subjective revolution initiated by the Cartesian *cogito*. Descartes rethinks vitality in a way that drains Aristotelian life from it."[4] Laurie Shannon makes a similar point by describing Descartes's move in terms of the solipsistic claustrophobia—characterized by the peculiar circularity of "I am what I am"—that comes to define Descartes's idea of the human. "Animal soul/mind is at stake in this trial, but no form of testimony exists by which it might be affirmed . . . Cartesian method, then, makes no offer of a method concerning other minds" beyond the "closed sphere of a self testifying only to itself idiolectically."[5] Taking a cue from Sullivan and Shannon, *The Two-Soul'd Animal* has attempted to recuperate, and indeed linger, in early modern literary conceptions of the subject that are not recursively knotted in Cartesian "I am that I am" statements. The authors that we have read embraced and accounted for a composite model of the soul that embeds psychological difference and a diversity of faculties at the core of the human. Problematically, however, these early modern positions that adopt a psychological "vantage that is incompletely human" have been abandoned in modernity as "a practice that Cartesianism would successfully shame as heretical."[6]

But perhaps the door that Descartes closed on these "incompletely human" inflections of the soul was not as decisively sealed as we have assumed. Thomas Willis's *De Anima Brutorum* (*The Soul of Brutes*), which we considered in the introduction, was first published in English in 1683, over forty years after the declaration of the Cartesian cogito. Willis considers, and anguishes over, the "two souls in man" in great depth, but does so in a markedly different context from the discourses of the soul we have considered in the early modern period. The subtitle of Willis's treatise delineates his purpose as "Pathological, which unfolds the diseases which Affect it and its Primary Seat; to wit, The *Brain* And *Nervous Stock*, And Treats Of Their Cures." The puzzle of "two souls in man" lived on well past Descartes and his flattening of the soul, but in the domain of medical pathology and not in the positive definition of the human's spirituality and psychology. Indeed, Willis's logic admits that the paradox of two souls in one body is an anxiety-provoking problem writ large, but these puzzlements notwithstanding, his taxonomy of the animal faculties of the soul provides him with a novel methodology in "our Pathology or Method or Curing." And so the bulk of his treatise shifts from *defining* the function of the two souls in humans and animals, to *curing* nervous diseases: headaches, lethargy, insomnia, nightmares, and vertigo. Willis does recognize the theological and ontological problems entangling the two souls, but he abandons the hope of reconciling classical and Christian psychologies. He prefers instead to find an incomplete resolution to the problem in the practical domain of "Medical Science": "Altho it is neither our Hope or Ambition that these should be pleasing to all; yet (what is my last wish) I doubt not, but that this may be an help to many for the illustrating the Medical Science, and for the more happy Curing of Cephalick Diseases." And so from Donne and Milton's ambitious efforts to salvage a positive, generative definition of the creation, the fall, our death, and our salvation through the labyrinth of the two-souls problem, we come to Willis's rather modest goals. He limits his scope and has no such pretensions of elucidating a comprehensive solution that could define the human. For him, the negative definition of the animal soul as the basis of understanding pathology and diseases is a sufficient end in itself.

The historical shift from the early modern aspiration to carve out a positive definition of the human based upon the two-souls problem that had been inherited from the classical and Christian traditions, to the appropriation of classical faculty psychology as a diagnostic index for treating "Cephalick Diseases," represents the intellectual context that we inherit today. The twentieth-century philosopher Ian Hacking's work on "Two Souls in One Body" illustrates this shift to our contemporary intellectual context. Hacking focuses his attention on the case of Bernice R., a "retarded child" who "suffered from multiple personality disorder" that dissociated her "core personality."[7] Her story prompts Hacking to meditate upon the soul as the basis of the self in a modern context. But his methods differ little from Willis's, evinced by his emphasis on "clinical reports," "medical" questions, and the "diagnostic" parameters of defining her selfhood.[8] Such a diagnostic definition of the human in its pathological fragmentation can only repeat what Shannon has vividly described as the Cartesian "closed sphere of a self testifying only to itself idiolectically."

By contrast, the counter-narrative I have recounted seeks value in the historical and literary efforts of authors who embraced, however tentatively, a definition of the soul as the basis of human "self-identification" (to borrow Hacking's phrase) in a way that could account for "incompletely human" models of the subject. In the historical story that has largely come to be accepted, Descartes closed the possibility of these imaginings as either flights of literary fancy, or as something "heretical for modernity." The remainder of "two souls in one body" persists today as the assumption that diagnosis of the corrosive power of diseases, rather than the vitality of the self, defines the sciences of life. To this extent, the generative models of the soul we have examined, and the patient refinement of the soul along the "tract of time" to which Milton aspires at the end of his epic poem and the early modern period, shall remain unfinished.

NOTES

Introduction

EPIGRAPHS: Walter Benjamin, "Critique of Violence," in *Selected Writings, Volume 1, 1913–1926*, ed. Marcus Bullock and Michael Jennings (Cambridge, Mass.: Belknap/Harvard University Press, 2004), 251; Giorgio Agamben, *The Open: Man and Animal*, trans. Kevin Attell (Stanford, Calif.: Stanford University Press, 2004), 16.

1. Setti Rengachary, Andrew Xavier, Sunil Manjila, Usha Smerdon, Brandon Parker, Suzan Hadwan, and Murali Guthikonda, "The Legendary Contributions of Thomas Willis: The Arterial Circle and Beyond," *Journal of Neurosurgery* 109, no. 4 (October 2008): 765–75; Zoltan Molnar, "Thomas Willis, the Founder of Clinical Neuroscience," *Nature Reviews Neuroscience* 5 (April 2004): 329–35.

2. Thomas Willis, *Two Discourses concerning the Soul of Brutes* (London: Thomas Dring, 1683), 4.

3. Guido Giglioni, introduction to *Renaissance Averroism and Its Aftermath*, ed. Ana Akasoy and Guido Giglioni (Dordrecht: Springer, 2013), 17.

4. The problem of "two souls in one body" has previously been associated with Saint Augustine's critique of the Manichean position that the human is composed of a good soul created by God and an evil soul created by the "people of darkness" (*gente tenebrarum*). For this, see R. Ferwerda, "Two Souls: Origen's and Augustine's Attitude to the Two Souls Doctrine," *Vigiliae Christianae* 37 (1983): 360–78.

5. Aristotle, *On the Soul*, in Aristotle, *On the Soul, Parva Naturalia, On Breath*, trans. W. S. Hett (Cambridge: Loeb Classical Library, 1936), 402a6–8.

6. Aristotle, *On the Soul*, 412a27–413b14.

7. Aristotle, *On the Soul*, 412a5–412a20.

8. As the Vatican affirmed in 1993 in its doctrinal definition, the "'soul' signifies the spiritual principle in man." *Catechism of the Catholic Church* (Vatican City: Libreria Editrice Vaticana, 1993), para. 363.

9. Martin Luther, "Disputation of Doctor Martin Luther on the Power and Efficacy of Indulgences," in *Works of Martin Luther*, ed. Adolph Spaeth, L. D. Reed, and Henry Eyster Jacobs (Philadelphia: A. J. Holman, 1915), Thesis 4. See also Martin Luther, "The Bondage of the Will," in *Erasmus and Luther: Discourse on Free Will*, ed. Ernst Winter (New York: Continuum, 2005).

10. Robert Mason, *Reasons Academie* (London: Thomas Creede, for John Browne, 1605), 28–29. The poem was originally attributed to Sir John Davies.

11. Robert Burton, *The Anatomy of Melancholy* (New York: New York Review of Books, 2001), 154–55.

12. Elizabeth Harvey has phrased the issue to frame the related problem of the Pythagorean soul and transmigration in terms of similar questions: "Was the

rational soul unique to human beings? Did the vegetative and sensitive soul join human beings to plant and animal life in ways that changed their connection to the environment?" For this, see Elizabeth D. Harvey, "The Souls of Animals: John Donne's *Metempsychosis* and Early Modern Natural History," in *Environment and Embodiment in Early Modern England*, ed. Mary Floyd-Wilson and Garrett Sullivan (London: Palgrave Macmillan, 2007), 55.

13. Throughout the English Renaissance, the parts of the classical soul were called "faculties," "souls," or "powers," depending on the author. For uniformity of style, I will use the term "faculties," while specifying when the author cites Aristotle's *De Anima* specifically (i.e., the Aristotelian soul) or the "classical" idea of the organic soul more generally. Throughout this book, I will use Katharine Park's definition of the "organic" soul, locating the principle of life in the union of the body's organs and the soul's faculties. (For this, see Park, "The Organic Soul," in *The Cambridge History of Renaissance Philosophy*, ed. C. B. Schmitt, Quentin Skinner, and Eckhard Kessler [Cambridge: Cambridge University Press, 1988], 464.)

14. Park, "The Organic Soul," 467.

15. Caroline Walker Bynum, *The Resurrection of the Body in Western Christianity, 200–1336* (New York: Columbia University Press, 1995), 261.

16. Walker Bynum, *Resurrection of the Body*, 272.

17. Walker Bynum, *Resurrection of the Body*, 66.

18. St. Augustine of Hippo, *The City of God*, trans. Marcus Dods (Peabody, Mass.: Hendrickson, 2009), book 22, chapter 24.

19. Walker Bynum, *Resurrection of the Body*, 10.

20. St. Thomas Aquinas, *Summa Contra Gentiles*, trans. Charles O'Neil (South Bend, Ind.: University of Notre Dame Press, 1975), 4.81.

21. Eleonore Stump, *Aquinas* (London: Routledge, 2003), 10–11.

22. Alessandro Achillini, *De Elementis* (Venice: Giovanni Antonio de Benedetti, 1505), fol. 127b, in Giglioni, introduction to *Renaissance Averroism*, 13. The parenthetical comment is Giglioni's.

23. Giglioni, introduction to *Renaissance Averroism*, 13.

24. Jacopo Zabarella, "Liber de Mente Humana," in *De Rebus Naturalibus* (Frankfurt: Lazar Zetzner, 1607), c. 965A, in Giglioni, introduction to *Renaissance Averroism*, 15.

25. Paul of Venice, *Libros de Anima Explanatio* (Venice: Heirs of Ottaviano Scoto, 1504), fol. 46, in Giglioni, introduction to *Renaissance Averroism*, 13.

26. Agostino Nifo, *De Immortalitate Anime Libellus* (Venice: Ottaviani Scoto, 1518), c. 4, in Giglioni, introduction to *Renaissance Averroism*, 13.

27. Giglioni, introduction to *Renaissance Averroism*, 14.

28. Marsilio Ficino, *Platonic Theology, Volume 5* (Cambridge, Mass.: Harvard University Press, 2005), 121.

29. Giglioni, introduction to *Renaissance Averroism*, 14.

30. Marsilio Ficino, "Five Questions concerning the Mind," in *The Renaissance Philosophy of Man*, ed. Ernst Cassirer, Paul Oskar Kristeller, and John Herman Randall (Chicago: University of Chicago Press, 1948), 196.

31. Ficino, "Five Questions," 202.

32. Mary Thomas Crane, *Shakespeare's Brain: Reading with Cognitive Theory* (Princeton, N.J.: Princeton University Press), 120.

33. Heinrich Plett, "Rhetoric and Humanism in the Renaissance," in *The Oxford Handbook of Rhetorical Studies*, ed. Michael MacDonald (Oxford: Oxford University Press, 2014).

34. Giorgio Agamben, *Homo Sacer: Sovereign Power and Bare Life*, trans. Daniel Heller Roazen (Stanford, Calif.: Stanford University Press, 1998), 7.

35. Pierre de la Primaudaye, *The Second Part of the French Academie, as It Were a Naturall Historie of the Bodie and Soule of Man*, trans. Thomas Bowes (London: Bishop Ralph Barker, 1594), 89–90.

36. Martin Luther, "Against Latomus 1521," in *Selected Writings of Martin Luther*, ed. Theodore Tappert (Philadelphia: Fortress, 1967), 197–98.

37. William Perkins, *An Exposition of the Symbole or Creede of the Apostles* (Cambridge: John Legat, 1600), 255; John Woolton, *A New Anatomie of Whole Man, As Well of His Body As of His Soule* (London: Thomas Purfoote, 1576), 16–17.

38. John N. King, "The Light of Printing: William Tyndale, John Foxe, and Early Modern Print Culture," *Renaissance Quarterly* 54, no. 1 (spring 2001): 83.

39. Tessa Watt, *Cheap Print and Popular Piety, 1550–1640* (Cambridge: Cambridge University Press, 1994); Jaime Goodrich, *Faithful Translators: Authorship, Gender, and Religion in Early Modern England* (Evanston, Ill.: Northwestern University Press, 2013); Brian Cummings, *The Literary Culture of the Reformation: Grammar and Grace* (Oxford: Oxford University Press, 2002).

40. Sir Walter Ralegh, "A Treatise of the Soul," in *The Works of Sir Walter Ralegh* (Oxford, 1829), 574.

41. Francis Bacon, "The Advancement of Learning," in *The Collected Works of Francis Bacon*, vol. 4, ed. J. Spedding (London: Routledge, 1996), 396.

42. Crane, *Shakespeare's Brain*, 119; see also Susan James, *Passion and Action: The Emotions in Seventeenth-Century Philosophy* (Oxford: Oxford University Press, 1997).

43. William Shakespeare, *Twelfth Night, or What You Will*, in *The Complete Works of Shakespeare*, ed. David Bevington, 7th ed. (New York: Pearson, 2016), 2.3.54–57.

44. John Donne, "The Extasie," in *The Major Works*, ed. John Carey (Oxford: Oxford University Press, 1990), 42.

45. Ramie Targoff, *John Donne: Body and Soul* (Chicago: University of Chicago Press, 2009); N. K. Sugimura, *"Matter of Glorious Trial": Spiritual and Material Substance in Paradise Lost* (New Haven, Conn.: Yale University Press, 2009); Garrett A. Sullivan, *Sleep, Romance, and Human Embodiment: Vitality from Spenser to Milton* (Cambridge: Cambridge University Press, 2012).

46. Gail Kern Paster, *Humoring the Body: Emotions and the Shakespearean Stage* (Chicago: University of Chicago Press, 2010), 7 and 14.

47. Michael C. Schoenfeldt, *Bodies and Selves in Early Modern England: Physiology and Inwardness in Spenser, Shakespeare, Herbert, and Milton* (Cambridge: Cambridge University Press, 1999), 1 and 74.

48. Jonathan Sawday, *The Body Emblazoned: Dissection and the Human Body in Renaissance Culture* (London: Routledge, 1996); and Richard Sugg, *The Smoke of the Soul: Medicine, Physiology and Religion in Early Modern England* (London: Springer, 2013), 6; Richard Sugg, "Donne and the Uses of Anatomy," *Literature Compass* 1 (2004): 2; and Richard Sugg, *Murder after*

Death: Literature and Anatomy in Early Modern England (Ithaca, N.Y.: Cornell University Press, 2007).

49. Paster, *Humoring the Body*, 150. See also Karen Raber, *Animal Bodies, Renaissance Culture* (Philadelphia: University of Pennsylvania Press, 2013); and Erica Fudge, *Brutal Reasoning: Animals, Rationality and Humanity in Early Modern England* (Ithaca, N.Y.: Cornell University Press, 2006).

50. Laurie Shannon, *The Accommodated Animal: Cosmopolity in Shakespearean Locales* (Chicago: University of Chicago Press, 2013), 2 and 3.

51. Leslie Lockett, *Anglo-Saxon Psychologies in the Vernacular and Latin Traditions* (Toronto: University of Toronto Press, 2011); Masha Raskolnikov, *Body against Soul: Gender and "Sowlehele" in Middle English Allegory* (Columbus: Ohio State University Press, 2009); Sarah Rivett, *The Science of the Soul in Colonial New England* (Chapel Hill: University of North Carolina Press, 2011).

52. Fernando Vidal, *The Sciences of the Soul: The Early Modern Origins of Psychology* (Chicago: University of Chicago Press, 2011); James, *Passion and Action*.

53. James, *Passion and Action*; Philip Pettit, *Made with Words: Hobbes on Language, Mind and Politics* (Princeton, N.J.: Princeton University Press, 2009); Jonathan Lear, "Integrating the Non-Rational Soul," *Proceedings of the Aristotelian Society* 114, no. 1 (2013); Jacques Derrida, *The Animal That Therefore I Am* (New York: Fordham University Press, 2008).

54. Examples of this methodology include Victoria Kahn, *Wayward Contracts: The Crisis of Political Obligation in England, 1640–1674* (Princeton, N.J.: Princeton University Press, 2009); John Rogers, *The Matter of Revolution: Science, Poetry and Politics in the Age of Milton* (Ithaca, N.Y.: Cornell University Press, 1998); Ann Hartle, *Montaigne and the Origins of Modern Philosophy* (Evanston, Ill.: Northwestern University Press, 2013), 57 and 66.

55. Barbara Fuchs, "Recent Studies in the English Renaissance," *Studies in English Literature 1500–1900* 55, no. 1 (2015).

56. Katharine Craik and Tanya Pollard, eds., *Shakespearean Sensations: Experiencing Literature in Early Modern England* (Cambridge: Cambridge University Press, 2013), 4.

57. Stephen Greenblatt, *Shakespeare's Freedom* (Chicago: University of Chicago Press, 2012); Joshua Scodel, "Finding Freedom in *Hamlet*," *Modern Language Quarterly* 72, no. 2 (2011): 163–200.

58. Giorgio Agamben, *The Open*, trans Kevin Attell (Stanford, Calif.: Stanford University Press, 2003), 13.

59. Agamben, *The Open*, 14.

60. Agamben, *The Open*, 15.

61. Agamben, *The Open*, 15.

Chapter 1

1. Pietro Pomponazzi, "On the Immortality of the Soul," in *The Renaissance Philosophy of Man*, ed. Ernst Cassirer, Paul Oskar Kristeller, and John Herman Randall (Chicago: University of Chicago Press, 1948), 377.

2. Mandell Creighton, *A History of the Papacy during the Period of the Reformation: The Italian Princes, 1464–1518* (London: Longmans and Green, 1887), 239.

3. For an overview of the Pomponazzi incident, see Eckhard Kessler, "The Intellective Soul," in *The Cambridge History of Renaissance Philosophy*, ed. C. B. Schmitt, Quentin Skinner, and Eckhard Kessler (Cambridge: Cambridge University Press, 1988), particularly, 500–507. See also M. L Pine, *Pietro Pomponazzi: Radical Philosopher of the Renaissance* (Padua, 1986).

4. Walker Bynum, *Resurrection of the Body*, xviii.

5. Walker Bynum, *Resurrection of the Body*, 126.

6. Walker Bynum, *Resurrection of the Body*, 147–51.

7. Walker Bynum, *Resurrection of the Body*, 231.

8. St. Thomas Aquinas, *Summa Theologiae*, ed. Dominican Fathers (London, 1964–80); James, *Passion and Action*, 47.

9. James, *Passion and Action*, 47.

10. Aquinas, *Summa Theologiae*, 1a.77.3.

11. Aquinas, *Summa Theologiae*, 1a.78.4.

12. Aquinas, *Summa Theologiae*, 1a.79.3 and 1a.79.3.

13. Aquinas, *Summa Theologiae*, Suppl.IIIae.92.2.6.

14. P. O. Kristeller, "Paduan Averroism and Alexandrism in the Light of Recent Studies," in *Aristotelismo Padovano e Filosofia Aristotelica* (Florence, 1960), 114–15.

15. Sachiko Kusukawa, *The Transformation of Natural Philosophy: The Case of Philip Melanchthon* (Cambridge: Cambridge University Press, 1995), 7.

16. Paul of Venice, *Libros De Anima Explanatio* (Venice: Heirs of Ottaviano Scoto, 1504), fol. 46, in Giglioni, introduction to *Renaissance Averroism*, 13.

17. Jacopo Zabarella, "Liber de Mente Humana," in *De Rebus Naturalibus libri XXX* (Frankfurt: Lazar Zetzner, 1607), c. 965A, in Giglioni, introduction to *Renaissance Averroism*, 15.

18. Pomponazzi, "On the Immortality of the Soul," 296.

19. For this, see Aristotle, *On the Soul*, 403a3–25, and 431a1–432a15.

20. Pomponazzi, "On the Immortality of the Soul," 288.

21. Pomponazzi, "On the Immortality of the Soul," 282.

22. Pomponazzi, "On the Immortality of the Soul," 282.

23. Pomponazzi, "On the Immortality of the Soul," 348.

24. Pomponazzi, "On the Immortality of the Soul," 375.

25. Pomponazzi, "On the Immortality of the Soul," 377.

26. Pomponazzi, "On the Immortality of the Soul," 376.

27. Pomponazzi, "On the Immortality of the Soul," 381.

28. Although Pope Leo X officially condemned Pomponazzi's work, Leo is thought to have enjoyed a good controversy, and he fanned the flames of the debate by encouraging some of Pomponazzi's fiercest critics to publish their work. For this, see Don Cameron Allen, *Doubt's Boundless Sea: Skepticism and Faith in the Renaissance* (Baltimore, Md.: Johns Hopkins University Press, 1964), 31.

29. Norman Tanner, "Fifth Council of the Lateran," in *Decrees of the Ecumenical Councils: From Nicaea I to Vatican II* (Washington, D.C.: Georgetown University Press, 1990). For general background on the Fifth Lateran Council, see O. de la Brosse et al., *Latran V et Trente, Histoire des conciles oecumeniques, 10* (Paris: Editions de l'Orante, 1975), 13–114; and Nelson H. Minnich, *The Fifth Lateran Council (1512–17): Studies on Its Membership, Diplomacy and Proposals for Reform* (Aldershot, Eng.: Variorum, 1993).

30. The Lateran Council's position has traditionally been understood as a refutation of the doctrine of "double truth" developed by medieval Averroists, who claimed that a premise could be "true in philosophy but false in theology, and vice versa. They could therefore quite literally claim that the truth of philosophy was mortality while the truth of theology was immortality" (Martin Pine, "Pomponazzi and the Problem of 'Double Truth,'" *Journal of the History of Ideas* 29, no. 2 [1968]: 163). For a more recent evaluation of the doctrine of double truth, see Eric Constant, "A Reinterpretation of the Fifth Lateran Council Decree *Apostolici regiminis* (1513)," *Sixteenth Century Journal* 33, no. 2 (2002).

31. William Wright, *Martin Luther's Understanding of God's Two Kingdoms* (Grand Rapids, Mich.: Baker Academic, 2010), 76.

32. For this, see Robert Kolb, *Martin Luther: Confessor of the Faith* (New York: Oxford University Press, 2009), 24.

33. Martin Luther, "Lectures on Galatians," in *Luther's Works*, ed. Jaroslav Pelikan and Helmut T. Lehmann (St. Louis, Mo.: Concordia, 1955–76), xxvii, 364.

34. Kusukawa, *Transformation of Natural Philosophy*, 99.

35. Luther, "Bondage of the Will."

36. Martin Luther, *Christian Liberty* (Philadelphia: Lutheran Publication Society, 1903), 5–6.

37. Luther, *Christian Liberty*, 17–19.

38. This mode of psychological slavery is not limited to the theological discourse of the time, since we find its traces pervading the literary culture of Elizabethan England as well, with the most vivid example found in Sir Philip Sidney and Arthur Golding's translation of De Mornay's *Worke concerning the Trewnesse of the Christian Religion*.

> We be free to followe out owne Nature; and our Nature is becomme euill through sinne. O wretched fréedome, which bringeth vs vnder such bondage! And afore this nature of ours, we can neither shun it nor driue it from vs: for we be bonslaues to it, and it to sinne, and there behoueth a stronger than our selues to rid vs thereof. Therefore let vs pray God to bring the fréedome of our wills in bondage to his will, and to frée our soules from this hard and damnable kind of fréedome, and to graunt vs by his grace, not as to the wicked, to doe his will in béeing vnwilling to do it; but as to his Children, at least wise to be willing to doe it euen in not doing it.

In this cruel and peculiar logic, Sidney and Golding translate DeMornay as suggesting that the human condition of "wretched freedome" can only slip into a state of abject "bondage to his will." Phillippe de Mornay, *A Worke concerning the Trewnesse of the Christian Religion, Written in French: Against Atheists, Epicures, Paynims, Iewes, Mahumetists, and Other Infidels* (London: John Charlewood and George Robinson for Thomas Cadman, 1587), 224. See also Étienne de La Boétie, *Discours de la servitude volontaire* (Paris: Éditions Flammarion, 1993).

39. Philip Melanchthon, *Corpus Reformatorum* (Halle: C. A. Schwetschke and Son, 1843), XI, 281.

40. Kusukawa, *Transformation of Natural Philosophy*, 82–83.

41. Kusukawa, *Transformation of Natural Philosophy*, 88.

42. Kusukawa, *Transformation of Natural Philosophy*, 99.

43. Kusukawa, *Transformation of Natural Philosophy*, 90.

44. Philip Melanchthon, *A Melanchthon Reader*, ed. Ralph Keen (New York: Peter Lang, 1988), 273–75.

45. Luther, "Bondage of the Will." For a detailed explanation of the anxiety provoked by this ironic self-binding freedom, see Victoria Kahn, *Wayward Contracts: The Crisis of Political Obligation in England, 1640–1674* (Princeton, N.J.: Princeton University Press, 2004), 57–79.

46. Martin Luther, "Assertio omnium articulorum M. Lutheri per Bullam Leonis X novissimam damnatorum," in *The Works of Martin Luther Volume 3*, trans. Henry Eyster Jacobs (Philadelphia: A. J. Holman, 1930).

47. John Schofield, *Philip Melanchthon and the English Reformation* (London: Ashgate, 2006), 61.

48. Schofield, *Philip Melanchthon*, 63.

49. Schofield, *Philip Melanchthon*, 63–64.

50. John Woolton, *A Treatise of the Immortalities of the Soule* (London: John Shepperd, 1576); and John Woolton, *A New Anatomie of Whole Man, As Well of His Body As of His Soule* (London: Thomas Purfoote, 1576).

51. Woolton, *Immortalities of the Soule*, "Epistle," fol. 6.

52. For the "image of God in man" as the harmony of the faculties, see also Woolton, *Anatomie of Whole Man*, fol. 9.

53. Woolton, *Anatomie of Whole Man*, fol. 13.

54. See "Faculty," *Oxford English Dictionary*, 2nd ed., 1989. "An ability or aptitude, whether natural or acquired, for any special kind of action; formerly also, ability, 'parts,' capacity in general"; "Facultās and facilitās were originally different forms of the same word; the latter, owing to its more obvious relation to the adj., retained the primary sense of 'easiness,' which the former had ceased to have before the classical period."

55. Woolton, *Anatomie of Whole Man*, fols. 16–17.

56. William Perkins, *An Exposition of the Symbole or Creede of the Apostles* (Cambridge: John Legat, 1600), 255.

57. Richard Hooker, *Of the Laws of Ecclesiasticall Politie* (London: 1604), 56–57.

58. For an excellent account of the relationship between print and literacy, see Heidi Brayman Hackel, *Reading Material in Early Modern England: Print, Gender, and Literacy* (Cambridge: Cambridge University Press, 2005).

59. For example, Woolton's printer John Charlewood was responsible for producing translations of Virgil (1575) and Plato (1592), the Protestant sermons of Calvin (1578) and Theodore Beza (1576), Tyndale's translation of the Epistle to the Romans (1564) and John Foxe's *Principles of Christian Religion* (1587), and from the angle of expanding English literary culture, Sir Philip Sidney's *Astrophil and Stella* (1591), Thomas Nashe's *Anatomie of Absurditie* (1589 and 1590), and William Webbe's *Discourse of English Poetrie* (1586). Equally active in expanding the range of English vernacular print culture was Hooker's printer John Windet, who published George Chapman's translation of Homer (1598), Calvin's sermons (1584 and 1592), and Blundeville's *Arte of Logike* (1599), which makes a point of emphasizing that it is "plainly taught in the English tongue." The texts of William Perkins are an interesting wrinkle on this vernacular print culture,

since his theological treatises were largely first written in Latin and printed by John Legat, the stationer of Cambridge University, were translated thereafter by Thomas Tuke (1606 and 1607) and Robert Hill (1591), and subsequently enjoyed remarkable popularity in thirteen editions of the translated versions between 1591 and 1621.

Chapter 2

1. Although the curriculum of Shakespeare's grammar school in Stratford is not extant, the study of grammar and rhetoric is programmatically outlined in William Kempe, *The Education of Children in Learning* (London: Thomas Orwin for John Porter and Thomas Gubbin, 1588); and Roger Ascham, *The Scholemaster* (London: John Daye, 1570).

2. For this point, see Victoria Kahn, "The Passions and the Interests in Early Modern Europe: The Case of Guarini's *Il Pastor Fido*," in *Reading the Early Modern Passions: Essays in the Cultural History of Emotion*, ed. Gail Kern Paster, Katherine Rowe, and Mary Floyd-Wilson (Philadelphia: University of Pennsylvania Press, 2004), 217–19.

3. Jonathan Bate, *The Genius of Shakespeare* (Oxford: Oxford University Press, 1998), 261; and Marjorie Garber, *Shakespeare After All* (New York: Pantheon Books, 2004), 4.

4. Samuel Johnson, *The Works of Samuel Johnson, Volume 2*, ed. Arthur Murphy (New York: Harper and Brothers, 1857), 491.

5. The earliest interpretations of Hamlet's interiority as the feature of his subjectivity can be found in Samuel Taylor Coleridge's *Treatise on Method*, where he extols the character's "internal activity of mind in reflecting and generalizing" (Samuel Taylor Coleridge, *Treatise on Method as Published in the Encyclopaedia Metropolitana*, ed. Alice D. Snyder [London: Constable, 1934], 29), and in Hegel's *Aesthetics*, where he admires Hamlet's romantic "absolute inwardness" (1.519). For examples of the critical vogue that defined Hamlet as the first modern subject, see Francis Barker, *The Tremulous Private Body: Essays on Subjection* (London: Methuen, 1984); Catherine Belsey, *The Subject of Tragedy: Identity and Difference in Renaissance Drama* (London: Methuen, 1985); Christopher Pye, *The Vanishing: Shakespeare, the Subject, and Early Modern Culture* (Durham, N.C.: Duke University Press, 2000); John Lee, *Shakespeare's "Hamlet" and the Controversies of Self* (Oxford: Oxford University Press, 2000); Eric Levy, *Hamlet and the Rethinking of Man* (Madison, N.J.: Fairleigh Dickinson University Press, 2008); and J. K. Harmer, "Hamlet's Introspection," in *Essays in Criticism* (2011). Critics identifying the Shakespearean corpus in general as the origin of subjectivity include Joel Fineman, *Shakespeare's Perjured Eye: The Invention of Poetic Subjectivity in the Sonnets* (Berkeley: University of California Press, 1986); and Harold Bloom, *Shakespeare: The Invention of the Human* (New York: Riverhead Books, 1998). A "new wave" has read *Hamlet* in terms of cognitive models: Crane, *Shakespeare's Brain: Reading with Cognitive Theory*; Ellen Spolsky, *Word vs. Image: Cognitive Hunger in Shakespeare's England* (London: Palgrave Macmillan, 2007); Amy Cook, "Staging Nothing: Hamlet and Cognitive Science," *SubStance* 35, no. 2 (2006): 83–99.

6. Paster, *Humoring the Body*, 28; and Schoenfeldt, *Bodies and Selves in Early Modern England*, 10.

7. Richard Sugg, "Flame into Being: Spirits, Soul, and the Physiology of Early Modern Devotion," *Journal of Medieval and Early Modern Studies* 46, no. 1 (2016): 141–42; Donovan Sherman, "Governing the Wolf: Soul and Space in *The Merchant of Venice*," *Journal of Medieval and Early Modern Studies* 43, no. 1 (2013): 100; Christopher Crosbie, "*Oeconomia* and the Vegetative Soul: Rethinking Revenge in *The Spanish Tragedy*," *English Literary Renaissance* 38, no. 1 (2008): 4.

8. Stephen Greenblatt, *Hamlet in Purgatory* (Princeton, N.J.: Princeton University Press, 2013), 252–53.

9. For an evaluation of Jonson's claim, see Leonard Barkan, "What Did Shakespeare Read?" in *The Cambridge Companion to Shakespeare*, ed. Margreta de Grazia and Stanley Wells (Cambridge: Cambridge University Press, 2001).

10. As Debora Shuger suggests, the "Renaissance tends to make emotional power, Cicero's *movere*, the aim of all rhetorical discourse," thus reducing the importance of the other two goals of Ciceronian eloquence: *docere* (to instruct) and *delectare* (to delight). For this, see Debora Shuger, *Sacred Rhetoric: The Christian Grand Style in the English Renaissance* (Princeton, N.J.: Princeton University Press, 1988), 120.

11. Stephen Greenblatt, *Shakespeare's Freedom* (Chicago: University of Chicago Press, 2012); and Joshua Scodel, "Finding Freedom in Hamlet," *Modern Language Quarterly* 72, no. 2 (2011): 163–200.

12. Richard Strier, "Against the Rule of Reason: Praise of Passion from Petrarch to Luther to Shakespeare to Herbert," in *Reading the Early Modern Passions: Essays in the Cultural History of Emotion*, ed. Gail Kern Paster, Katherine Rowe, and Mary Floyd-Wilson (Philadelphia: University of Pennsylvania Press, 2004), 23–42.

13. T. S. Eliot, "Hamlet and His Problems," in *The Sacred Wood: Essays on Poetry and Criticism* (New York: Alfred A. Knopf, 1921).

14. James, *Passion and Action*, 1.

15. Paster, *Humoring the Body*, 1–2.

16. Ambrosius Autpertus, *A Monomachie of Motives in the Mind of Man* (London: H. Denham, 1582), 3.

17. Pierre de la Primaudaye, *The French Academie Fully Discoursed and Finished in Foure Bookes* (London: John Legat for Thomas Adams, 1618), 21–22. Note that Legat was the printer at Cambridge University, and was responsible for producing the theological texts of William Perkins and the rhetorical treatises of Henry Peacham, along with translations of Cicero. Where possible, I will cite early modern translations of classical and Continental texts rather than modern editions, in order to frame the context of the books that were in circulation in English at the time. As we shall see, this context is an important part of the story itself.

18. There were various ways to enact this voiding of the soul in Shakespeare's time, but one of the most notable, and congruent with the playwright's own practice, was from an early 1528 compendium translating Aristotelian philosophy into vernacular English, which recommended theater: "For the minde being occupied and intentiue to the words, dooth feele the griefe lesse. And therefore Comedies and stage playes were inuented in times past, to withdrawe the minde. . . . and this is Galens meaning, for by the expressing of the tongue, many actions of diuers passions are made manifest." According to this vernacular

account of Aristotle, words and speech, and particularly language performed on stage, serve as a particularly appropriate vehicle for soothing the perturbations of the passionate soul. For this, see Aristotle, *The Problems of Aristotle* (Edinburgh: Robert Waldgrave, 1595), 19.

19. Jeff Dolven and Sean Keilen, "Shakespeare's Reading," in *The New Cambridge Companion to Shakespeare*, ed. Margreta de Grazia and Stanley Wells (Cambridge: Cambridge University Press, 2010), 18.

20. Rolf Soellner, "Shakespeare, Aristotle, Plato, and the Soul," *Deutsche Shakespeare-Gesellschaft West. Jahrbuch* (1972): 56–71; David N. Beauregard, "Shakespeare and the Passions: The Aristotelian-Thomistic Tradition," *The Heythrop Journal* 52, no. 6 (2011): 912–25.

21. Stephen Greenblatt, "The Traces of Shakespeare's Life," in De Grazia and Wells, eds., *The New Cambridge Companion*, 4.

22. Brian Vickers, *In Defense of Rhetoric* (Oxford: Oxford University Press, 1989), 229–30; Lawrence Green, "Aristotle's Rhetoric and Renaissance Views of the Emotions," in *Renaissance Rhetoric*, ed. Peter Mack (London: Palgrave Macmillan, 1994), 11, 15; Quentin Skinner, *Reason and Rhetoric in the Philosophy of Hobbes* (Cambridge: Cambridge University Press, 1996), 37.

23. Cicero, *De Officiis (On Duties)*, trans. Walter Miller (Cambridge, Mass.: Harvard University Library, 1913), 54–55.

24. Cicero, *The Orations of Marcus Tullius Cicero*, trans. C. D. Yonge (London: George Bell, 1890), 439.

25. Cicero, *On the Orator (De Oratore)*, trans. E. W. Sutton (Cambridge, Mass.: Harvard University Press, 1942), 41, 143, 159.

26. Cicero, *On the Orator*, 332–33. Cicero's quotation is cited from Pacuvius, in his tragedy *Hermione*.

27. Plato, *Euthyphro, Apology, Crito, Phaedo, Phaedrus*, trans. Harold North Fowler (Cambridge, Mass.: Harvard University Press, 1914), 548–53.

28. Plutarch, *The Lives of the Noble Grecians and Romanes*, trans. Thomas North (London: Thomas Vautroullier and John Wright, 1579), 177.

29. Barkan, "What Did Shakespeare Read?" 7.

30. John Walker, *Shakespeare and the Classical Tradition: An Annotated Bibliography, 1961–1991* (Oxford: Taylor and Francis, 2002), 280.

31. Peter Stallybrass, Roger Chartier, Franklin Mowery, and Heather Wolfe, "Hamlet's Tables and the Technologies of Writing in Renaissance England," *Shakespeare Quarterly* 55, no. 4 (2004): 379–419.

32. Aristotle, *On the Soul*, 412a6–412b6.

33. Cicero, *On the Orator*, 466–67; see also Raphael Lyne, *Shakespeare, Rhetoric and Cognition* (Cambridge: Cambridge University Press, 2011), 90.

34. Greenblatt, *Hamlet in Purgatory*, 151–257.

35. Edmund Chambers, *William Shakespeare: A Study of Fact and Problems* (Oxford: Clarendon, 1930); and Ernst Honigmann, *Shakespeare: The Lost Years* (Manchester: Manchester University Press, 1985).

36. Claire McEachern, "Shakespeare, Religion and Politics," in *The New Cambridge Companion to Shakespeare*, ed. Margreta de Grazia and Stanley Wells (Cambridge: Cambridge University Press, 2010), 195–96.

37. At another level, Hamlet's confusion about his two very different souls hinges on the paralyzing ethical dilemma his father has forced upon him. Ironically,

after painting a terrifying picture of the punitive consequences of breaking God's law, the ghost commands his son to murder Claudius so as to avenge his death, ordering his son to break God's commandment forbidding murder. After telling his son how God violently punishes those who break his law, he asks his son to break it. Therefore Hamlet's most famous speeches after his interaction with the ghost can certainly be read as lofty metaphysical meditations, but ones that struggle with the ethical dilemma posed by his father's order to murder and break God's law. With this understanding, Hamlet's soliloquies read very differently. For example, the famed "To be or not to be" soliloquy is not so much about being and nothingness, but rather struggles with the raw deal Hamlet is confronted with, of exchanging one system of punishment in life for another, more painful punishment in death: "That dread of something after death . . . makes us rather bear those ills we have / Than to fly to others that we know not of?" (*Hamlet* 3.1.78–82). As Murray Bundy has noted, in the "To be or not to be" soliloquy, "the deterrent to suicide is not, as some think, moral scruple, but the vivid imagination of the penalty of the guilty" (Murray W. Bundy, "Shakespeare and Elizabethan Psychology," *The Journal of English and Germanic Philology* 23, no. 4 [1924]: 516–49). Therefore, Hamlet's paralysis after his encounter with his father's ghost is not caused by a philosophical conflict between thought and action, as has been conventionally argued by countless readers of the play.

38. Aristotle, *The Ethiques of Aristotle* (London: Richard Grafton, 1547), 10–11.

39. Aristotle, *Rhetoric*, trans. John Henry Freese (Cambridge, Mass.: Harvard University Press, 1926), 1356a7.

40. Cicero, *Marcus Tullius Ciceroes Three Bokes of Duties to Marcus His Sonne*, trans. Nicholas Grimalde (London: Richard Tottel, 1556), 6, emphasis mine.

41. Skinner, *Reason and Rhetoric in the Philosophy of Hobbes*, 35–37.

42. For a survey of this reading, see Robert Miola, "Aeneas and Hamlet," *Classical and Modern Literature* 8 (1988): 281–86. Carl Schmitt has famously read Hamlet as an allegory of the Tudor succession crisis. For this, see Carl Schmitt, *Hamlet or Hecuba: The Intrusion of Time into the Play* (New York: Telos, 2009).

43. For this, see Paster, *Humoring the Body*, 42–43, and Gilles Deleuze and Felix Guattari, *A Thousand Plateaus: Capitalism and Schizophrenia*, trans. Brian Massumi (Minneapolis: University of Minnesota Press, 1987), 153.

44. Paster, *Humoring the Body*, 43.

45. Aristotle, *On the Soul*, 412a27–412b9.

46. As Greenblatt notes, "there is a striking link between Hamlet's description of the player" and "the Ghost's description of the effect that his tale of torment would have on Hamlet" (Greenblatt, *Hamlet in Purgatory*, 252–53).

47. Paster has read the act of "tenting" in this scene as a "humoral therapeutic" used to "express corrupt bodily matter" (Paster, *Humoring the Body*, 52).

48. James, *Passion and Action*, 11.

49. J. L. Austin, *How to Do Things with Words* (Cambridge, Mass.: Harvard University Press, 1975).

50. Paul Kottman, ed., *Philosophers on Shakespeare* (Stanford, Calif.: Stanford University Press, 2009), 8; and Johann Wolfgang von Goethe, *Wilhelm Meister* (New York: Collier, 1962), 234–36.

51. For a detailed reading of Shakespeare's neologism of "enacture" here, see Crane, *Shakespeare's Brain*, 132–33.

52. The most important of these readings are Jacques Lacan, "Desire and the Interpretation of Desire in *Hamlet*," *Yale French Studies* 56 (1977): 11–52; and Janet Adelman, *Suffocating Mothers: Fantasies of Maternal Origin in Shakespeare's Plays* (New York: Routledge, 1991).

53. "Apoplexy," *Oxford English Dictionary*, Second Edition, 1989.

54. Shakespeare's definition of apoplexy as a disease of the Aristotelian faculties parallels Thomas Adams's description in *Diseases of the Soule* of the sickness as specifically disrupting the proper functioning of the faculties of movement, sense, affection, reason, and memory: "The Apoplexie is a disease, wherin the fountain & originall of all the finewes being affected, euery part of the body loseth both mouing & sense; all voluntary functions hindred . . . The parish of his affections is extremely out of order; because Reason his Ordinary doth not visite; nor Memorie his Churchwarden present; (or if it at all, Omnia bene.) Neither doth Understanding the Iudge censure and determine." Thomas Adams, *Diseases of the Soule* (London: George Purslowe, 1616).

55. For the relation of rhetorical "daggers" to Hamlet's conception of theater, see Bruce Danner, "Speaking Daggers," *Shakespeare Quarterly* 54, no. 1 (2003): 23–62.

56. Claudius laments such an internal division of the self in his description of Ophelia's madness in 4.5.83–84: "poor Ophelia / Divided from herself and her fair judgment, / Without the which we are pictures, or mere beasts." Where Claudius grieves over such a division, Hamlet attempts to provoke such a self-division precisely through the description of "pictures."

57. Garrett Sullivan emphasizes the importance of sleep in relation to classical faculty psychology in *Sleep, Romance and Human Embodiment: Vitality from Spenser to Milton* (Cambridge: Cambridge University Press, 2012).

58. We shall revisit this theme in a sustained way in the final chapter of this book, on John Milton.

59. Cicero, *On the Orator*, 334–35.

60. Alan Sinfield. *Faultlines: Cultural Materialism and the Politics of Dissident Reading* (Berkeley: University of California Press, 1992), 222–30.

61. Skinner, *Reason and Rhetoric in the Philosophy of Hobbes*, 126.

62. Michel de Montaigne, *Shakespeare's Montaigne: The Florio Translation of the Essays*, ed. Stephen Greenblatt (New York: New York Review of Books, 2014), 166.

63. J. Dover Wilson, *What Happens in "Hamlet"* (Cambridge: Cambridge University Press, 1995), 268.

64. Margreta De Grazia, *"Hamlet" without Hamlet* (Cambridge: Cambridge University Press, 2007), 152.

65. De Grazia, *"Hamlet" without Hamlet, 203*.

66. For other readings of Hamlet's particularly metalinguistic play, see James Calderwood, *Shakespearean Metadrama: The Argument of the Play in Titus Andronicus, Love's Labour's Lost, Romeo and Juliet, A Midsummer Night's Dream, and Richard II* (Minneapolis: University of Minnesota Press, 1971); and James Calderwood, *To Be and Not to Be: Negation and Metadrama in "Hamlet"* (New York: Columbia University Press, 1983).

67. De Grazia, *"Hamlet" without Hamlet*, 8.
68. De Grazia, *"Hamlet" without Hamlet*, 8–9.

Chapter 3

1. Stanley Kunitz has called Davies's *Orchestra* a "neglected Elizabethan masterpiece." For this, see Rebecca Rush, "Making Order in John Davies's *Orchestra*," *Modern Philology* 114, no. 2 (2016): 243.

2. From the "Notes of the Life of Sr John Davys," in Bodleian MS. Carte 62, fol. 590–91.

3. This interpretation of Davies's career gained momentum in J. G. A. Pocock's well-known work on common law, where he identifies Davies as an important counterpart to Sir Edward Coke in defining an ancient tradition of English law (J. G. A. Pocock, *The Ancient Constitution and Feudal Law* [Cambridge: Cambridge University Press, 1957]). More recently, Bradin Cormack has reconfirmed Davies's prominent position in the seventeenth-century common law tradition in *A Power to Do Justice: Jurisdiction, English Literature, and the Rise of Common Law, 1509–1625* (Chicago: University of Chicago Press, 2007). Other important examples evaluating Davies's role in the history of common law and empire include Hans Pawlisch, "Sir John Davies, The Ancient Constitution, and Civil Law," *The Historical Journal* 23, no. 3 (1980); Hans Pawlisch, *Sir John Davies and the Conquest of Ireland: A Study in Legal Imperialism* (Cambridge: Cambridge University Press, 1985); Anthony Pagden, *Lords of All the World: Ideologies of Empire in Spain, Britain and France, c. 1500–c. 1800* (New Haven, Conn.: Yale University Press, 1994); Patricia Palmer, *Language and Conquest in Early Modern Ireland: English Renaissance Literature and Elizabethan Imperial Expansion* (Cambridge: Cambridge University Press, 2001); Brian Lockey, "Conquest and English Legal Identity in Renaissance Ireland," *Journal of the History of Ideas* 65, no. 4 (October 2004); and Ian Campbell, "Aristotelian Ancient Constitution and Anti-Aristotelian Sovereignty in Stuart Ireland," *The Historical Journal* 53, no. 3 (2010).

4. David Hadas, "Review of *Sir John Davies*," *Renaissance Quarterly* 29, no. 3 (1976): 447–48.

5. Wilkes suggests: "*Orchestra* holds its special place in Elizabethan verse not as an exposition of the world order, but as a poem in which ideas are used for a purpose best described as 'aesthetic,' as materials for the fashioning of a work which has no end but its own excellence, and the pleasure its cleverness may give." Although Wilkes's use of the term "aesthetic" precedes the eighteenth-century definition of the concept, it is nonetheless illustrative for my purposes here. For this, see G. A. Wilkes, "The Poetry of Sir John Davies," *Huntington Library Quarterly* 25, no. 4 (1962): 289–90. See also Sarah Thesiger, "The *Orchestra* of Sir John Davies and the Image of the Dance," *Journal of the Warburg and Courtauld Institutes* 36 (1973): 277.

6. E. M. W. Tillyard, *The Elizabethan World Picture* (London: Chatto and Windus, 1948), 99–101. Along similar lines, Roy Strong has suggested that Davies's poetry represents "the final poetic cadences of the Eliza-cult." See Roy Strong, *The Cult of Elizabeth: Elizabethan Portraiture and Pageantry* (Berkeley: University of California Press, 1977), 46. For the opposing view, see Robert Krueger, introduction in *The Poems of Sir John Davies* (Oxford: Clarendon, 1975), xlviii and lxiv.

7. Rush, "Making Order," 243; Wilkes, "Poetry of Sir John Davies," 283.

8. Elias Sneath, *Philosophy in Poetry* (New York: Scribner's, 1903); Margarete Seemann, *Sir John Davies* (Leipzig: W. Braymuller, 1913); L. I. Bredvold, "The Sources Used by Davies in Nosce Teipsum," *PMLA* 38 (1923): 745–69; G. T. Buckley, "The Indebtedness of Sir John Davies's *Nosce Teipsum* to Philip Mornay's *Trunesse of the Christian Religion*," *Modern Philology* 25 (1927): 67–78.

9. Pawlisch, *Sir John Davies and the Conquest of Ireland*, 161–75.

10. Wilkes, "Poetry of Sir John Davies," 283 and 298.

11. Throughout my analysis, I will be citing Sir John Davies, *Nosce Teipsum: This Oracle Expounded in Two Elegies: Of Humane Knowledge, Of the Soule of Man, and the Immortalitie Thereof* (London: Richard Field, 1599).

12. For this point, see Christopher Crosbie, "*Oeconomia* and the Vegetative Soul: Rethinking Revenge in the Spanish Tragedy," *English Literary Renaissance* 38, no. 1 (February 2008); and Kurt Singer, "Oikonomia: An Inquiry into Beginnings of Economic Thought and Language," in *Aristotle (384–322 BC)*, ed. Mark Blaug (Brookfield, Vt.: Edward Elgar, 1991).

13. Davies, *Nosce Teipsum*, 53.1–3.

14. We have already considered Aristotle's figure of the "seal in wax impression" in detail in the previous chapter on Hamlet. For Aristotle's original use of the figure, see Aristotle, *On the Soul*, trans. W. S. Hett, 412a6–412b6.

15. Davies, *Nosce Teipsum*, 5.4–6.2.

16. Aristotle, *Politics*, 3.4.1277b24; *Nicomachean Ethics*, 8.7.1158b11 and 8.11.1161a22; *Rhetoric* 1.5.1361a4–10. See also Robert Mayhew, *The Female in Aristotle's Biology: Reason or Rationalization* (Chicago: University of Chicago Press, 2004), 92–98; and Sophia Connell, "Aristotle and Galen on Sex Difference and Reproduction: A New Approach to an Ancient Rivalry," *Studies in History and Philosophy of Science* 31, no. 3 (2000).

17. Martin Luther, *Treatise on Christian Liberty* (1520).

18. Davies, *Nosce Teipsum*, 18.4.

19. Davies, *Nosce Teipsum*, 18.5–19.2.

20. Davies, *Nosce Teipsum*, 18.3.

21. Thomas Wright's *Passions of the Minde in Generall* (1604) gives one of the most famous accounts of this psychological rebellion, framing it as one in which the faculties rebel not just against their ruler, but also fight amongst each other:

> Our senses were joint-friends in such sort with Passions, that whatsoever delighted sense, pleased the passions; and whatsoever was hurtfull to the one, was an enemy to the other; and so, by long agreement and familiarity, the passions had so engaged themselves to sense, and with such bonds and seals of sensual habits confirmed their friendship, that as soone as reason came to possession of her kingdome, they began to presently make rebellion; for right reason oftentimes deprived sense of the pleasures he had of long time enjoyed, as by commanding continencie, and fasting, which sense most abhorred: then passions repugned, and very often haled her by force, to condescend to that they demanded . . . Moreover, after that men, by reason, take possession over their soules and bodies, feeling this war so mightie, so continuall, so neare, so domesticall, that either they must consent to do their enemies will, or still be in conflict. . . . By two wayes the subjects of every

> Common-weale, usually disturbe the State, and breede civil broyles therein: The first is, when they rise up and rebel against their King: the second is, when they brawle one with another, and so cause riots and tumults: the former is called Rebellion, the latter sedition. After the same manner, Passions either rebell against Reason their Lord and King, or oppose themselves one against another . . . For these rebellious Passions are like crafty pioneers, who, while souldiers live carelesly within their Castle, or at least not much suspect, they undermine it, and breake in so upon them, that they can hardly escape: in like manner these affections undermine the understandings of men.

For this, see Wright, *The Passions of the Minde in Generall* (London: Valentine Simmes, 1604), 9–10.

22. Davies claims that the soul is an ember buried under ash, barely glowing: it "is now become a Sparkle, which doth lie / Under the Ashes, halfe extinct, and dead" (Davies, *Nosce Teipsum*, 3.5).

23. Davies opposes the Calvinist model of election in *Nosce Teipsum*: "For what is Man without a moving Mind, / Which hath a judging Wit, and chusing Will? / Now, if God's Pow'r should her Election bind, / Her Motions then would cease, and stand all still . . . / Love must free-hearted be, and voluntary; / And not inchanted, or by Fate constrain'd" (47.1–3).

24. Davies, *Nosce Teipsum*, 43.5–44.2.

25. Herbert Davidson, "Averroes and Narboni on the Material Intellect," *Association for Jewish Studies Review* 9, no. 2 (1984): 179; and Richard Taylor, "Separate Material Intellect in Averroes' Mature Philosophy," in *Words, Texts and Concepts Cruising the Mediterranean Sea* (Leuven: Peeters, 2004).

26. Giglioni, introduction to *Renaissance Averroism*, 16–17.

27. Davies, *Nosce Teipsum*, 83.4–86.2.

28. Davies, *Nosce Teipsum*, 21.4–5; 65.2.

29. See Pawlisch, *Sir John Davies and the Conquest of Ireland*, 15–28.

30. Focused readings of Davies's *Orchestra* are relatively rare. The three most sustained analyses of the poem are Rush, "Making Order"; Thesiger, "The Orchestra of Sir John Davies and the Image of the Dance"; and R. J. Manning, "Rule and Order Strange: A Reading of Sir John Davies's *Orchestra*," *English Literary Renaissance* 15, no. 2 (March 1985).

31. Davies's friend John Hoskins claimed that *Orchestra* was constructed around a single premise: "This only trick made up J.D's poem of dancing; all danceth, the heavens, the elements, mens minds, commonwealths, and so by parts all danceth" (Hoskins, *Directions for Speech and Style*, ed. H. H. Hudson [Princeton, N.J.: Princeton University Press, 1935], 23).

32. Sir John Davies, *Orchestra; or A Poeme of Dauncing* (London: I. Robarts, 1596), stanzas 78–79, 96, 102.

33. Aristotle, *Aristotles Politiques, or Discourses of Government*, trans. John Dickenson (London: Adam Islip, 1598), 209–10.

34. Scholars have recently demonstrated how dance served as an important Renaissance metaphor for describing the social and cosmic order. For this, see Blair Hoxby, "The Wisdom of Their Feet: Meaningful Dance in Milton and the Stuart Masque," *English Literary Renaissance* 37, no. 1 (2007); Judith

Bryce, "Performing for Strangers: Women, Dance, and Music in Quattrocento Florence," *Renaissance Quarterly* 54, no. 4 (2001): 1074–1107; and Jennifer Nevile, "Dance and the Garden: Moving and Static Choreography in Renaissance Europe," *Renaissance Quarterly* 52, no. 3 (1999): 805–36.

35. Davies, *Orchestra*, stanzas 69–70.

36. Davies, *Orchestra*, stanza 92.

37. Davies, *Orchestra*, stanzas 126–30.

38. Krueger, *The Poems of Sir John Davies*, xlviii and lxiv; and Pawlisch, *Sir John Davies and the Conquest of Ireland*, 24.

39. Sir John Davies, *A Discoverie of the True Causes of Why Ireland Was Never Entire Subdued, nor Brought under Obedience of the Crowne of England* (London: John Jaggard, 1612).

40. Davies, *A Discoverie of the True Causes*, 219–20.

41. Davies, *A Discoverie of the True Causes*, 284.

42. Davies applies the same metaphor of musical harmony to the English government, in a 1613 speech to the Irish Parliament: "These Parliaments, thought they consist of three different estates—the King, the Nobility, and the Commons—yet as in music distinct and several notes do make a perfect harmony, so these Councils, compounded of divers states and degrees, being well ordered and timed, do make a perfect concord in a Commonwealth" (Davies, *The Works in Verse and Prose, Vol. 3*, ed. Alexander Grosart [Blackburn: Fuller Worthies' Library, 1876], 223, from the Sloane MSS 4793, fol. 57).

43. Davies, *A Discoverie of the True Causes*, 126–27.

44. Rush, "Making Order," 252–56.

45. Davies, *A Discoverie of the True Causes*, 103–4.

46. Davies, *A Discoverie of the True Causes*, 168–69.

47. Davies, *A Discoverie of the True Causes*, 271–72.

48. Davies, *A Discoverie of the True Causes*, 176–77.

49. Pawlisch, *Sir John Davies and the Conquest of Ireland*, 8.

50. Davies, *A Discoverie of the True Causes*, 280–81.

51. Davies, *A Discoverie of the True Causes*, 281.

52. Davies, *A Discoverie of the True Causes*, 30.

53. Tertullian, "A Treatise on the Soul," in *The Ante-Nicene Fathers*, ed. Alexander Roberts and James Donaldson (Grand Rapids, Mich.: Eerdmans, 1977), XLVIII; Ronald Heine, *Origen: Scholarship in the Service of the Church* (Oxford: Oxford University Press), 123–26; Jean Bodin, *On the Demonomania of Witches* (Toronto: Centre for Reformation and Renaissance Studies, 1995), 129; Johannes Dillinger, "'Species,' 'Phantasia,' 'Raison': Werewolves and Shape-Shifters in Demonological Literature," in *Werewolf Histories*, ed. Willem de Blecourt (London: Palgrave Macmillan, 2015), 151.

54. Pawlisch, *Sir John Davies and the Conquest of Ireland*, 14.

55. Sir John Davies, *Nosce Teipsum: This Oracle Expounded in Two Elegies 1. Of Humane Knowledge. 2. Of the Soule of Man, and the Immortalitie Thereof. Hymnes of Astraea in Acrosticke Verse. Orchestra, or A Poeme of Dauncing. In a Dialogue betweene Penelope, and One of Her Wooers. Not Finished* (London: Augustine Mathewes, 1622).

56. "Reason's Moane" is the poem concluding Robert Mason's *A Mirrour for Merchants: With an Exact Table to Discouer the Excessiue Taking of Vsurie,*

against the Lawes Manifested in This Treatise of Reasons Academy (London: R. Mason, 1609).

57. Sir John Davies, *The Question concerning Impositions, Tonnage, Poundage, Prizage, Customs, &c. Fully Stated and Argued, from Reason, Law, and Policy Dedicated to King James in the Latter End of his Reign* (London: S.G. for H. Twyford, 1656), 3.

58. Bodleian MS. Carte 62, fol. 590b.

Chapter 4

EPIGRAPH: John Donne, "Sermon Preached to the King, at Whitehall, April 1, 1627," in *The Sermons of John Donne*, ed. George Potter and Evelyn Simpson, 10 vols. (Berkeley: University of California Press, 1953–62), vol. 7, no. 16. All subsequent quotations of Donne's sermons are from this edition and will be cited by sermon title and volume.

1. John Carey, introduction to John Donne, *The Major Works*, ed. John Carey (Oxford: Oxford University Press, 1990), xxx.

2. Carey, in Donne, *Major Works*, xxxi.

3. Ramie Targoff, *John Donne: Body and Soul* (Chicago: University of Chicago Press, 2009), 1.

4. Richard Wollman, "'The Press and the Fire': Print and Manuscript Culture in Donne's Circle," *Studies in English Literature, 1500–1900* 33.1 (1993): 94.

5. For these two positions, see Elizabeth L. Eisenstein, *The Printing Press as an Agent of Change*, vol. 1 (Cambridge: Cambridge University Press, 1980); and Adrian Johns, *The Nature of the Book: Print and Knowledge in the Making* (Chicago: University of Chicago Press, 1998). Harold Love and Arthur F. Marotti have described the press as a fixing agent that stripped the reader of the power to reshape the text: "Print replaced manuscript with an objectivity that was both a remoteness and a fixity. . . . Readers of a printed text could not . . . have any way of altering [its] condition." Love and Marotti, "Manuscript Transmission and Circulation," in *The Cambridge History of Early Modern English Literature*, ed. David Loewenstein and Janel Mueller (Cambridge: Cambridge University Press, 2002), 57, 58. In the specific case of Donne, Ted-Larry Pebworth asserts that he uncomfortably viewed printed texts as immutable "objects destined to endure" and as "stable artifacts," whereas manuscript afforded him the "freedom of treating texts as scripts for performance" and a level of "flexibility and impermanence." Pebworth, "John Donne, Coterie Poetry, and the Text as Performance," *Studies in English Literature, 1500–1900* 29 (1989): 61–75.

6. Alvin Kernan, *Samuel Johnson & the Impact of Print* (Princeton, N.J.: Princeton University Press, 1989), 55. For a response to Kernan, see David McKitterick, *Print, Manuscript and the Search for Order, 1450–1830* (Cambridge: Cambridge University Press, 2003).

7. Donne, "The Extasie," in *The Major Works*, ed. John Carey (Oxford: Oxford University Press, 1990), 42. All subsequent references to Donne's *Songs and Sonnets* and *Anniversaries* are from this edition and will be cited parenthetically within the text by poem and line. The dates of specific poems are disputed because they were distributed in manuscript form.

8. For recent readings of Donne's debt to Galenism, see Kate Narveson, "Flesh, Excrement, Humors, Nothing: The Body in Early Stuart Devotional Discourse,"

Studies in Philology 96 (1999): 313–33; and Margret Fetzer, "Donne, Devotion, and Digestion," in *The Pleasures and Horrors of Eating*, ed. Norbert Lennartz and Marion Gymnich (Bonn: Bonn University Press, 2010), 143–64. See also Gail Kern Paster, "Nervous Tension: Networks of Blood and Spirit in the Early Modern Body," in *The Body in Parts: Fantasies of Corporeality in Early Modern Europe*, ed. David Hillman and Carla Mazzio (London: Routledge, 1997); and Schoenfeldt, *Bodies and Selves in Early Modern England*.

9. John Freccero's reading has argued that the compass image forwards a "vortical reconciliation of body and soul" in the Neoplatonic model of the spiral motion or *motus obliquus* (Freccero, "Donne's Valediction: Forbidding Mourning," *ELH* 30 [1963]: 337). In contrast to Freccero, I argue that the compass figures the relation of two souls (and not the body and soul) in the Aristotelian and not the Platonic tradition and cannot be read as a "reconciliation," since the compass legs are mechanically codependent but not physically unified.

10. Jonathan Sawday, *The Body Emblazoned: Dissection and the Human Body in Renaissance Culture* (London: Routledge, 1996), 122; and Richard Sugg, "Donne and the Uses of Anatomy," *Literature Compass* 1 (2004): 2. See also Sugg's *Murder after Death*.

11. Donne persistently figures the anatomization of the soul into the Aristotelian faculties and its "bony" structure in his later sermons: "The soul hath bones as well as the body. And in this Anatomy, and dissection of the soul, as the bones of the soul, are the constant and strong resolutions thereof, and as the seeing of the soul is understanding, so the hearing of the soul is hearkning" ("The Second Sermon Preached by the Author After He Came to St. Dunstanes, 25 April 1624," vol. 6, no. 4).

12. Donne articulates an analogous process of transplanting or "delivering" the writing self into the reading other in a letter to Sir Henry Goodyer: "I make account that this writing of letters, when it is with any seriousness, is a kind of ecstasy, and a departure and secession and suspension of the soul, which doth then communicate itself to two bodies. And as I would every day provide for my soul's last convoy, though I know not when I shall die, and perchance I shall never die, so for these ecstasies in letters, I oftentimes deliver myself over in writing when I know not when those letters shall be sent to you" (Donne, "A Letter to Sir Henry Goodyer, 9 October 1607," in *Letters to Severall Persons of Honour: Written by John Donne* [London: J. Flesher for Richard Marriot, 1651], 11).

13. Donne, *The Major Works*, 462.

14. I agree with Ramie Targoff's statement that while "the complexities of the *First Anniversary* have been thoroughly considered, the radical nature of *The Second Anniversary* has been almost completely neglected" (Targoff, *John Donne: Body and Soul*, 81).

15. Targoff states that "Donne seems here at once to anticipate and to rebut Descartes's *cogito*, the supreme isolation of mind as the exclusive sphere of thinking" (Targoff, *John Donne: Body and Soul*, 98). Sawday states that instances in Donne's poetry such as the "body thought" and the "Extasie's" "subtle knot, which makes us man," link the body and soul in a manner similar to Descartes's identification of the pineal gland as the "place where the soul exercised its functions within the body" (Sawday, *The Body Emblazoned*, 146).

16. This specific passage has been a favorite of anatomical readings: Sawday, *The Body Emblazoned*, 18 and 122; and Sugg, "Donne and the Uses of Anatomy," 2. See also Jonathan Sawday, *Engines of the Imagination* (London: Routledge, 2007), 213; Sugg, *Murder after Death*; Don Cameron Allen, "John Donne's Knowledge of Renaissance Medicine," *Journal of English and Germanic Philology* 42 (1943): 331–33; and Donne, *The Major Works*, ed. Carey, 247: "to a Baconian Donne's list would constitute a programme for future research."

17. For an explanation of early modern debates over the classification of hair and nails in the sensitive and nutritive faculties, see Allen, "John Donne's Knowledge of Renaissance Medicine," 333.

18. The only reading suggesting the two-sided textual soul is that of A. Raspa, "Theology and Poetry in Donne's Conclave," *ELH* 32.4 (1965): 478–89. Raspa avers, "As a synthesis of this human typology, Elizabeth Drury had two 'soules' and was like paper written on both sides, on one her history as a created being and on the other her mystical significance as the law of God" (481).

19. For an account of Donne's use of these conventions, see Raymond B. Waddington, "'All in All': Shakespeare, Milton, Donne and the Soul-in-Body Topos," *English Literary Renaissance* 20 (1990): 40–68.

20. Donne's "Funeral Elegy," written in honor of Drury two years prior to the *Progress of the Soul*, sets the terms for the later poem's reconstitution of the soul as a two-sided sheet: "She hath yielded to too long an ecstasy, / He which not knowing her sad history, / Should come to read the book of destiny . . . Should turn the leaf to read, and read no more, / Would think that either destiny mistook, / Or that some leaves were torn out of the book. / But 'tis not so" (ll. 81–91). In the earlier poem, Donne argues that the "ecstasy" of Drury's soul is an interrupted reading of a text: either the reader attempts to "turn the leaf to read" but stops reading, or tears the leaves out of her book. The conclusion of the later poem completes the interrupted reading of the "Funeral Elegy" by finishing the act of "turning the leaf to read" onto the second side of Drury's soul.

21. Arthur Marotti, *John Donne, Coterie Poet*, 2nd ed. (Eugene, Ore.: Wipf and Stock, 2008), 15.

22. Wollman, "'The Press and the Fire,'" 93.

23. Wollman, "'The Press and the Fire,'" 91–92.

24. Donne, *The Major Works*, ed. Carey, 10–11.

25. Genesis 1:26–27.

26. John Donne, "Sermon Preached to the King, at the Court," vol. 9, no. 2.

27. Aristotle, *On the Soul*, 424a17–20, and 412b5–7.

28. Aristotle, *On the Soul*, 414a29–414b19.

29. Aquinas, *Summa Theologiae*, I.QQ76.A4.

30. St. Augustine, *The Confessions of St. Augustine*, ed. Temple Scott (New York: E. P. Dutton, 1900), 237.

31. See also St. Augustine, *On the Trinity*, ed. Gareth B. Matthews and Stephen McKenna (Cambridge: Cambridge University Press, 2002), specifically books 11 and 12; Eugene Vance, "Seeing God: Augustine, Sensation, and the Mind's Eye," in *Rethinking the Medieval Senses: Heritage / Fascination / Frames*, ed. Stephen G. Nichols, Andreas Kablitz, and Alison Calhoun (Baltimore, Md.: Johns Hopkins University Press, 2008), 13–29.

32. John Donne, "Sermon Preached at Lincolns Inne," vol. 3, no. 3.

33. John Donne, "Sermon Preached at St. Dunstanes upon Trinity Sunday," vol. 8, no. 1.

34. John Donne, "Sermon Preached upon All Saints Day," vol. 10, no. 1.

35. Walter J. Ong, *Orality and Literacy* (London: Routledge, 2002), 129. According to Marotti and Love, readers of "a printed text could not . . . have any way of altering the condition" of its language ("Manuscript Transmission and Circulation," 58).

36. Johns, *The Nature of the Book*, 175.

37. John Donne, "Sermon Preached at White-Hall," vol. 8, no. 7.

38. The word "dissolve" suggests the chemical process of a copper plate covered in wax and washed in acid to reveal the inscribed etching (Charles Harrison, "The Printed Picture in the Renaissance," in *Making Renaissance Art*, ed. Kim Woods [New Haven, Conn.: Yale University Press, 2007], 214–26).

39. John Donne, *Poems by J.D. with Elegies on the Author's Death* (London, 1635), A4^{v}. All subsequent references to this edition will be cited parenthetically within the text by signature.

40. David Scott Kastan, "The Body of the Text," *ELH* 81 (2014): 455.

Chapter 5

1. For a comparison of Donne and Milton in the face of censorship, see Achsah Guibbory, *Returning to John Donne* (London: Ashgate, 2015), in particular, 235–36. See also Jeanne Shami, *John Donne and Conformity in the Late Jacobean Pulpit* (Suffolk, Eng.: D. S. Brewer, 2003); and Richard McCabe, "'Right Puisante and Terrible Priests': The Role of the Anglican Church in Elizabethan State Censorship," in *Literature and Censorship in Renaissance England*, ed. Andrew Hadfield (Basingstoke, Eng., 2001), 75–94. The Folger Shakespeare Library's manuscript V.b.201 contains a petition by Donne's son, John Donne Jr., in which he "claims that the chaplains of William Laud, Archbishop of Canterbury, demanded major excisions and revisions to [his father's] sermons, which he refused to make." For this, see Daniel Starza Smith, "Attempting to Censor John Donne," The Collation: Research and Exploration at the Folger, http://collation.folger.edu/2013/11/attempting-to-censor-john-donne/.

2. John Milton, "Areopagitica," in *Complete Poems and Major Prose*, ed. Merritt Hughes (Indianapolis, Ind.: Hackett, 2003), 720.

3. Milton, "Areopagitica," 744.

4. Milton, "Areopagitica," 745.

5. Tobias Gregory, "In Defense of Empson: A Reassessment of *Milton's God*," in *Fault Lines and Controversies in the Study of Seventeenth-Century English Literature*, ed. Claude Summers and Ted-Larry Pebworth (Columbia: University of Missouri Press, 2002), 78–79.

6. Paul Cefalu, *Moral Identity in Early Modern English Literature* (Cambridge: Cambridge University Press, 2005), 168.

7. John Milton, *The Complete Prose Works, Volume 6, Christian Doctrine*, ed. Maurice Kelley (New Haven, Conn.: Yale University Press, 1973), 222. In a similar moment of Milton's rationalism, the *Christian Doctrine* denies the possibility of contradiction in God's work: "everyone agrees that an exception must be made to God's omnipresence, namely that he cannot do things which, as it is put, imply a contradiction" (148).

8. For this, see Richard Strier, "Milton's Fetters, or Why Eden Is Better Than Heaven," in *The New Milton Criticism*, ed. Peter C. Herman and Elizabeth Sauer (Cambridge: Cambridge University Press, 2012), 26. In a similar line of reasoning, Stephen Fallon suggests that Milton "was confident" in his "attempts to subject God's justice to rational evaluation" (Stephen Fallon, *Milton's Peculiar Grace: Self-Representation and Authority* [Ithaca, N.Y.: Cornell University Press, 2008], 184).

9. William Kolbrener, *Milton's Warring Angels: A Study of Critical Engagements* (Cambridge: Cambridge University Press, 2008), 69. In Milton's time, Hobbes and Bramhall stood at the two poles of the rationalist spectrum, with Hobbes asserting that "the power which is absolutely irresistible, makes him that hath it above all law, so that nothing he doth can be unjust," while the Bishop Bramhall viewed God's power as intrinsically reasonable, countering that Hobbes's "greatest error" was to "make justice to be the proper result of power . . . Power does not measure and regulate justice, but justice measures and regulates power." For this, see Thomas Hobbes, "The Questions concerning Liberty, Necessity, and Chance," in *The English Works of Thomas Hobbes*, ed. William Molesworth (London: John Bohn, 1840), 146. For Bramhall, see *The English Works of Hobbes*, 136. William Empson famously described Milton's God as one that almost "turns into the God of the Cambridge Platonists" (Empson, *Milton's God* [London: Chatto and Windus, 1965], 132).

10. Ralph Cudworth, *The True Intellectual System of the Universe* (London: Richard Royston, 1678), 717.

11. Cudworth, *The True Intellectual System of the Universe*, 721.

12. Cudworth, *The True Intellectual System of the Universe*, 12.

13. Thomas Hobbes, *Leviathan*, ed. J. C. A. Gaskin (Oxford: Oxford University Press, 1996), 15. See also Philip Pettit, *Made with Words: Hobbes on Language, Mind, and Politics* (Princeton, N.J.: Princeton University Press, 2008), 42–45.

14. Hobbes, *Leviathan*, 27–28.

15. Henry More, *The Immortality of the Soul, So Farre Forth As It Is Demonstrable from the Knowledge of Nature and the Light of Reason* (London: William Morden, 1659), 51.

16. Henry More, *An Antidote against Atheisme, or, An Appeal to the Natural Faculties of the Minde of Man* (London: Roger Daniel, 1653), 16–18.

17. For some recent examples of Milton's wide-ranging engagement with the legacy of humanist rhetoric, see Victoria Kahn, *Wayward Contracts: The Crisis of Political Obligation in England, 1640–1674* (Princeton, N.J.: Princeton University Press, 2004), 171–222; and Daniel Shore, *Milton and the Art of Rhetoric* (Cambridge: Cambridge University Press, 2012).

18. I am gesturing to several twentieth-century theories of cognition, which posit that the human mind is structured by language. For some of the most prominent examples of this, see Martin Heidegger, *Being and Time* (New York: Blackwell, 1996); Edward Sapir, *Language: An Introduction to the Study of Speech* (New York: Harcourt, Brace, 1921); Benjamin Whorf, *Language, Thought, and Reality: Selected Writings of Benjamin Lee Whorf* (Cambridge, Mass.: MIT Press, 1956); George Lakoff and Mark Johnson, *Metaphors We Live By* (Chicago: University of Chicago Press, 1980); and George Lakoff, "The Contemporary Theory of Metaphor," in *Metaphor and Thought*, ed. Andrew Ortony (Cambridge: Cambridge University Press, 1992).

19. Strier, "Milton's Fetters," 26.

20. Milton, *The Complete Prose Works, Volume 6, Christian Doctrine*, 322.

21. Aristotle, *On the Soul*, 412a6–21.

22. Milton, *The Complete Prose Works, Volume 6, Christian Doctrine*, 308.

23. For this, see also Thomas Aquinas, *Commentary on Aristotle's Physics*, ed. Kenneth Thomas (New York: Bloomsbury, 2003).

24. Milton, *The Complete Prose Works, Volume 6, Christian Doctrine*, 309.

25. Milton, *The Complete Prose Works, Volume 6, Christian Doctrine*, 317.

26. Francis Bacon, "De Augmentis Scientiarum," in *The Works of Francis Bacon*, ed. James Spedding (New York: Hurd and Houghton, 1879), IV.iii.

27. Milton, *The Complete Prose Works, Volume 6, Christian Doctrine*, 317–18.

28. Hobbes, *Leviathan*, 15.

29. Milton, *The Complete Prose Works, Volume 6, Christian Doctrine*, 318.

30. We see resonances of this phenomenon in Adam's first moments of reason as a mode of naming in language: "But who I was, or where, or from what cause, / Knew not; to speak I tri'd, and forthwith spake, / My Tongue obey'd and readily could name / What e're I saw" (*Paradise Lost* 8.270–73) and "I nam'd them, as they pass'd, and understood / Thir Nature, with such knowledg God endu'd / My sudden apprehension" (8.338–54).

31. Milton, *The Complete Prose Works, Volume 6, Christian Doctrine*, 324.

32. Milton, *The Complete Prose Works, Volume 6, Christian Doctrine*, 319.

33. More, *The Immortality of the Soul*, 52.

34. Milton, *The Complete Prose Works, Volume 6, Christian Doctrine*, 324–25.

35. Milton, *The Complete Prose Works, Volume 6, Christian Doctrine*, 318.

36. Milton, *The Complete Prose Works, Volume 6, Christian Doctrine*, 317.

37. The only reader of Milton who specifically identifies the "living soul" as the Aristotelian soul, and not the "soul" in general, is George Williamson. He claims: "Milton's 'living soul' and Hobbes's 'living creature' ought to be defined in the light of Aristotle's view of the soul." Ironically, like my own argument, Williamson finds an unexpected link in the thinking of Milton and Hobbes in their shared appropriation of the Aristotelian soul as the principle of life. For this, see George Williamson, "Milton and the Mortalist Heresy," *Studies in Philology* 32, no. 4 (1935): 553–79.

38. A programmatic statement of this conventional Aristotelian psychological hierarchy can be found in More: "*A Subject therefore from whence is both Vegetation and Sensation is the general notion of the Soule of a Brute*. Which is distributed into a number of kindes, the effect of every *Intrinsecal power* being discernible in the constant shape and properties of every distinct kind of Brute Creatures. If we adde to *Vegetation* and *Sensation Reason* properly so called, we have then a setled notion of the Soule of Man; which we may more compleatly describe thus: *A created Spirit indued with Sense and Reason, and a power of organizing terrestrial matter into humane shape by vital union therewith*" (More, *The Immortality of the Soul*, 52).

39. A particularly striking example of this crossing of the chemical and the transcendental for our purposes lies in the work of Thomas Willis:

> But indeed, the Intellect presiding o're the Imagination, beholds all the Species deposited in it self, discerns and corrects their obliquities or hypocrisies

> the Phantasie there drawn forth sublimes, and divesting it from matter formes universal things from singulars; Which discerns the errors of this. Moreover, it frames out of these some other more sublime Thoughts, not Competent for the Corporeal Soul: so it speculates or Considers both the nature of every substance, and abstracted from the Individuals of Accident, Sublimates its notions, & divests them from Matter. viz: Humanity, Rationality, Temperance, Fortitude, Corporeity, Spirituallity, Whiteness, and the like; besides, being carried higher, it Contemplates God, Angels, It self, Infinity, Eternity, and many other notions, far remote from Sense and Imagination. And so as our Intellect, in these kind of Metaphysical Conceptions, makes things almost wholly naked of matter, or carrying it self beyond every sensible Species, consider or beholds them wholly immaterial, this argues certainly, that the Substance or Nature of the Rational Soul is Immaterial and Immortal: Contemplates immaterial Substances. Because, if this Aptness or Disposition were Corporeal, as it can conceive nothing Incorporeal by Sence, it should suspect there were no such thing in the World. (Willis, *Two Discourses concerning the Soul of Brutes* [London: Thomas Dring, 1683], 38–39)

Despite man's fallen, monstrous disposition as a "two-soul'd animal," Willis suggests that the path to salvation lies in the manifold valences of the word "sublime." The description of a substance that is "divested of matter" and turned "wholly immaterial" certainly gestures to the chemical process of converting a massy solid into a gaseous vapor—sublimation—while the spiraling register of "being carried higher" to "Metaphysical Conceptions" and "Infinity, Eternity" invokes the potent aesthetic experience of the sublime that we find in Boileau, and later in Addison, Burke, and Kant.

40. For example, drawing from just a few prominent readings, John Rogers influentially describes Milton's monism as a politically inflected engagement with "natural philosophy"; Stephen Fallon suggests that the soul for Milton is a question of the "corporeal" versus the "incorporeal"; William Kolbrener argues that Milton's work performs an oscillation between the poles of dualism and monism; and N. K. Sugimura posits that Milton's commitment to monism is "fragmentary" and "illusory" at best. These subtle readings have done much to illuminate Milton's intervention in the scientific debates of his time, and all suggest that his philosophical positions informed his poetic practice, but my own argument proposes that Milton was much more literal about his linguistic understanding of the soul. For this, see John Rogers, *The Matter of Revolution* (Ithaca, N.Y.: Cornell University Press, 1998); Stephen Fallon, *Milton among the Philosophers: Poetry and Materialism in Seventeenth-Century England* (Ithaca, N.Y.: Cornell University Press, 1991); William Kolbrener, *Milton's Warring Angels*; and N. K. Sugimura, *Matter of Glorious Trial: Spiritual and Material Substance in "Paradise Lost"* (New Haven, Conn.: Yale University Press, 2009).

41. "discourse, n.," OED Online, September 2016, Oxford University Press, http://www.oed.com/view/Entry/53985.

42. More differs from Milton in this key respect: to his mind, angels cannot be born in "terrestrial" form and subsequently convert to a more "aereal or aethereal" one (More, *The Immortality of the Soul*, 52).

43. Milton's emphasis on patience and the slow unfolding of time differs markedly from the other major articulation of the "tract of time" by Thomas Sprat: "And I will also add; that, if such a course had been at first set on foot, Philosophy would by this means have been kept closer to material things; and so, in probability, would not have undergone so many Eclipses, as it has done ever since. If we reckon from its first setting forth in the East; we shall find, that in so long a *Tract of Time*, there have not been above four, or five hundred years, at several intervals, wherein it has been in any request in the World. And if we look back on all the alterations, and subversions of States, that have hapned in Civil Nations, these three thousand years: we may still behold, that the Sciences of mens brains, have been alwayes subject to be far more injur'd by such vicissitudes, than the Arts of their hands" (Thomas Sprat, *The History of the Royal-Society of London, for the Improving of Natural Knowledge* [London, 1667], 118). For Sprat, the "Tract of Time" represents a too-long history of delayed human progress, of periods of frequent "Eclipses" which could have been remedied by a "closer" study of "things" and not "words." The tract of time represents slowness, and the frustrating crawl of human knowledge that is unfortunately "so long." If Milton's "tract of time" is a cry for patience, Sprat's "tract of time" is precisely the opposite, declaring that human time has been too slow in unfolding, and that the rise up the "chain" of faculties to a scientific vantage point where "secrets are open to our minds" needs to be accelerated.

44. Genesis 3:3–6.

45. "attend, v. To stretch to (still in Old French); *hence*, to direct the mind or observant faculties, to listen, apply oneself; to watch over, minister to, wait upon, follow, frequent; to wait for, await, expect. In almost every variety of meaning it is, or has been, both *trans.* and *intr.*, the latter construed with *to*, *unto*, *on*, *upon*, and having indirect passive, as: we must *attend to* this, this must be *attended to*. To wait for, await, expect" (OED Online, September 2016, Oxford University Press, http://www.oed.com/view/Entry/12780).

46. Strier, "Milton's Fetters," 27.

47. Milton, *Complete Prose Works*, 317.

48. Milton, *Complete Prose Works*, 321–22.

49. Milton, *Complete Prose Works*, 321.

Coda

1. Rene Descartes, *Discourse on Method and Meditations on First Philosophy*, ed. David Weissman (New Haven, Conn.: Yale University Press, 1996), 4.

2. Descartes, *Discourse on Method*, 28–29.

3. Descartes, *Discourse on Method*, 21.

4. Sullivan, *Sleep, Romance, and Human Embodiment*, 8.

5. Shannon, *The Accommodated Animal*, 15.

6. Shannon, *The Accommodated Animal*, 28.

7. Ian Hacking, *Rewriting the Soul: Multiple Personality and the Sciences of Memory* (Princeton, N.J.: Princeton University Press, 1998), 246–66.

8. Ian Hacking, "Two Souls in One Body," *Critical Inquiry* 17, no. 4 (summer 1991): 839.

INDEX